GUARDIANS OF THE
An Ethnography of a Jain Ascetic Community

Itinerant, white-robed ascetics represent the highest ethical ideal among the Jains of rural Rajasthan. They renounce family, belongings, and desires in order to lead lives of complete nonviolence. In their communities, Jain ascetics play key roles as teachers and exemplars of the truth; they are embodiments of the *lokottar* – the realm of the transcendent.

Based on the author's thirteen months of fieldwork in the town of Ladnun, Rajasthan, India, among a community of Terapanthi Svetambar Jains, *Guardians of the Transcendent* explores the many facets of what constitutes a moral life within the Terapanthi ascetic community, and examines the central role ascetics play in upholding the Jain moral order. Focusing on the Terapanthi moral universe from the perspective of female renouncers, Anne Vallely considers how Terapanthi Jain women create their own ascetic subjectivities, and how they construct and understand themselves as symbols of renunciation. The first in-depth ethnographic study of this important and influential Jain tradition, this work makes a significant contribution to Jain studies, comparative religion, Indian studies, and the anthropology of South Asian religions.

ANNE VALLELY is a part-time lecturer in the Departments of Anthropology and Religion at Concordia University, and in the Faculty of Religious Studies at McGill University.

ANTHROPOLOGICAL HORIZONS

Editor: Michael Lambek, University of Toronto

This series, begun in 1991, focuses on theoretically informed ethnographic works addressing issues of mind and body, knowledge and power, equality and inequality, the individual and the collective. Interdisciplinary in its perspective, the series makes a unique contribution in several other academic disciplines: women's studies, history, philosophy, psychology, political science, and sociology. For a list of the books published in this series see page 297.

Guardians of the Transcendent

An Ethnography of a Jain Ascetic Community

ANNE VALLELY

UNIVERSITY OF TORONTO PRESS
Toronto Buffalo London

© University of Toronto Press Incorporated 2002
Toronto Buffalo London
Printed in Canada

ISBN: 0-8020-3545-0 (cloth)
ISBN: 0-8020-8415-X (paper)

Printed on acid-free paper

National Library of Canada Cataloguing in Publication Data

Vallely, Anne, 1966–
  Guardians of the transcendent : an ethnology of a Jain ascetic community

  (Anthropological horizons)
  Includes bibliographical references and index.
  ISBN 0-8020-3545-0 (bound).   ISBN 0-8020-8415-X (pbk.)

  1. Terapanth (Jain sect)   2. Jain women – India – Ladnun.
  3. Asceticism – Jainism.   4. Ascetics – India – Ladnun.   5. Ascetics –
  India – Ladnun.   6. Ethnology – India – Ladnun.   I. Title.   II. Series.

  BL1380.T4V34 2002   294.4'9   C2002-900232-X

This book has been published with the help of a grant from the Humanities
and Social Sciences Federation of Canada, using funds provided by the Social
Sciences and Humanities Research Council of Canada.

University of Toronto Press acknowledges the financial assistance to its
publishing program of the Canada Council for the Arts and the Ontario Arts
Council.

University of Toronto Press acknowledges the financial support for its publishing activites of the Government of Canada through the Book Publishing
Industry Development Program (BPIDP).

For my father and for Kenny

Contents

Acknowledgments

This book would not have been possible without the help and guidance of a great number of people. My first thanks must go to the Terapanthi Jain community for its immense generosity. A special thanks goes to the late Ganadhipati Guru Dev Tulsi, whose support opened so many doors that would otherwise have remained closed to an outsider. I also wish to thank Acharyasri, Sadhvi Kanak Prabha, Niojikaji, Samanji, the Sadhvis, Samanis, Mumukshus sisters, Munis, and Samans; without their warm welcome this research would not have been possible. I am deeply indebted to my dear friends in the Samani order who made my experience such a memorable one. I will always remember your good humour, patience, and endless kindness. *Dhanyavad!*

I am privileged to have had the affection and guidance of Professor A.N. Pandeya, who treated me as a family member during my brief sojourns in Delhi and provided me with invaluable suggestions in the early stages of my fieldwork.

Of those people in Canada to whom I owe great thanks, four stand out in particular. First is Michael Lambek, whom I was fortunate to have as my supervisor. His guidance and encouragement provided the foundation for this work. I am deeply indebted to him. I would like to thank Professor Joseph T. O'Connell for his insightful and meticulous reading of the book, as well as for his kindness. I am grateful to Patrick Vallely, who rigorously and painstakingly critiqued the language of the text and who was available any time I needed someone to act as a sounding board. *Go raibh maith agat!* It is no exaggeration to say that this work may never have come to pass without the support of Ken Kaplan; his understanding and boundless patience were a steadfast support for my sometimes flagging spirits and energy.

I am very grateful to the following agencies, which supported me financially during my doctoral studies. The Shastri Indo-Canadian Institute provided me with a Hindi-language training grant prior to my fieldwork. Travel to India and living expenses while I was there were financed by the Shastri Indo-Canadian Institute and the Commonwealth Institute. Upon my return to Canada, the Social Sciences and Humanities Research Council of Canada provided me with support for the writing stages of the book. Lastly, I am deeply appreciative of James Leahy's scrupulous review of the manuscript.

PART ONE
THE ETHICS OF RENUNCIATION

1

Introduction

Reeboks and Renunciation in Rajasthan

Like an ungainly acrobat on a tightrope, she fought to keep her balance before the curious onlookers. Determined not to use her hands, she struggled to pry off her right sneaker with her left foot, but the velcro straps were snug and secure, preventing an easy release. Back home this would be less of a big deal, since one's hands play a less central role in bodily maintenance – more like aloof middlemen than active participants in the feeding and cleaning of the body. But here, bare hands *sans instrument* are the big players in daily nourishing and ablutions. The importance of their cleanliness must be unconditional! Ms. Veena,* who had effortlessly stepped out of her *chappals* (sandals) stood calmly waiting for me to finish my ordeal.

Ms. Veena, a middle-aged woman from the Punjab, dressed in a floral-patterned sari, continued to watch my animated feet. I felt that she had by now become involved in the struggle and was aligning herself with the Reeboks. Perhaps she thought this was the standard way Westerners remove their shoes! And what shoes! What had I been thinking when I bought them? Simplicity was not in fashion in Montreal the day I purchased sneakers for my trip. My only criterion had been that they not be made of leather, since, for Jains, eating animals and wearing their skins are unnecessary forms of violence. Their motto *ahimsa paramo dharma,* which translates as 'nonviolence is the highest form of religion,' is applied to every aspect of life. I succumbed to the first pair of non-

*Pseudonyms are used throughout. However, actual names are used for well-known personages.

leather Reeboks the breezy clerk suggested. He assured me that the Big Sneaker look is not just American hype-aesthetics, but a global phenomenon. I can report that it hadn't reached Ladnun by the time I had. Here, my Reeboks were categorically absurd.

The small but growing crowd of spectators paid little attention to my particular struggle, more interested as it was in the general package. Finally I surrendered and with an air of apology darted over to the cement steps in front of the nun's residence to sit and remove the shoes the only way I knew: with both hands. As I had feared, my fingertips were soon gritty from the Rajasthani sand, which, like an endless beige blanket, is everywhere, and in everything, dulling and adding a matte finish to the harsh shadows of the desert. The shoes finally off, I took them to the surprisingly orderly pile of *chappals* huddled together fraternally by the steps of the nuns' residence. Most were of the simplest style, with just one tiny strap for the large toe. I placed mine on the left side in the shadow of the steps.

The jet lag and intensity of the past few hours were taking their toll on my sobriety. From the time it took me to travel from Montreal, Canada, to Ladnun, India, I had been transformed from being something of an outsider within my own culture to being its celebrated representative. I now stood as its living exemplary in a part of rural Rajasthan not familiar with foreigners. My views and actions were no longer my own, nor my dress, nor even the way I walked: all carried piercing insights into Western ways of being. But I was the reluctant emissary; I sought to dodge this fiction, to eclipse it somehow. I yearned to merge with the greys and browns of the Indian winter; to walk unselfconsciously through the narrow village streets, past the itinerant cows and wretched dogs, and among the spirited crowds at the marketplace. I looked down at my stubborn sneakers: who was I kidding? The velcro and the stripes stared back mockingly, and I realized how much they encapsulated my own awkwardness. A beacon brighter than the star of Bethlehem, they announced a foreign presence with all the subtlety of American jingoism. This image clung to me like a huge shadow in the dusk of early evening. I had wanted to enter this culture with reserve, sensitivity, and openness, but as I stepped hesitantly, the shadow ridiculed me by racing ahead and announcing itself assuredly.

'Miss Anne, let us enter now." Ms.Veena was waiting for me at the top of the steps. I followed directly behind her. She was taking me to meet a young and junior nun in the order, Sadhvi Prasandji. We continued down a corridor, which opened on one side to face the barren courtyard. On the other side were a series of small, dark, windowless rooms. A hefty middle-aged man in a *dhoti* was moving brusquely down the hall behind us, darting in and out of the small rooms as if he were in a big hurry to find something. Mumbling, he pushed ahead into the room nearest us and flicked on the light. Then he disappeared.

Jain ascetics are not allowed to use electricity because they believe it to be alive. Animals, plants, water, soil, air, and fire are all considered sentient beings with souls identical in every way to those of humans. For lay Jains, a distinction is made between necessary and unnecessary violence; the eating of plants for survival is a form of violence that leads to the accumulation of bad karma, but it is necessary. However, the ascetics attempt to exist in an environment of complete nonviolence, or *ahimsa*. They never prepare any food for themselves, and only 'beg' for what they need. In this way, they argue, they are not implicated in the violence. They will not accept offerings of foods that are 'alive': all vegetables, fruit, and water must have been boiled, and hence dead, before they can accept them. In addition, the food must never have been prepared expressly for them. Only if the ascetics are sure of this, will they accept the offerings. In reality, they depend on the lay community to commit some 'necessary' violence on their behalf, which the laity do with great enthusiasm. It is an honour to have monks or nuns come to one's home for alms, and, to boot, it leads to the accumulation of good karma. The turning of a light switch on and off, which involves the destruction of innumerable living souls, is unnecessary violence. The devoted lay community willingly does this 'killing' for their revered ascetics, who would otherwise sit in the dark and be unable to provide them with religious instruction.

With the light on, I could see Sadhvi Prasandji. She looked to be in her late teens. She sat cross-legged on the cement floor, her bare feet weathered from the sun. The group following behind now rushed in ahead of us, stooped over in supplication. They lowered themselves to their knees, and bowed deeply before her. She raised her hand gently as a sign of acknowledgment. Light stubble peaked out from under the hood of her sari. Her huge eyes appeared jovial, but with half her face hidden under the *muhpatti*, I could only guess. The mouth covering, or *muhpatti*, distinguishes her as a Jain ascetic in a country with no shortage of saints and holy men. It is at once practical and symbolic: worn to prevent the accidental swallowing of tiny living creatures, but also to avoid causing injury to the air itself. I was also told that it serves as a reminder to speak only when necessary, and then only in gentle words.

Ms. Veena and I moved forward, our hands joined in *namaste.* When Ms.Veena lowered herself to kneel, I bowed my head and sat down quietly in a cross-legged position. Immediately, I knew I had done something terribly wrong. Eyes that had been focused on the young *sadhvi* were now on me again. Ms.Veena lowered her head ceremoniously.

Then, from a deep bow, she raised herself with graceful control and turned her head toward me. Her face was sedate but severe. All she said was 'This is how we show respect to our *maharajas.*' She bowed deeply again in the direction of the *sadhvi,* touching her forehead on the floor before her. This was my cue, though I was reluctant to take it up. Such self-effacing seemed altogether inappropriate before a pubescent teen, her pimples peering over her *muhpatti.* Reckoning that a little ego-debasing was better than being perceived as a cultural dolt, I prostrated myself.

Ms. Veena said a few words in Hindi by way of introduction. She used a cotton handkerchief as a makeshift *muhpatti.* The nun nodded, and then settled herself more securely in her lotus position, one hand grasping the big toe of her left foot and the other resting on her knee.

'You have come from far to learn about Jainism.' Her words were flattened and muffled under her *muhpatti,* but her English was good. I then realized why I was taken to see so junior a nun. Most of the nuns of the Terapanthi Jains spoke Rajasthani and Hindi, but very few spoke English. For the most part, the girls came from conservative merchant families and received little education before entering the order. Here they learned to read the ancient Jain scriptures in their original Sanskrit and Prakrit, and to study the great traditions of Indian philosophy. Of Sadhvi Prasandji, I was later told that she 'comes from south India' as a short-hand way of explaining why her English was so fluent. Of the others who had come that evening for her *darshan,* mostly middle-aged women in colourful saris and a few men, several knew a little English. The others didn't appear troubled at all; the main thing was to be in the presence of a 'saint.' All were eager to hear the young nun's words.

We all sat crossed-legged on the second floor of a large, whitewashed, cement building built several hundred years ago by Jain merchants working the trade routes in and out of the Middle East. Some years ago, descendants of those merchants donated the building to the Jain monastic order. The rooms were austere. Except for a few miniature desks, which the nuns used for scripture study, and a cupboard for books, the rooms were empty. The nuns studied, ate, and slept on the hard cement floors.

'I will tell you the story of Isu. We also know about Isu here,' Sadhvi Prasandji said. Ms. Veena quickly leaned over to me, saying, 'You say Jesus, we say Isu.'

'Jesus?' I whispered back at her in amazement. I was hoping for something more exotic: the Jain saint Lord Mahavir and his heroic fasts in the forest or an exhilarating Hindu tale of Kali or Vishnu. Sadhvi Prasandji continued:

'One day a blind man asked Isu to help him. He told Isu that he was unable to have a family of his own or to work since he was blind. Isu felt pity for the man and so he touched his eyes with both his hands. Then the man could see. He thanked Isu and went away very happy. Many months later, when Isu was walking through the bazaar, he was surprised to see the same man in a brothel. The man, seeing Isu, came out to pay his respects. Isu asked him, "Why are you at this bad place? I helped you not long ago and this is how you thank me?" The man then replied, "Isu you gave me eyes so that I could see, but you did not show me the right path to follow." '

After some whispers of translation, everyone was soon nodding in acceptance of its profundity, aligning themselves with those 'in the know.' I, however, sat blank-faced as I searched my mental repertoire of children's bible stories. Could it be that I simply never heard this one? There was Jesus and Lazarus, Jesus and the fish, the water into wine story ... I distrusted my memory. The young *sadhvi* went on:

'In the West you make a big mistake. You confuse the body and the soul. The body is just body!' she exclaimed, emitting a huge breath of air from the sides of her *muhpatti*. She stared down at her folded legs wrapped in white cotton sari and mock-hit her knee with contempt, 'One day – no more. It will die. To heal *it* is not religion. For religion, you must heal the soul.'

There was a moment's silence. Then she asked:

'What is your country?'

'Canada.'

It was obvious that this meant nothing. She turned towards another *sadhvi* for help, but none was forthcoming. Ms.Veena looked as though she was about to come to the rescue when a man's voice from the back of the room called out 'America.' Instantly, order was restored.

'Well, *north* of America" I added, but no one heard the detail. The young *sadhvi* had heard all she needed to continue and, perhaps armed with this new ammunition, she asserted:

'You are very lost.'

'I'm sorry?' I said.

'You are *lost.*' She emphasized the word 'lost,' assuming, I suppose, that I was having some difficulty understanding her accented English, 'like the blind man.'

Amazed at her words, I forced a smile, hoping that the seriousness of moment was in my own mind and that it might quickly evaporate. But the young *sadhvi*'s eyes were without humour. My smile dropped. What was this, I thought? Where was all that 'feel-good' stuff associated with *darshan*? I had been to spiritual gatherings back home, even to ones with jet-set gurus flown in from India. This bore no resemblance to those outpourings of affection in which the banal was transformed into sublime epiphanies, simply through a smile or totter of the swami's bearded head, and where everyone left feeling sanctified.

'You are here because you are lost *spiritually.*' She clarified, looking very matronly. Then she turned to Ms.Veena and asked her in Hindi how long I would be staying. 'Several months,' Ms.Veena answered. The *sadhvi* rocked backed on her rump, one hand still grasping her bare foot.

'Oh ... you will learn *so* much here. In the West you say, "Eat, drink, be merry," yes? This is not good. You will learn that you too have a soul, not just a body and then you can teach this in your country.'

She appeared happy with her counsel. Her *muhpatti* strained across her cheeks as she evinced a broad smile beneath. She raised her palm to us to signal the end of our *darshan*. The edifying lecture was over.

We all filed out of the room. The others went to pay their respects to other, more senior, *sadhvis*, but Ms.Veena and I left the residence. I looked at my watch: 8: 10 p.m. I had only been in the town five hours and already I wanted to flee! My anxieties had not been unfounded: the *sadhvi* saw me not as an individual eager to learn about Jainism, but as a representative of a caricatured culture known for its crassness, selfishness, and unspirituality. And without her even seeing my shoes! I looked down at my feet: smothered beneath something so showy and cumbersome, they longed, like the ascetics, for release.

Never having married, my wonderful companion Ms. Veena was something of an oddity herself. She chose to devote herself to her guru, as she put it, but not to become a *sadhvi*. This was a risky and uncommon path for a woman in India, and she would tell me in later months that she considered her life to be far more difficult than those of the ascetics. She seemed totally unconcerned with her appearance, in distinct contrast to the typically wealthy lay Jain women on their annual pilgrimages to receive Guru Dev's blessing. Ms.Veena's laxity also made her distinct from the ascetics, whose 'neglect' of their bodies was cultivated and, in fact, a daily preoccupation. In the course of my stay I came to the conclusion that they renounce the world, society, and their families to pursue the ascetic path of nonviolence, but their bodies become the templates upon which they demonstrate and judge the success of their efforts.

We were on our way to visit Ganadhipati Guru Dev Tulsi[1] himself, the gentle and charismatic leader of the Terapanthi Jains. His devotees loved to recount miracles associated with him, insisting that he had tremendous spiritual power. I was often told of how, when Guru Dev wanders from place to place under the scorching Rajasthani sun, the clouds are eager to shelter his path so that his journey is always in shade. I was more interested in his fifty years of relentless campaigns for nonviolence, for which he is justly famous throughout India. Although he renounced the world when he took his monastic vows he remained actively involved in efforts to make it a less violent place. I had been eager to meet him for years, but now I was feeling utterly exhausted and discouraged, and would have preferred to return to my room.

The *galis* (paths) that Ms.Veena shepherded me through seemed narrower and smellier than before, and the open sewers that lined them, more menacing. It was dark and only the bulbs dangling from the makeshift shop stalls lighted our way. Horses free of their *tonga*-carts stood meekly in the dwarfed grass awaiting sunrise and another day's work. The shopkeepers squatted comfortably on their haunches, resting their upper arms on their angular knees. Disenchanted, I resented their stares, which I assumed to be mocking. We walked slowly, careful not to step into the mounds of horse droppings dotting our path. With each shuffle of Ms. Veena's *chappals*, the parched sand would rise up in a big beige cloud, sometimes as high as our eyes. In a world of dulled and muted hues, the ascetics in their impossibly white saris were visions of purity and 'otherness.' They too liked to describe themselves this way: 'like beautiful white lotuses that float on top of the water, only barely touching it and never contaminated by it.'

With the monks' residence in view, I rushed ahead to remove my sneakers, getting a head start on the confrontational velcro. All pretence at Indian protocol abandoned, my already filthy hands went to work. It was late and the monastery was nearly devoid of devotees, as Ms.Veena had hoped it would be. This would give us a greater chance to pay our respects, she said. We entered the spacious and barren room with our heads lowered and hands joined: I immediately recognized Guru Dev from the many photos I had seen of him, though I hadn't expected him to be quite so small or old. He sat in a lotus position on top of a low wooden dais that elevated him slightly above those around him. Here was the man that had led the Terapanthi Jains since he was just twenty-five years old, controlling one of the largest ascetic communities in all of India, with nearly 800 monks and nuns.

Several monks (*munis*) sat near or moved quietly behind him. Two looked very young – no older than eleven or twelve. All in white, and gliding across the marble floor with their *rajoharan* (whiskbrooms) clearing the way before them, they looked like dreamy little Chagall angels. All Jain ascetics carry *rajoharan*, which they use to gently sweep away any insects or critters that may be in harm's way. Most of the lay devotees present were also wearing the *muhpatti*. They were there for *darshan* (to be in the presence of the holy one), not for discussion. But one stout man in his fifties with well-oiled, dark hair was busy recounting a tale to Guru Dev when we walked in. He held his right hand an inch or so away from his mouth as a quickly improvised but untrained *muhpatti*: his words were faster than his well-intentioned hand, which moved up and down like a piston out of control. His hand would flutter before a silent mouth, only to drop as a torrent of words gushed forward again. It was not a well-synchronized performance, but the intent was there.

Guru Dev noticed our entrance, and before we could move to the back of the room, he gestured for us to come forward. We came within two feet of him and then bowed deeply three times, as is the custom. I had heard that he eschewed formality and was oblivious to status. Without delay, he asked me in Hindi why I had come to study Jainism. There was no interrogation; his dark eyes were smiling above his *muhpatti*.

'I've known about Jainism since I was a child, and have always been interested in its teachings,' I answered in a Hindi–English hybrid.[2] He called one of the youngest monks to come forward. His name was Amit Muni and he too 'came from south India.' He would serve as our interpreter. Translating Guru Dev's words, Amit Muni asked in a surprisingly loud and clear voice beneath his *muhpatti*,
'Why did you come to Ladnun?'

'By chance,' I answered. 'I met a Jain family when I was in Canada and they suggested I come here. I was planning on coming to India, but at that time I didn't know where in India to come.' Guru Dev had closed his eyes and was nodding his head meditatively even before the translation came back. He asked another muffled question through Amit Muni.

'Are you vegetarian?' Vegetarianism is so central a practice in Jainism, and widespread in Hinduism and Buddhism as well, that it is often simply taken for granted. But Jains know of Westerners as voracious meat eaters.

'Yes, for a long time.'

Guru Dev, smiling broadly, gestured around the room when he spoke in a Hindi tailored for me:

'*Yahan ... ahimsa*,' he said, allowing Amit Muni to then elaborate: 'Everything here is done for nonviolence.'

Guru Dev continued (in translation) – 'There is so much violence in the world today, people hurt people, people hurt animals. We spend so much money and so much time thinking about ways to destroy living beings, if only we could put this energy into peace. Imagine what we could do! We must change people's hearts so they know what a terrible thing violence is.'

'It is my dream,' I answered in English.

'Do you eat cake?' Amit Muni interjected with his own question.

'Cake?' I remember smiling, wondering if perhaps I misheard him.

'Yes, cake,' he persisted, 'Cake has eggs and eggs are non-veg.'

In India there are two main categories of food: 'veg' and its negation, 'non-veg,' leaving no doubt which commands the moral high ground. I enjoyed the idea of being part of a universe where the default was to vegetarianism, and where it was the meat eaters who were called upon to explain themselves. But now was I going to be grouped with the dreaded cake eaters?

Guru Dev started to laugh heartily at the over-zealousness of the little monk. His laugh was contagious and soon everyone was smiling. He was nothing like the waif-like *swamis* with Mona Lisa smiles and oxygen-deprived voices that the West has caricatured as India's spiritual teachers. He had a powerful presence that was at once intellectual and pragmatic. His eyes exuded such tremendous warmth that I felt relaxed for the first time since leaving Canada and knew I was privileged to be exactly where I was at that moment. He began to speak directly to me again in Hindi:

'You are home, you have come home.'

Before I could react, he turned to Acharyasri Mahaprajna, the second in command, and said something I could not follow. Acharyasri nodded his bald head, his eyes becoming smaller as they scrunched up into smiling creases. I looked around at the laity to find them beaming back at me. There was a buzz of Hindi in the room until the man with the oily hair, forever impatient, blurted out loudly, and without his hand-*muhpatti*:

'His Holiness says that you were a Jain in a past life, and now you have come home.' I felt colour race across my face and I smiled widely as I looked back at Guru Dev. Ms.Veena leaned forward to me and whispered, 'It is a great honour for you. Guru Dev knows so many things.' I lowered my head in a deep bow of thanks and respect.

Outside the monk's residence, Ms.Veena was smiling when she asked me if I remembered the way back to my room. I wasn't certain, but told her I did. I was happy to be alone with my thoughts. A Western reincarnation of a former Jain! (Later on in my stay, this status would be further elevated to that of a former Jain ascetic!) What sins must I have committed to deserve my present incarnation, I mused light-heartedly. No doubt it was another classification, another fiction, but one that I delighted in because it was a *Jain* fiction. I had been invited to join their drama, to dream using their idioms, and to share in their reveries. For a fraction of a moment I floated like a white lotus on a pond.

The exposed lightbulbs jutting out of the low cement buildings transformed the shadows of the passers-by into enormous animated goblins: a sweeper-woman's long broom of uneven twigs cast a deranged image as she hurried by, and a distorted shadow of a mangy dog told of its fear. The difficulties of the day were wiped away. I had crossed a line from outsider to friend, and was joyous even though I knew it would be a bridge I would have to cross daily. That was fine. I didn't yearn to be a Jain, even if their teachings were the most virtuous I had heard. The crossing itself was exhilarating. I had feared that I would be prevented from taking the first step; that the bridge would be permanently closed, but within a few short moments Guru Dev paved the way for me. With his benison, I could walk less hesitantly. I watched my shadow as it moved ahead of me: things were going to be all right. The sneakers, casting their enormous shadow, would definitely have to go. I would liberate them.

Background

I first learned about Jainism from my father when I was a child. In the course of his work at the National Film Board of Canada, he had come upon a short film on the tradition, and found it compelling enough to bring home for family viewing. I still recall my astonishment at watching holy men sweep aside tiny insects from their path so as not to harm them. Jains appeared to be a sort of magical, enchanted people – certainly a world apart from the playground of my school, where kids pulled insects apart for fun. The film constituted both the beginning and end of my early Jain education, but it had the immediate effect of making me feel less self-conscious about my own regard for creepy-crawlies (which, I suspect, was the real reason my father had me watch it). The impressions it left me of the possibility of a less violent world were enduring.

It was not until graduate school that I again gave serious thought to the Jain tradition. But this time it was an interest in gender that drew me back. Like many women of my generation, my first exposure to feminist thought came at university. I became intrigued with (and disturbed by) the ubiquitous asymmetrical valuation of women, and with the historical and cross-cultural persistence of gender stratification. Again, like many women first learning about female discrimination, I was anxious to know the causes and deep structures that sustained it, and to work towards social and political strategies to end it.

However, the 1990s was a curious time in feminist studies. The search for a single, comprehensive account of women's subordination was no longer fashionable. The poststructural, postmodern critique of theory as totalizing and essentialist had had its effect. Many feminists who had previously concerned themselves with explanations and origins of female subordination now retreated from such grand theorizing to focus on the great diversity of women's experiences. Assumptions of a commonality in women's experiences, even of the category of 'woman,' were challenged. Feminist concerns fragmented, and the idea of establishing feminism as a single unity seemed fanciful, if not misguided.

Feminism shared postmodernism's concern with local, particular, and multiple human experiences, and had long presaged its critique of the dualistic, androcentric, and rationalistic foundations of Western thought. The postmodern critique influenced a shift away from treating women as passive victims of patriarchy, to exploring women's competing discourses, strategies of resistance, and own forms of self-representation. Nevertheless, feminism's relationship with the postmodernist approach remains ambivalent, and its distrust of theory has been far more equivocal. Feminism is inherently theoretical – to the extent that it conceptualizes female subordination as systematically interconnected – and, therefore, antithetical to epistemological relativism. Disavowing the possibility of generalizing about women is counterproductive to the social and political goals of most feminists, and counterintuitive in the face of women' s common experiences.

The postmodern concern with the ways in which discourses create their own definitions of truth – their own subjects, objects, knowledge, and power structures – sensitizes us to the multiplicity of ideologies about women, and the diversity and uniqueness of women's experiences. But it does not preclude the recognition of patterns. Unique cultural expressions and generalized patterns of social phenomenon require alternate, but corresponding, forms of analysis. Both interpretative and causal understanding is necessary. As Weber established over a hundred years ago, the two need not be antagonistic: social phenomena must be understood both subjectively and objectively. The Enlightenment discourse on rationality, for instance, created woman as an irrational and emotional counterpart to rational man; the Jain discourse on nonviolence and nonattachment, likewise, creates women as the more violent and 'attached' counterpart to men. In each, the discourse creates its own peculiar truths, values, and asymmetries – but in each, the asymmetries are gendered in like manner. In the dominant public ideology, as Michelle Zimbalist Rosaldo argued in the 1970s, women are perceived as less capable of achieving the cultural ideal – no matter what form it takes. The dominant cultural ideal remains the male ideal.

In South Asian traditions, asceticism is overwhelmingly perceived as a male ideal. In Hinduism, monastic orders have traditionally been closed to women, and female asceticism has only on rare occasions been organized into self-sustaining institutions. 'More often,' writes Clementin-Ojha, 'female ascetics have to survive within the framework of systems that are essentially male-orientated and have been designed and refined by males for other males' (1988: 34). Elizabeth Nissan (1983), in her essay on Buddhist nuns in Sri Lanka, writes that asceticism is seen as a male vocation in Sri Lanka because of the belief that men are more suited to monastic life than women. In Jainism, however, women dominate religious practices. Twice as many women as men pursue the ascetic path, and women are considered better suited to monastic life. In addition, female ascetics enjoy a status that is unparalleled among other religious traditions in the Indian subcontinent. In spite of this, in the dominant public ideology, asceticism is conceived of as a male ideal.

The high status of female ascetics appears to controvert the prevailing ideology of female inferiority and the practice of gender stratification in Jain lay society. A far more common pattern found cross-culturally is one in which religious systems *reinforce* cultural values and patterns of social organization, and in which women's positions in religion reflect their status in society. As such, Jainism appears to be something of an anomaly within the anthropological literature.

Jainism is an ancient and enduring tradition. Like Buddhism, it rejected the authority of the Vedas – the ancient Hindu scriptures – and denied the caste system any legitimacy. In addition, it opposed the authority and privilege of the Brahmans, and claimed, contrary to the conventional wisdom of the times, that it was possible for all humans to achieve liberation through their own efforts (Folkert, 1987). Mahavir (c. 599–527 BCE),[3] a historical figure and contemporary of the Buddha, usually represents the starting point in the historical study of Jainism, but to Jains, he represents the final great spiritual teacher of our present cycle of time (he is alternatively called *Tirthankara* and *Jina*).[4] Jains, like Hindus, conceive of time in grand cosmic cycles of moral and physical ascent and decay, and claim that their tradition has no beginning and no end. Like the universe, it is eternal and uncreated; it is simply a set of 'truths' that has always existed and always will be true (Dundas, 1992; Folkert, 1987).[5]

Jainism bases its teachings on a fundamental division of all existing things into two classes: *jiv* – that which is sentient – and *ajiv* – a nonsentient, material component that is connected with the soul (also called karma). The soul's association with *ajiv* prevents it from realizing its true and omniscient nature. Because it is understood as a physical substance, it is subject to, and governed by, individual human agency; liberation becomes a battle between the individual (*jiv*) and karma (*ajiv*) on the battleground of worldly existence (*samsar*) (see Goonasekera, 1986). A consequence of this 'concrete' cosmology is that crucial differences between individuals are sought in behaviour, not in inherited qualities. It is the great warriors of *samsar* – the ascetics – who are Jainism's cultural heroes (see Babb, 1996).

Since the fourth century BCE, the Jain community has been divided into two major branches: the Svetambar ('white clad') and Digambar ('sky clad') (Dundas, 1992: 43). One of the major disputes between the two sects centres on the attire of the ascetics; the Svetambar ascetics wear white robes, whereas the Digambar are naked ascetics. There are many other areas of contention between the two sects, but the one that concerns us most here is that of female spirituality. The debate centres on the question of whether or not *moksa* (liberation) can be attained following a life in a female body (Balbir, 1994; Jaini, 1991). Since nudity is not 'feasible' for women, the Digambar argue that liberation is not possible following a life in a female body – that a woman would have to be reborn as a man before liberation could occur. The Svetambar, who do not see garments as an obstacle to liberation, argue that women can attain salvation (Balbir, 1994; Banks, 1986; Jaini, 1991; Shântâ 1985).

The practical consequence of this doctrinal divide is that fully fledged female ascetic orders exist among the Svetambar sect, which admits women to full monastic vows. The Terapanthi Jains, with whom I conducted my fieldwork in 1996, are a branch of the Svetambar sect and have the largest order of female ascetics (nearly 600 nuns) under a single leader (*acharya*). Among the Digambar, however, women are not permitted to take full monastic vows and therefore can attain only the quasi-ascetic status of *aryika* meaning 'noble woman' (Babb, 1996; Jaini, 1991; Shântâ, 1985: 483–517).

Although the Svetambar and Digambar are often depicted as opposites with respect to their views on female religiosity, the ideas they share in common are as important as those on which they differ. Both hold the same negative understanding of female nature as flawed and associated with sexuality and sin. The connections postulated in the anthropological literature between female subordination and women's association with sexuality, corporeality, and emotion are widespread. Women's physicality and sexuality are common themes in the world's religious traditions, too, and are of particular concern among the ascetic traditions of South Asia. The vigour and persistence of these ideas inform practices of gender socialization, and form the basis of a religious imagination which problematizes the female form as a symbol of renunciation in the Jain religious tradition.

Clearly, religion plays a key, yet complex and ambiguous, role in maintaining gender inequality. It 'authenticates' a particular understanding of reality, usually reinforcing existing social values, giving them preternatural authority. In so doing, it can serve to naturalize sexual inequalities. But it can also be a liberating and creative force in women's lives, a source of great strength and pride, and a tool with which to create competing discourses. Its dual, controlling/enabling nature – much like gender identity itself – presents a challenge for scholars who have traditionally focused on religion as a constraining force.

Religion has been at the very centre of anthropology's 130-year history. Yet, until recently, anthropology did not concern itself with studying the ways individuals value, judge, act, and transform their worlds. Its primary interest was in the ways religion functions within society. Religion was always 'about' something else, standing in for a 'truer' level of social reality. Generally speaking, in the dominant anthropological approaches – whether materialist or ideational – individuals are passive recipients of, or vehicles for, social, psychological, or materialist structures in the guise of religion. In the 1870s, Edward Burnett Tylor's interest in cultural evolution led him to argue that religion evolved from early humans' efforts to make sense of death, illness, and dreaming; he surmised that the 'function' of religion is to assuage intellectual curiosity and existential angst. Durkheim saw religion as the expression of the collective consciousness, a force with the necessary moral authority and coerciveness to ensure social cohesion. Structuralists have used religious symbols to explain the structure of the human mind, and structural functionalists are interested in religion's capacity to maintain social cohesiveness. And typically, in the hands of Marxist anthropology, religion becomes a form of ideological fancy, tied to and reflecting the (presumed to be more foundational) 'means of production.' In these traditional approaches to the study of religion, the anthropologist stands above and beyond the native, as an objective, dispassionate purveyor of truth; the privileged voice of science silences the perceptions, affections, critiques, and values of the people studied.

Beginning in the 1970s, the scientific model upon which anthropology (and the anthropological study of religion) had been based, came under sustained attack. Its comparative cross-cultural methodology, cause-and-effect explanations, and claims to objectivity were challenged. The most damning critique centred on the construction of the exotic in its representation of others. Anthropology was born of the colonialist, imperialist imagination, and its creation of the Other as a mute, exoticized, and essentialized caricature, served to dichotomize humanity into 'us/them' contrasts, and to justify the colonialist enterprise that nourished it. Talal Asad (1973) has called the anthropological project a form of Western colonialism; James Clifford (1986) contends that ethnography is more about invention than representation; and Edward Said has described anthropology's representation of others as 'neither science, nor knowledge, nor understanding; it is a statement of power and a claim for relatively absolute authority' (1985: 19).

Whether or not we can ever truly escape from representing other peoples and cultures in essentialized, stereotyped ways is a matter of debate. But most would agree the challenge is worth the effort. The gradual wearing away of the foundations of the positivist approach have opened a clearing ground in which new approaches are taking root, approaches that focus on an interpretative, experiential model of religion, and concern themselves with the way people value, judge, create, and make sense of their world.

Van Maanen described ethnography as 'the peculiar practice of representing the social reality of others through the analysis of one's own experience in the world of these others' (1988: ix). His definition points to a way out of the 'representational impasse' in its recognition that the subjectivities of others should be our primary concern, and that our representations of others are inescapably shaped by our own views and experiences of the world. The shift away from *explaining* religion to trying to *understand* it as an experiential phenomenon has precedents in the German sociological tradition of Max Weber. Weber's methodology, *Verstehen*, stresses the important role that meaning plays in sociological analysis, and recognizes the need for empathetic understanding in order to get some sense of how others subjectively interpret their own behaviour. In more contemporary language, Caroline W. Bynum, in her justly praised work on medieval Christian female asceticism, writes: 'If symbols are in fact multivocal, condensing and lived, we will understand them only when we look with as well as over and beyond the participants who use them, feeling as well as knowing their dramas in their own context' (1994: 51).

James Clifford suggests a dialogical approach that centres on the relationships between (and constituting) self and other (1989: 562). Michael Jackson's 'radical empiricism' invites anthropologists to 'make ourselves experimental subjects and treat our experiences as primary data' (1989: 4). In like manner, the 'ethno-hermeneutic' approach of Armin Geertz (1994) draws attention to theories and models proposed by both scholars and native thinkers, and is concerned with the meanings and relevance of these models to the people studied. June O'Connor, the feminist anthropologist of religion, splendidly captures the ethno-hermeneutic ideal in her description of the anthropological project as 'an effort to expand our horizons to see what others see, to expand our affections to feel something of what they feel, and to expand our valuations to empathize with what they value – long enough at least to understand these horizons, affections, and valuations in terms that our research partners (the subjects of our research) themselves would recognize' (1994: 9).

I consider these dialogical models to be the most sensible and honest approaches to the study of religious phenomena – that is, to the exploration of the way people conceive, value, and transform their worlds. The dialogical approach focuses on the experiential dimensions of religion and the participatory nature of anthropological inquiry. It neither elevates representation to truth status nor strives to forsake it altogether (for an example of this approach, see Tyler, 1978, 1987). Instead, it recognizes that representations of cultural others are situated and partial interpretations emerging from a dialogue between insider and outsider perspectives.

I bring a Western anthropological and feminist perspective to this dialogue with Jain ascetic women, with the recognition that my interests in gender, ethics, and nonviolence inform my queries and, inescapably, shape my interpretations. Extracting or banishing the outsider/ethnographer from the representation of others – whether with the romantic goal of letting the voices of others speak or through the pose of scientific detachment is a genre of fiction, a pretence and a deceit. The ethnographer is, of course, ever-present and omnipresent. And surely it is far better to make this presence explicit and recognize the epistemological limitations it brings than to create an authenticity that is feigned.

This is a focused study on a little-known sect within a comparatively understudied religious tradition. It is essentially an account of Jain ascetic women of the Terapanthi sect, and their uniqueness. It is also an effort to understand – in theoretical terms how the Jain discourse of asceticism creates its own power relations and gender asymmetries. Colleagues have drawn my attention to parallels that exist between the religious experiences of Jain ascetic women and those of other traditions (e.g., in such works as Bynum on medieval Christian asceticism, Grimshaw on Buddhism, Menelely as well as Metcalf on Islam, and Narayan on Hindu narrative, among others). The comparative literature reveals striking but complex resemblances that warrant investigation. However, such an undertaking has largely been beyond the scope of this book, and I draw upon this literature in a very limited way.

This study is first and foremost an account of the ways in which Jain religious ideals relate to the lives of the women who profess them. I attempt to accurately, and with empathy, represent the Jain moral universe from the perspective of the female renouncers with whom I lived. It attempts to elucidate how Jain women of the Terapanthi sect create their own ascetic subjectivities and competing discourses, and how they construct and understand themselves as symbols of renunciation.

Symbols of Renunciation: Women and the Ascetic Ideal

The late Jain scholar Kendall Folkert described Jain studies as 'bedeviled by the perceived split between the *sadhus* and the community' (1993: 172), in recognition of the fact that, in reality, it is interaction and interdependence between the laity and *sadhus* that characterize the Jain community. His study suggests that what is paramount is an understanding of why this split is 'perceived' to exist and why it is vehemently maintained and defended, in the face of its 'real' (i.e., day-to-day) transgression. From the perspective of Jains themselves, the split reflects the ontological separation of *jiv* and *ajiv* at the centre of their worldview.

I explore how the 'split' is used rhetorically in the construction of the Jain moral universe, and how the ascetic embodies this 'split.' Throughout this study, I use the word 'rhetorical' to describe the way in which the ideological split between the worldly (*laukik*) and the transcendent (*lokottar*) realms is used persuasively in the construction of Jain reality. It is only through persuasive or 'rhetorical' means that the *laukik* and *lokottar* are constructed and maintained as separate, since daily life is characterized by their interdependence. As a means of persuasion, rhetorical techniques are not meant to be challenged or validated. Instead, the context in which they are used supplies its own answer through suggestion. In particular, I look at how this embodied subjectivity is structured and experienced, from the perspective of women. Throughout, I attempt to consider the interaction between abstract ideals and empirical realities, without privileging either. Jain ascetics embody the cultural ideals of world renunciation and understand themselves as such. And it is on this ideological level that they find personal and *social* legitimacy. Therefore, this is necessarily a study of both ideology and practice, and the dynamic dialectic between them.

Renunciation constitutes a breach between the *laukik* (worldly) and the *lokottar* (spiritual). The ascetic is the great divider, demarcating the separate realms, and the exalted symbol of transcendence. Jain renunciation does not act as a social feedback system whereby ascetic values infuse and legitimate worldly life, as is the case with Hindu asceticism, according to Louis Dumont (1960; 1980).[6] Rather than a temporary suspension of social and normative structures, Jain renunciation is a state of permanent 'outsiderhood' or fixed 'liminality.' Its referents are society's norms and values; but rather than a temporary inversion of them, renunciation seeks to unmask them as illusory, once and for all. The ideological rupture to society's norms and values is permanent, and it is the ascetic who is the agent.

I set out to examine how women create ascetic subjectivities and how they construct and understand themselves as symbols of renunciation. Josephine Reynell's (1985a) rigorous study on lay Jain women in Jaipur explored the relationship between women and religion in Jainism. It prompted me to look at this relationship among the nuns, who, as renunciants, epitomize the tradition's highest ideal. I was interested in looking at the ways in which Jain social and religious ideals are embodied in the role of the female ascetic, and in examining how religion serves as both a creative and conservative force in women's lives.

Reynell's work outlines the close affinities that exist between Jain religious beliefs and economic practices where family prestige depends on the sexual honour of its women, and where the control of female sexuality is central to the control of wealth. It demonstrates that religious activity is the primary means whereby women publicly demonstrate their sexual purity. In Jainsim, lay female spirituality is an essential aspect of the pan Indian female ideal of *stridharma* (woman's duty), whereby a woman's primary purpose is to dedicate herself to the service of others, first as daughter, then as wife and mother. I set out to explore the lives of the female ascetics who renounce the world for their own spiritual advancement and who, therefore, represent a challenge to the dominant female ideology. Clementin-Ojha notes that female asceticism in Hinduism is outside the orthodox feminine norm. She writes,

> From the orthodox point of view as it is outlined in the vast corpus of texts of dharma, known collectively as the Dharma Sastras, there is no possible existence for a woman outside of marriage. The practice of world renunciation is a masculine pattern of life ... Marriage and married life are thus viewed as a road to salvation, they are *sadhana*, a method of spiritual achievement. (1988: 35)

Since female asceticism has been an institutionalized feature of Jainism since the time of Mahavira, it cannot be considered 'outside the norm' as female asceticism is in Hinduism. I assumed, however, that the ideas and understandings of what constitute a meaningful life to be profoundly different for lay and ascetic women. Reynell describes the disjuncture between lay and ascetic female religiosity thus:

> Whilst women's fasts and religious activities are seen by the community as an extension of their duties within the domestic sphere, and whilst the women themselves engage in religious activities in the belief that they are furthering their family's fortunes, they also see religion as something which they do for their own pleasure, as a vocation consuming their interest and creative energies. It brings with it far more self esteem and prestige from their peers and the community than the women gain from their domestic work. Taken to its extreme, this culminates in nunhood. At this point we reach an aspect of Jainism which has vital repercussions for women. (1985: 242)

I was interested in exploring the lives of female ascetics and the relationship between lay and ascetic women, who, I believed, embodied conflicting cultural ideals. The Terapanthi Jain ascetic order offers an interesting opportunity through which to explore the relationship between religion and gender: it has the largest order of female ascetics of any Jain sect, and, consistent with Jain orders in general, female ascetics greatly outnumber the monks.[7] Furthermore, its insistence on *self* realization as the sine qua non of ascetic life seemed to offer a direct challenge to the pan-Indian cultural female ideal of *stridharma*.

The Terapanthi are a non-idolatrous branch within the Svetambar Jain tradition, emerging as a distinct sect in the eighteenth century. A fuller discussion of Terapanthi social organization is presented in chapter 3.

My fieldwork among the Terapanthi ascetics of Rajasthan, however, challenged some of my early assumptions. I learned that, in practice, the differences between lay and ascetic women are less stark than their different orientations (worldly/spiritual) might suggest. In spite of renouncing the world by becoming renunciants, ascetic women, like lay women, are 'perceived as intimately connected to both the physical material world and the spiritual world and ... in a sense they mediate between the two' (Reynell, 1985a: 241). The popular story of the renowned female ascetic Candanvala illustrates this nicely. Believed to be one of the first nuns ordained by Mahavir, she remains an enduring role model for women aspiring to the ascetic path. I paraphrase Reynell's account of her life story:

Candanvala was a very religious princess who was taken by a merchant's family and made to work as a maidservant, but the merchant's wife was jealous of her beauty. When her husband left on business, she shaved off Candanvala's hair, bound her in chains and left her without food or water. When the husband returned he was shocked to see her in this state. He offered her some food, but she refused to eat until she first gave alms to an ascetic. She sat on the threshold of the house, with one foot inside and one foot outside, repeating the namaskar mantra as she sorted through the black lentils, which were the only food that was available. Mahavir then appeared. He had just completed a fast of five months and twenty-five days and vowed not to break the fast until certain conditions were met. He specified that 'the donor should be a royal woman yet working as a maidservant, she should be cleaning grains at the threshold of the house with one foot inside the house and one foot outside. Her hair should be shaved, she should just have undergone a three-day fast, she should be unmarried, learning the *namaskar mantra* by heart, and weeping.' Candanvala fulfilled all these conditions save that she was not weeping, so Mahavir passed her by. This upset her so greatly that she began to weep, at which point Mahavir returned to break his fast ... She then renounced the world and became Mahavir's chief disciple, leading an order of 36,000 nuns. On death, she achieved moks. (Reynell, 1985a: 240)

Like Candanvala, with one foot in and one foot out of the house, ascetic women are perceived by the community as 'liminal' beings. Even in the Terapanthi order, with its insistence on a rigid demarcation between the *laukik* and the *lokottar*, female ascetics continue to be seen (in part) as extensions of the social sphere, by both lay and ascetic society; they are considered less able to completely break with the *laukik*. The powerful symbols and rhetorical tools of the *lokottar* – namely, nonviolence, nonpossession, celibacy, independence, detachment, etc – are less available to ascetic women than to their male counterparts.

The gendered universe from which women 'opt out' is implicated in their relationship to the ascetic ideal and shapes the way in which they come to understand themselves as symbols of purity and detachment. This book is a story of how women use the dominant symbols of renunciation in the creation of themselves as ascetics and what makes their ascetic lives meaningful to them.

Fieldsite

From December 1995 to January 1997 I lived in the ancient town of Ladnun in the Nagaur district of Rajasthan, India. Once an important trading town along the caravan routes of the Thar desert, today it is a small, quiet market town with a population of under 40,000. Digambar, Murtipujakas, and Terapanthi Jains comprise roughly a third of Ladnun's population, and Hindu and Muslim communities represent another third each (Goonasekera, 1986). For Terapanthis, Ladnun has special significance because it is the birthplace (in 1914) of Ganadhipati 'Guru Dev' Tulsi. The Terapanthi Jains are distinct from other Jain sects in their allegiance to one leader, or *acharya*. This has led to a far greater centralization of control than is common among Jain ascetic orders. In addition, it has led to the unique development of a devotional cult around the leader, which bears more resemblance to the 'god-man' traditions of Hinduism than anything found elsewhere in Jainism (see

24   The Ethics of Renunciation

Babb, 1991; Fuller, 1992). The Terapanthi Jains are also distinct from other sects in their conservative, scripture-based interpretation of Jain ethics – an interpretation that many non-Terapanthi Jains consider to be overly rigid.

After Guru Dev Tulsi's accession to acharyship in 1936, the small town of Ladnun became an important spiritual base for the order. In 1948, on the recommendation of Guru Dev, the *Parmarthik Shikshan Sanstha* (PSS) was established in Ladnun. It is an institute designed primarily to provide training for young women who aspire to become nuns[8] (Shântâ, 1985).

In the early decades after Independence, a wealthy devotee donated sixty acres of land to the Terapanth Mahasabha (national lay organization) for the purpose of establishing a Jain learning centre. This had long been a dream of Guru Dev, and in 1970, under his spiritual guidance, the Jain Vishva Bharati (JVB) was established. It presently includes a learning institute, and the JVBI (Jain Vishva Bharat Institute) – 'the first ever Jain university'[9] – which offers degree programs in Non-Violence and Anuvrat, Jainology, Prakrit Language, Preksha Meditation, and, since 1996, Social Work. The JVB also has a small library, an ayurvedic clinic, a meditation centre, a video centre, and a publishing house. However, the dynamism and raison d'être behind the JVB comes largely from the ascetic community's presence there, and the ascetics (especially the *samanis*) form a good proportion of the student population at the Institute. At the centre of the JVB campus is the *munis'* residence and a large open-air assembly hall that extends from it. To the south, and connected by a long stretch of sand, is the *samanis'* residence. The *samans'* tiny quarters, attached to a building for lay workers, are to the east of the *munis'* residence. The *sadhvis'* residences, like the PSS, are outside the JVB grounds.

In 1996, Guru Dev was too fragile to make his *vihar* (pilgrimage) and therefore spent the entire year in Ladnun with approximately 200 ascetic disciples. Given the large number of ascetics and the constant flow of pilgrims, the JVB was, for all intents and purposes, transformed into a quasi-'monastery,' and I refer to it as such throughout this book.* At the start of 1997, after the Maryada Mahotsva (annual 'Festival of Restraint' in which all Terapanthi ascetics take part), Guru Dev and his *raj*[10] travelled to Gangashar, where on June 23 of that year, he died.

---

*The Terapanthis are opposed to ascetics living in dwellings built especially for them, and therefore it is unlikely they would define it this way.

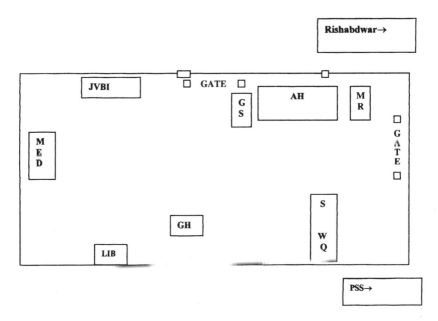

Sketch of Jain Vishva Bharati grounds
GH = guest house; **MED** = meditation centre; **JVBI** = Jain Vishva Bharati Institute; **GS** = Gautam Shalla. Samani's residence; **S** = Saman's room; **AH** = Assembly Hall; **MR** = monks' residence; **LIB** = Library; **WQ** = Workers' Quarters; **RISHAB-DWAR** = nuns' residence in the town of Ladnun; **PSS** = Parmarthik Shikshan Sanstha, training school for nuns in Ladnun

Organization of This Book

The book is divided into three sections. Part One, 'The Ethics of Renunciation' (comprising this chapter and the next), provides a general introduction to the theoretical interests that frame the study, as well as an overview of Terapanthi Jain ethics. Part Two, 'The Rituals of Separation' (chapters 3, 4, and 5), looks at the ascetics' conceptual universe, which is largely concerned with separating and maintaining boundaries between *laukik* (social or worldly) and *lokottar* (transcendent) realms. In Part Three, 'Being of the World' (chapters 5, 6, and 7), I look at how the *laukik* and *lokottar* realms are, in many important ways, inseparable, and how the ascetics negotiate and reconcile the worldly in their midst. After an examination of the ways in which the *laukik* and *lokottar* are symbolically constructed and separated in Jain religious life, I consider why women remain, to a considerable degree, a link between the two.

My interest in conducting fieldwork among the Terapanthi Jains was to explore the ascetic ideal from the domain of the women who profess it – namely from that of the *sadhvis, samanis, mumukshus,* and *upasikas.* Out of a total of 81 *samanis,* approximately[11] half were present in Ladnun during the year I was there.

This book, as well as my most enduring friendships, grew out of interactions with this group. Throughout, I explore similarities and differences between our different world experiences on the premise that the possibility for understanding arises from within one's own experiences.

Following anthropologist Michael Jackson, I define the research field as one of interactions and intersubjectivity, and treat my work as a product of my participatory experience with the Terapanthi community, with whom I lived and studied. I have done my best to portray a view of the Jain tradition that is faithful to the nuns who were my teachers and from whom I have learned so much.

2

Ethics and the Ascetic Ideal

I remember the afternoon at my elementary school when the priest coolly informed our class that animals do not go to heaven. Our anxious, hopeful faces had not deterred him from bringing us his enlightenment. I can hear his voice echoing in the bewildered silence of the room: 'They don't have souls,' he explained. My early exposure to Jain ethics left me with the hope that maybe the priest at my school had made a mistake. Today, I would say that this was my first real experience of 'decentration' – the process of having one's viewpoint shaken up, and of coming face to face with the relativity of one's own comfortable sense of reality (see Corin, 2001). Many years later, among the Jain ascetic women of Rajasthan, I would encounter this feeling repeatedly. Jainism can be difficult to one steeped in Judaeo-Christian lore, and trying to make sense of each other's ethical worldviews became our indefatigable, daily challenge. The discussion that follows reflects this challenge; rather than a compendium of Jain ethical beliefs and practices, it is a conversation between and about different ways of being in the world.

According to Jainism, all living beings have consciousness and a soul. Respecting all life forms, and not causing them any harm, is the golden (and only) road to salvation. Although an abiding interest in Jain ethics underpinned my desire to pursue research among the community, it was not a formal or explicit part of my original research goals. I considered it a personal curiosity, and not connected with my academic interest in gender and female religiosity. But the women of the Terapanthi order were not especially interested in talking gender, nor were they particularly concerned about their relatively subordinate position vis-à-vis the monks in the order. Ironically, what they were keen to talk about was ethics, and it was not until I had lived among them for several months that I came to learn how closely intertwined the issues of gender and ethics are in Jain cosmology. As will become obvious throughout the book, ethics are understood, negotiated, and constituted in relation to the gendered spaces individuals occupy.

The Jain tradition is often encapsulated in the aphorism '*ahimsa paramo dharma*' ('nonviolence is the highest form of religious conduct'). Its ethical commitment to nonviolence is integral to its unique cosmology, which emphasizes the common fate of all living beings. In Padmanabh Jaini's words:

> This awareness of the basic worth of all beings, and of one's kinship with them, generates a feeling of great compassion (*anukampa*) for others. Whereas the compassion felt by an ordinary man is tinged with pity or with attachment to its object, anukampa is free of such negative aspects; it develops purely from wisdom, from seeing the substance (dravya) that underlies visible modes, and it fills the individual with an unselfish desire to help other souls towards moksa. If this urge to bring all tormented beings out of samsara is particularly strong and is cultivated, it may generate those auspicious karmas that later confer the status of Tirthankara upon certain omniscients. When present to a more moderate degree, anukampa brings an end to exploitative and destructive behaviour, for even the lowest animal is now seen as intrinsically worthwhile and thus inviolable. (Jaini, 1990: 150)

Ethics is the gateway into a culture's worldview, in that our morals reveal our notions of what it is to be truly human and why humans are worthy of respect. The philosopher Charles Taylor argues that a community's ethics represents the best mode of access to its reality. 'Our moral reactions,' he writes, 'involve claims, implicit and explicit, about the nature and status of human beings' (1989: 5). In Jainism, the highest cultural ideals revolve around nonviolence, nonpossession, and nonattachment, and are embodied in the ascetics (see Babb, 1996, for a discussion of the veneration of ascetics). Ascetics acquire tremendous respect because they have renounced the world to pursue ethical ideals totally. Yet, all humans have the power to partake of this ideal, and herein lies our potential for greatness.

A central focus of all cultural life is to establish what it is to be properly human; the attempt to establish human uniqueness in contradistinction to the 'otherness' of the environment appears to be fundamental to self-definition. I eventually came to understand the Jain ideal of asceticism in these terms – that is, as the classification of a unique place for humanity in the universe. I had originally considered Jainism to be a profoundly non-anthropocentric, non-speciesist, even biocentric, worldview, in which all living beings are considered as onto-logically *moral* equivalents. I understood the Jain ethic of nonviolence to be an expression of its altruism for all living beings, and its desire to make the world a better place. I had got it only partially right.

Although Jain teachings are deeply compassionate, they are not pri-marily sociocentric. By 'sociocentric,' I mean an ethic that is concerned principally with social morality, social mobility, and fulfilment of one's social obligations – as is, for instance, the *Dharmasastras* (Jhingran, 1989: 73). The sociocentric alternative to the ascetic ethic finds expression in much of Indian thought. Saral Jhingran elaborates:

> The term *dharma* is derived from the root *dhr* meaning to sustain or sup-port; that is, *dharma* is what sustains or supports the society. This definition of *dharma* has given a slight bias to the entire Hindu thought in favour of social stability. The main emphasis of Hindu Law-givers has been on those duties of the individual which directly contribute to the stability and har-monious preservation of the social order. (1989: 74)

Jain compassion is not directed so much at the suffering *in* social life, but at the suffering *of* social life; it arises from observing worldly life itself. The message of the *Tirthankaras* is that all human beings are capa-ble of conquering the bondage of physical existence and achieving freedom from the cycle of rebirth (Folkert, 1987). *Ahimsa*, as Jains for-mulate it, is not concerned with social roles and obligations, and its teachings are not designed to remedy social ills so much as escape them. It reveals a perception of the world as inherently corrupt and in need of transcendence, and it leads to renunciation and the desire to help indi-viduals out of *samsara*, not to active social involvement. Writing on Jain cosmology, Dundas states:

> The world is characterized by ignorance, suffering and pain caused by action (AS 1.1.2.1). True understanding embodies itself in non-violence through an awareness that all living creatures, including oneself, do not wish to suffer in any way (SKS 2.11.9-10). As a broad ethical principle, this is fairly unexceptional and has to be fitted into a further series of concep-tions: action, whether done, caused or condoned by oneself, brings about rebirth (AS 1.1), and the world is in a state of suffering caused by actions of ignorant people (AS 1.2.1) who do not know that they are surrounded by

life-forms which exist in earth, water, air and fire, a true understanding of which can be gained from the teaching of Mahavira. (1992: 36–7)

Every soul is entrapped in worldly bondage, and will one day have to break those bonds if liberation is to be attained. Compassion means recognizing that all living beings are essentially similar – that all deserve respect and that none should be injured. It means noninterference in another's spiritual journey. Rather than helping others in worldly ways, which involves violence, ascetics teach primarily by example; they represent a way out of *samsar.* In Jainism, therefore, *ahimsa* is not a 'this worldly' ethic of active support, but an ethic of respect and nondisruption in the spiritual realm and noninvolvement in the world of passion and violence. Holmstrom summarizes:

> As *individuality* is ultimately a process of *separation,* so the dominant vow of *ahimsa,* separation from the social and the violence which everyday life involves, is also concomitant with the pursuit of individual enlightenment. The aim of compassion (*daya*) which informs *ahimsa* is not to ensure that beings live rather than die *per se,* but the task of purifying one's own soul from the contamination caused by violence, and to persuade others to do likewise; *ahimsa* is not, strictly, to do with life or death, but about freeing the soul from passions. (1988: 37; italics in original)

Likewise, Jaini explains how *himsa* (violence) is understood in Jainism as an obstacle to self-realization.

> *Himsa* has ordinarily been understood in India as harm done to others; for Jainas, however, it refers primarily to injuring oneself – to behaviour which inhibits the soul's ability to attain *moksa.* Thus the killing of animals, for example, is reprehensible not only for the suffering produced in the victims, but even more so because it involves intense passions on the part of the killer, passions which bind him more firmly in the grip of *samsara.* (Jaini, 1990: 167)

We see that in Jainism, nonviolence is intimately connected with nonaction. James Laidlaw in his book *Riches and Renunciation* insightfully describes *ahimsa* as an 'ethic of quarantine' (1995: 159). He argues that Jains' elaborate practices of nonviolence are about neither minimizing death nor saving life, but about keeping life 'at bay.' They essentially amount to an attempt at the 'avoidance of life.' Complete detachment (*vairagya*), from which *ahimsa* is but one part, is a key virtue or attitude that pervades and determines the entire morality of the philosophies of liberation (i.e., Jainism, Buddhism, Samkhya-Yoga). In a liberation-centric morality, philanthropic or humanitarian deeds are not considered to be relevant to the quest for liberation, even if they should be pursued by the laity as 'social duty.'

The Terapanthi Jains take this to its logical end, and the distinction they make between religion and social duty is sharper than within any other Jain community. They argue that the building of hospitals or animal shelters – activities which are typical for most Jain communities – must be seen as a form of *social* and not *religious* activity. If one is living 'in society,' such acts may be necessary, but they do not lead to good karma or the removal of bad karma; that is, they do not lead to any *spiritual* gains. Most Terapanthi ascetics are very careful not to praise or encourage these efforts for fear that they may be misinterpreted as spiritual acts, which their doctrines insist they are not. They continuously instruct the laity on the differences between *adhyatmik dharm*, which refers to those activities that benefit one's soul along the path to liberation, and *laukik dharm*, which comprises all dimensions of *social duty*. Jhingran, in her book *Aspects of Hindu Morality*, claims that the elevation of 'soul duty' over that of social duty is shared by all liberation-centric philosophies.

> The tradition of liberation or *nivrtti-marga* is, of course, primarily concerned with man's quest of liberation (*moksa*). Man is constantly exhorted to seek his individual liberation and not worry about his other socio-moral obligations. It is even asserted that a man need not wait to take up the quest of liberation till he has reached the last stage of renunciation (*samnyasa-asrama*); instead he can take up renunciation whenever the desire for liberation is aroused in his heart.[1] In contrast, the philosophy and worldview associated with the *pravrtti-marga* of Vedas and Dharamasastras, is socio-centric and stresses than a man must repay all his debts and fulfil all his obligations before commencing the quest for his salvation. The tradition of liberation is also world-and-life-negating, in that it conceives liberation as a state of transcendent being and consciousness, totally unrelated to this world and its values which are viewed as hindrances in a man's search for liberation. This is again in sharp contrast to the world-and-life-affirming ethos of the earlier or Vedic tradition, with its three values, [Kama = desire; Artha = wealth; Dharma = righteousness/duty] pertaining to the life-in-the-world. (1989: 115)

Ahimsa is primarily an ethic of noninterference and a method of disconnecting or separating oneself from the violence of everyday life.[2] *Ahimsa* is the central practice in the quest for liberation because it defines – negatively – a state of purity and detachment within a violent, passionate world. And in so doing it establishes *difference*. *Ahimsa* makes the human incarnation unique among all living beings by making it moral.

Egalitarianism with Hierarchy

The Jain construction of the moral self does not depend upon the sequestering of humanity from nature, nor upon the establishment of human superiority. This makes it radically distinct from the Judaeo-Christian and secular Western philosophical traditions, in which human dignity resides in that which *distinguishes* us from the nonhuman environment, in particular, from animals. Animals have always served as a contrast to illuminate human nature, and human worth, in Western ethics, is located in those areas that we believe we have a monopoly on – for example, a soul, rationality, language, morality, and so forth. Establishing uniqueness is not merely a philosophical concern – to be considered deserving of moral worth is dependent upon its existence.[3] The anthropologist Tim Ingold, in an essay entitled 'Humanity and Animality,' writes:

> For those of us reared in the tradition of Western thought, 'human' and 'animal' are terms rich in association, fraught with ambiguity, and heavily laden with both intellectual and emotional bias. From classical times to the present day, animals have figured centrally in the Western construction of 'man' – and we might add of Western man's image of woman. Every generation has recreated its own view of animality as a deficiency in everything that we humans are uniquely supposed to have, including language, reason, intellect and moral conscience. (1994: 14)

And, he continues:

> By and large, philosophers have sought to discover the essence of humanity in men's heads rather than in their tails (or lack thereof). But in seeking this essence, they did not ask: 'What makes human animals of a particular kind?' Instead they turned the question around, asking: 'What makes humans different in kind from other animals?' This inversion completely alters the terms of the inquiry. For once the question is posed in the latter

form; humanity no longer appears as a species of animality, or as one small province of the animal kingdom. It refers rather to the principle that, infused into the animal frame, lifts its possessors onto an altogether higher level of existence than that of the 'mere animal.' [Humanity] becomes the state or condition of being human, one radically opposed to the condition of animality. (1994: 19)

In sharp contrast to the dominant religious and secular traditions of Western thought, human value in Jainism is not contingent upon that which nonhumans lack. Human dignity and moral consideration are not rooted in a nature–culture distinction: Jainism does not dichotomize the universe in this manner since animals are no more 'matter' than are humans; both represent different formulations or 'modes' (*paryaya*) of spirit and matter. And although Jains treat the human incarnation as a privileged and exalted one, they don't believe that humans possess anything uniquely or exclusively which should entitle them to their superior status. There exist five types of living beings in the Jain universe, each type having either one, two, three, four, or five senses. These beings are arranged according to the following schema:[4]

Number and Type of Senses	Type of Beings
1. One-sensed beings called '*nigodas*' (touch)	earth-, water-, fire-, air- and plant-bodied.
2. Two-sensed beings (touch and taste)	worms, leeches, molluscs (oysters, mussels, snails etc.)
3. Three-sensed beings (touch, taste, smell)	small 'minibeasts' such as ants, fleas, plant-lice, cotton-seed insects, termites, centipedes.
4. Four-sensed beings (touch, taste, smell, sight)	some 'minibeasts' such as wasps, flies, gnats, mosquitoes, butterflies, moths, scorpions, etc.
5. Five-sensed beings (touch, taste, smell, sight, hearing)	larger animals such as fish, birds, and quadrupeds, humans, infernals, and gods

Source: *Tattvartha Sutra* (1994: 45)

The greater the number of senses, the greater the self-awareness and, therefore, the greater the ability to understand worldly existence as a state of bondage in need of escape. But an increase in the number of senses does not mean greater moral worth. Consciousness is the inalienable characteristic of every *jiva*, however undeveloped it may be. It is present even in the *nigodas* (the least-developed life form), and through its progressive development, it too may culminate in the supreme state of the soul, namely omniscience. Lawrence Babb provides an interesting discussion of Jainism's soteriological taxonomy, which he claims 'may be seen as a conceptual scaffolding for the Jain vision of creaturely bondage and the path to liberation' (1996: 44). Jains believe that the soul passes through an infinite number of states from the lowest to the highest state of spiritual development. These states have been classified into fourteen stages called *gunasthanas*, each of which is necessary to pass through to attain liberation (I have illustrated this in Appendix 1).

It is the possession of a soul, and not the stage of development or number of senses a being possesses that entitles one to a life of respect. (It should be noted that respecting other forms of life does not entail active efforts to befriend them; it means, above all else, not harming them, and not interfering in their spiritual path.) In Jainism, moral consideration does not hinge upon that which the human incarnation possesses alone, but on that which it shares with all other beings. In Jainism, human supremacy and distinction from the nonhuman environment are a matter of degree, not of kind; and importantly, it is established through ethical behaviour.

If, in fact, differences between all living beings do not reside in any essential quality, but instead lie in the degree of moral perfection – *demonstrable* only through behaviour – then ethical practice (of which asceticism is its highest expression) becomes a compelling and potent source of selfhood. It is my contention that ethics are a resource, and represent the primary method through which Jains define and maintain the human domain. *Ahimsa* becomes an active way to define human beings at the centre of a universe full of similar souls. Human worth is established through moral behaviour and not through any claim to being a privileged possessor of an essential characteristic. Voluntary restraint and ardent *ahimsa*, in a world characterized by meaningless activity and violence, establish the uniqueness of the human incarnation.

The foundation for the development of a moral self includes a classification of the world and a special status for human beings in it. No ontology considers human beings to be the same as other creatures. When Jains claim that all living beings are equal, they are referring to their belief that all living beings are equally endowed with souls, and that their spiritual journeys are of equal value to all others. Nevertheless, they consider human beings to be the finest of all possible incarnations. It is the human form, above all else, that is the most coveted because it is only from this incarnation that liberation can be attained, and virtually only in human life that, as a result of *samyak darshan* (correct view of reality), one can chart the course of one's future. Lawrence Babb explains:

> Almost everything he says [Muni Arunvijay, in a book he wrote on the soul's journey] converges on one fundamental assertion, namely that one's birth in a human body should not be wasted. This reflects the ascetics' view of things, a view that exists as a perpetual rebuke to the more comfortable lay view that routine piety is enough. It is possible, he says, for human births to be repeated; in theory it is possible to have seven or eight in a row. But this is very difficult and requires an immense amount of merit. Human birth is 'rare' (*durlabh*) and in this vast cosmos very difficult to obtain. Sin is so easy, and the sins of one life can pursue you through many births. Not only will sins send you to hell, but they will result in many births in the classes of two- to four-sensed creatures after you have emerged from below. Arunvijay reflects at length on the sin of abortion, and it is significant that, in his eyes, part of the horror of abortion is that it cuts the newly incarnated soul off from the possibility of human existence. (1996: 50–1)

In Jainism, human dignity is established and maintained through *ethical practice*, and *ahimsa* is the quintessential norm of Jain ethics. In the Jain universe, plants and animals are not believed to have autonomous and opposing existences, but rather form part of the same tragic drama of bondage and liberation that humans do, albeit with fixed roles and characters. They are all considered to be moral symbols and therefore they are also judged according to the same moral standards as are human beings. All things, animate and inanimate, are part of the same narrative. Jains have no nature–culture dichotomy because there is only one 'nature,' and it is the same for all. Jainism, for instance, is replete with stories of animals being inspired by ascetics to renounce the world, and even to commit *santara* (a fasting until death), so that their earthly bondage may one day be terminated. The story of the snake Chandakausika is typical:

Once Bhagavan Mahavira was walking through the hermitage of Kanaka-

khala. When some boys saw him, they came to him running and said, 'Sir
the path through which you are going is fraught with dangers. A little
ahead there is a snake called Chandakausika. The person on whom it casts
a glance will certainly be burnt to ashes.' They advised him to take another
route and not to play havoc with life on purpose. It was the correct advice
for those who long for life. But Mahavira had renounced his craving for
keeping himself alive. He had risen above life and death and become
totally immersed in his soul, and adopted an attitude of equanimity
towards all living beings. He did not heed the warning given to him by the
boys and proceeded forward.

The snake, upon seeing Bhagavan Mahavir, became suddenly enraged. It
could not tolerate anyone encroaching upon his domain. It spread its
hood, looked at the sun and then at Mahavira, and sprayed its poison,
which spread over the aura around Mahavira's body. The entire atmosphere became poisoned, but Mahavira remained unaffected. The snake
could not believe his eyes. He was convinced that the person at whom he
looked would be immediately burnt to ashes.

Chandakausika tried again to cast a dangerously poisonous glance. He
moved nearer Bhagavan Mahavira and bit his foot, but Mahavira remained
perfectly composed. To the snake's surprise, milk, instead of blood, oozed
from the foot. Next, he coiled himself around the body of Mahavira, but
was unable to upset him. Finally the snake lost its self-confidence: its anger
disappeared. When Mahavira's meditation was over, he saw the motionless
snake sitting docilely before him. He addressed the snake thus: 'Chandakausika, be calm! You are born as a snake because you had been a victim
of anger in your previous life. Two births ago, you were an ascetic. You had
once trampled to death a frog and one of your disciples had entreated you
to do a penance for the sin but you refused to do so. Enraged by the
repeated entreaties of the disciple, you tried to strike him and, having lost
the sense of balance you crashed against a pillar and cracked your skull. In
your next life, you became the head of this hermitage where the inmates
practised spiritual discipline. Again you were prone to great anger. Once
the Prince of Svetambi came to your hermitage and began plucking fruits
and flowers. You became so enraged that you ran after him with an axe in
your hand. You slipped on the ground and fell into a ditch and were fatally
injured by your own axe. After the death there, you are reborn as a deadly
poisonous serpent. You have already suffered much due to your passionate
nature. Leave the passion of anger like your worn-out skin and be peaceful
once and for all.'

Chandakausika began to remember his past lives. All the events of his past began to float in his memory. His heart changed and the seeds of equanimity for all living beings began to sprout in him. He sat motionless and performed *santara*. (Ganadhipati Tulsi, 1995: 30)

In the Jain universe, all creatures[5] are invested with the potential to realize their true nature – which is the same nature for all. The same ethical standards apply to *all* living beings: animals should ideally be renouncing the world and performing austerities too, just as Chandanbala did (Jainism has a number of stories in which animals are 'awakened' to do just this) but most souls trapped in animal bodies are simply too deep in their karmic quagmire to realize their misguided ways.

Thus, in a world where everything is classified and appraised according to a single ascetic ideal, all living beings are subject to the same totalizing moral discourse and necessarily serve as potent moral symbols. The universe is a catalogue of moral development, from the lowliest one-sensed *nigodas* to the five-sensed human beings at the apex of worldly existence. Because each living being is a moral symbol, all serve to instruct and admonish. Indeed, the motive behind the celebrated and ancient Jain inquiries into plant and animal existence, as well as the ardent desire among contemporary Jains to make their doctrines compatible with science, is likely a belief that the world is akin to a laboratory filled with myriad examples of bonded souls (see Babb, 1996, for a discussion of 'Jain Biology'). All are moral symbols, meaningful and of inherent pedagogic value.[6] We can therefore describe Jain attitudes towards all other beings as *metonymical* – that is, they serve as moral symbols in the same narrative, representatives of the whole, each denoting different levels of moral purity.[7] In place of the dominant individualistic and reductionistic metaphysics that underlies modern industrial society – in which things are symbols of nothing other than themselves – Jains live in a cosmic order where all things are imbued with meaning as they relate to the whole.

Whereas Jains espouse a belief in a larger cosmic order in which human beings are at the apex of all embodied creatures, they have never posited an adversarial relationship with nonhumans. Their preoccupation with *ahimsa* can be seen as their strategy to counter the blurring of classificatory difference in a metonymical world. In a moral cosmic order, where all beings are potent moral symbols, what makes humans worthy of special status is not the unique possession of a soul, or reason: it is the display of moral superiority evidenced in their practices.

The whole of existence is assumed to be ordered in a hierarchical scale, moving up to the Tirthankaras, and down from them, in what is regarded as diminishing degrees of perfection to ascetics, *shravaks*, animals, plants, and single-sensed beings.[8] As stated: the differences between beings lie in their moral purity, which is established primarily through ethical practice.

The Ascetic Ideal

Jainism's metonymical and nonadversarial relationship with the environment has important implications for the ascetic ideal. In a world where everyone and everything is hierarchically arranged, and where all classification is imbued with moral evaluation, the ascetic represents the symbolic apex of the society. In the eyes of the Jain laity, the ascetic is a window through which they can glimpse their own potential, and is the giver of truths needed to attain liberation.

The popular image of the *samavasaran*, or 'universal assembly hall,' illustrates the Jain understanding of the universe and the place of human beings in it. Those of us reared in Judaeo-Christian thought often turn to the story of Genesis to understand how we inherited our own particular understanding of ourselves and of our relationship with the world around us. We discover a divinely created special status for human beings within a subservient nature. The *samavasaran* is the Jain equivalent of the Genesis story, in that it sets out the ideal orientation human beings should have with the rest of the universe.[9]

In the innermost circle of the *samavasaran* diagram of concentric circles sits the Jina, encircled first by the ascetics – both nuns and monks sitting separately with hands joined in devotion. Following behind them are the Jina's devoted lay followers, and then there are circles of adoring animals. In the air above the Jina are gods and goddesses paying homage. The *Tattvartha Sutra* states:

> [E]ach unique soul possesses the inherent knowledge and intuition which can empower it to destroy the beginningless deluded world-view tormenting it. The enlightened world-view can arise at the appropriate moment in any form of life – infernal, subhuman, human or celestial – when the painful nature of life is realized, a vision of the Jina (omniscient founders of the Jaina religion) is seen, the teachings of the Jina heard or a past life remembered. (1994: 6)

In front of the Jina, the darkness of ignorance is banished, and creatures become aware of their true nature. This 'worldview' is critical in understanding the role of the ascetic ideal in the Jain tradition. The ascetics serve as exemplars and teachers, for a world full of bewildered beings in search of the same goal of liberation. In the Jain world, ascetics are indispensable as living exemplars for those who are on the path of liberation. They serve, through their own lives, to demonstrate what the ideal life ought to be. One has the choice to push forward along the spiritual path (to see one's human body as something earned from past auspicious lives) or to abandon the path and let oneself tumble into the downward spiral of worldly 'vomit' (a preferred metaphor of the late Ganadhipati Tulsi for the mess of worldly life). One does not have the choice to not be part of this forward and backward trajectory. The whole cosmic order is hierarchically classified according to its relation with the ascetic ideal; no one and nothing is left out.

PART TWO
THE RITUALS OF SEPARATION

3
Creation through Negation: The Rite of *Bhiksha*

Defence of the *Lokottar*

It was the commotion created by *bhiksha* rounds that would wake me up during the early weeks of my stay in Ladnun. The sounds of happy activity coming from just outside my room, near the kitchen, would rise and fall as the ascetics glided in for their alms collection and then were gone. Lay devotees (*shravaks*)[1] nearby would rush forward to show their respect and would often compete among themselves to serve the ascetics. Bapu, the Hindu cook who prepared the food,* looked indifferent to the drama and appeared glad to allow the lay devotees to serve the mendicants.

One day during the second week of my stay, I was awoken as usual by voices full of cheer and urgency, entreating the *maharajas* to approach; but the sounds were more numerous and more intense than on most mornings, and the excitement more prolonged. I peered out and saw Acharyasri Mahaprajna and several *munis* slowly entering the guest-house. The crowd of followers hindered their normally quick pace. As Acharyasri stepped forward, devotees rushed in front of him to touch his feet in veneration. Others stood to the side, lining the *munis'* path and prostrating themselves as the ascetics passed. I was surprised to spot the Hindu cook Bapu among the worshippers, pulling himself up after kneeling on the sandy ground. The ordinary *sadhvis* and *munis* that daily visited his kitchen did nothing to evoke his admiration, but clearly, the power and spiritual greatness associated with the senior ascetics

---

*Virtually none of the 'support staff' – the cooks, watchmen, sweepers etc. – at the Jain Vishva Bharati were Jain.

were awe-inspiring for Jain and non-Jain alike. Given Guru Dev's and Acharyasri's positions as leaders of the order, it was not often that they personally ventured out to collect alms, as this task was typically left to the more junior members. So when they did, there was always considerable excitement among the lay community. It had its effect on the ascetic community, too, according to Samani Urmilla Prajna, who once told me that if Guru Dev and Acharyasri could go for *bhiksha*, then no *muni* or *sadhvi* should consider themselves too senior to do so.[2]

With my door ajar, I watched the crowd grow around Acharyasri, who stood patiently and spoke gently with the gathering devotees. Today the alms would be offered by one of the families staying in the guesthouse, and not directly from Bapu's kitchen. The honoured family was frantically setting their full pots and containers on the cement floor outside their room, just several doors from mine. Since the rooms in the guesthouse are without kitchens, the family must have had Bapu prepare the enormous meal at sunrise. They could now generously offer some to the dispassionate *munis*. It is a sin for a *shravak* to prepare food specifically for the mendicants; it leads to the accumulation of *paap* – or bad karma. But it is also a duty of a religious *shravak* to offer alms to the ascetics, and this act leads to the accumulation of *punya* – or good karma. Very often the ascetics will ask the householders routine and general questions about the food's preparation – for example, for whom was it prepared, how was it prepared and so forth. The householders will emphatically reply that it was prepared for themselves alone and according to the strict code governed by the vow of *ahimsa*.

The elderly and gentle Muni Dulharaji (or 'Muniji') once told me that when he and a group of *munis* were travelling with Guru Dev and Acharyasri in Gujarat several years ago, they entered a village where everything appeared prearranged for their stay. And although it is common for the villagers to be notified of the approaching ascetics, on this occasion things appeared *overly* orchestrated. The mendicants went out for *bhiksha* and quickly returned with full *patras* (alms bowls).[3] Guru Dev suspected that the delicious foods had been prepared on account of their visit to the village, so before the monks gathered to eat, he called a snap meeting with the villagers. He asked if anyone had prepared food especially for the monks. After a moment of uneasy silence, a man stood up and admitted that he had. Guru Dev then thanked the villagers for their generosity but reprimanded them for their sinful acts. He told them that because of their misconduct, the monks would now have to go without the food. So instead of taking their meal, the monks had the food disposed of in a deep sandpit.[4] Muniji was wide-eyed and serious when he recounted the story – clearly the event impressed him as much as it was intended to impress me.

However, despite such occasional instances of vigilance, householders do indeed prepare food for the ascetics and it is hardly disguised. It seems obvious that either they do not take the threat of this form of accumulated *paap* very seriously or that they believe the *punya* gained from giving will outweigh any *paap* accrued in the process. The ascetics would not be implicated in this sin because they accept what the householders tell them as the truth. So long as the roles of the generous householder and restrained ascetic are well executed, rarely is any attention focused on the events which conspire to produce the exemplary encounter. The family down the hall from my room surely knew that monks would be collecting alms at the guest house – as they do nearly every day – otherwise they would not have had such a great quantity of food prepared so early. Whether or not they knew Acharyasri would be among the monks is another matter. I decided to join the gathering.

I stood off to one side where I could see all the activity. Acharyasri and the *munis* were now just outside the door of the family's room, removing their *patras* from the white *jholi* (sling made of cloth) in which they carry them. Acharyasri is often called a 'philosopher-saint' by his followers, and he has an air that befits that description. He stands taller than average, and the straightness of his posture and thinness of his body add to his already dignified appearance. His small, light blue eyes (made smaller still by thick, wide-framed glasses), bald head, and thin face, partly covered by the *muhpatti*, give him a severe and even glacial appearance that conceals a warmth that is immediately obvious when speaking with him. His movements appear calculated, as the ideal monk's should be. Guarded bodily movements ensure that karma is inhibited. The first of the five *Mahavratas* or 'Great Vows' that an ascetic accepts upon initiation is nonviolence[5] in action, speech, and thought. An aspect of this vow, condensed in the term *samitayah* compels an ascetic to 'walk, speak, seek alms, handle objects of daily use and dispose of excreta in the correct manner'[6] (*Tattvartha Sutra*, 1994: 220). I watched as Acharyasri made sure only a small quantity of rice was placed in his bowl by the attending woman. His reluctance to take alms appeared earnest, and, standing motionless in the midst of the excited crowd, he radiated a sense of 'otherness.'

In 1977, when he was still known as 'Muni Nathmal' (before being nominated as Yuvacharya (successor) in 1979 and then as Acharya in

1994, he was given permission from Guru Dev (then Acharya Tulsi) to leave monastic life for a year of solitude and study. That year, he was free from the many obligations associated with membership in a monastic community (e.g., group duties, *vihar* [pilgrimage]) and free from contact with lay followers.[7] He devoted himself to the study of Jain scriptures in the hope of reviving the ancient Jain practice of meditation, which, over the centuries, had largely been abandoned. Muni Nathmal was convinced that the Jains had their own meditation techniques, unique from Hindu and Buddhist ones, which deserved investigation. Through his research, he revived what he calls 'Preksha Dhyana'[8] or 'Insight Meditation,' in which one learns to 'engage the mind fully in the perception of subtle, internal and innate phenomena of consciousness' (cited in Dundas, 1992: 224). Muni Nathmal's research led to major changes in the training of ascetics; for example, it made Preksha Dhyana a major part of their *sadhana* (spiritual practices). Today all Terapanthi ascetics (except the elderly) including *samanis*, *samans*, and *mumukshus* are well trained in the techniques and rationale behind Preksha Dhyana. Indeed, for many, it was their attendance at summer Preksha Meditation camps that inspired them to join the ascetic order. One *mumukshu* sister whom I came to know well was so impressed with the technique that she decided to dedicate her life to mastering it. Also, many lay followers attend these camps and have made Preksha Dhyana an important part of their spiritual lives.[9] Lay and ascetic Terapanthis have worked together to promulgate the theory and practice of Preksha Dhyana in primary schools, camps, and health centres throughout India, with varying success. It, along with the Anuvrat Movement,[10] begun in 1949, has brought the Terapanthi community out of isolation and onto centre stage among Jain communities.

Standing at the back of the gathering, I watched as the monks resisted the family's onslaught of generosity. With one hand they each held their alms bowls cautiously close to their own bodies – so as to be able to withdraw them at any second, and held their free hand high in the air before them, palms upright and fingers outstretched as in a permanent yield sign. The family continued to implore them to accept ever more, and the lay spectators likewise urged them not to take so little. But they had had their share. Agilely, they placed empty *patras* over those filled with food and secured them in the *jholi*. The family continued their appeals even though the ascetics had turned to leave.

As Acharyasri and the *munis* approached, I lowered my head and pronounced aloud the words of respect I had recently memorized: 'Matthayena Vandami' ("I bow before your greatness"). I had met Acharyasri just a week earlier, on the second day of my stay. Mostly speaking through a translator, I had explained to him, as I did to Guru Dev, my long-term interest in the Jain doctrine of *ahimsa*, and my goal to learn more about the community. He had appeared happy with my interest and gave me his blessing. He had become the formal Acharya of the Terapanthi at the Maryada Mahotsav festival in 1994, when Guru Dev 'retired' from the position, but his status was clearly subordinate to that of his predecessor. Lay followers flocked from all over India to receive *darshan* from Guru Dev because they believed he had tremendous spiritual power. Innumerable miracles are associated with him. Acharyasri, though he is acclaimed for his sharp intellect, is more of an introverted thinker than a charismatic leader like Guru Dev. And now, since the recent death of Guru Dev Tulsi in the summer of 1997, Acharyasri will be without his mentor for the first time in sixty-six years. He was initiated into the order as 'Muni Nathmal' at the age of eleven and immediately came under the direction of the then seventeen-year-old Muni Tulsiji.[11]

Acharyasri appeared surprised to find me among the adoring followers, and raised his hand as in a blessing. Perhaps he thought I had been among the onlookers throughout the event, because he quickly turned to look back in the direction of the family and it became apparent to everyone (but me) that I was being offered an honour – he was allowing me to give him *bhiksha*.

Although at first I was hesitant about what to do, the surrounding crowd were not reticent in instructing me. We all moved towards the table, where the food was laid out in pots of various sizes, and I found myself standing among a vast selection of delicacies. Within closest reach was a bowl filled with peeled and halved bananas.[12] Amid sounds of agitated impatience, as well as encouragement, coming from the gatherers, I picked up a single piece and placed it into Acharaysri's *patra*. The householders were urging me to be more generous, but Acharaysri raised his hand in the yield gesture and was shaking his head, saying *'Bas'* ('enough'). I was unsure what to do. Under the vociferous pressure of the family, I placed another piece in Acharyasri's bowl but – inauspiciously – I did so with hesitation. He then pulled the *patra* away and with the *munis* left the guesthouse. There had been no haggling – no real resisting on Acharaysri's part and no beseeching on mine. The faces in the crowd around me were full of disappointment. Perhaps I had even put Acharyasri in an awkward position. I had had an opportunity to demonstrate my spirituality – through generosity – but had failed. To perform the perfect householder role, I should have tried to give everything in sight, against which Acharyasri could have been resolutely restrained and adamantly opposed. When not much was offered, the act of renunciation could not be fulfilled.

Through the ritual of alms-giving and alms-taking, renunciation is performed daily, and the roles of ascetic and householder are reinforced, and in fact, are created through it. Laidlaw describes the interaction between householder and ascetic at the juncture of *bhiksha* as 'the relationship which stands at the centre of Jainism' (1995: 320). Given its importance, its enactment is not usually left to chance or to the vagaries of individual aptitudes. Instead, it is a ritualized, codified, and compulsory performance for religious Jains. The *Atithisamvibhoga Vrata*, one of the twelve compulsory vows for lay Jains, states that it is the duty of every householder to offer alms to the ascetics (Jaini, 1990: 217–20). [13] The scriptures are specific about *what* should be given:

> Offering alms to ascetics must be undertaken with care to follow the strict prescriptions of the scriptures. The ascetics should be offered suitable food and drink with devotion and humility befitting the custom and etiquette of the place and occasion. The SS lists food, religious equipment, medicine and shelter as necessities to be offered to ascetics. The SBT recommends food, drinks, dainties, delicacies, clothes, towels, shelter, beds and medicine as alms that can be given. The householder observing these vows is described as partially self-restrained. (*Tattvartha Sutra [TS]*, 1994: 178) [14]

They also explain *how* alms should be given:

> The worth of a charitable act is determined by the manner of giving, the nature of the alms offered, the disposition of the giver and the qualification of the recipient. (*TS*, 1994: 178)

The translator's explanation follows:

> The giver's motives and enthusiasm and the quality of the alms offered determine the worth of the act of charity. The genuinely monastic life of the recipient adds dignity to the act. The worth of the charity is enhanced if the giver gives with a sense of duty and the recipient accepts what is a bare necessity of monastic life. (*TS*, 1994: 183)

Jain children grow up knowing the minute details of *bhiksha* protocol. They learn through observation – by watching family members interact with mendicants – and through instruction – most commonly through storytelling. The story of 'Sangam and the Muni' is one of the most popular tales told by both householders and ascetics, and it depicts their ideal encounter:

> There was once a very poor boy by the name of Sangam who lived in a small village. He faced many hardships in his childhood because of his family's lack of money. One day he watched a child eating *kheer* [a sweet mixture of rice, sugar, and milk] and longed for it himself. He returned home to his mother weeping, 'I want to eat *kheer*,' he demanded. The mother said, 'Dear son, how can I afford it? I am hardly able to get us enough food for our meals.' But Sangam wanted *kheer* so much he couldn't stop crying. The neighbours heard and asked, 'Why is your son crying so loudly?' His mother explained to them that he wanted *kheer* but that she could not afford it. The kind lady living next door was very fond of Sangam so she gave the mother milk, sugar, and rice to make the dish. When the mother was preparing *kheer* Sangam stopped crying and came to watch. She served it in a big dish and told him he could eat as much as he liked. Then she left for a while to fetch some water. But just as Sangam was about to start eating, he saw a monk passing by. Overcoming his own hunger and desire, he decided to offer the *kheer* to the *muni* as *bhiksha*. Sangam became filled with joy at the idea. He ran outside and asked the monk to come to his house and receive alms. When the *muni* saw his offering, he asked, 'Did you ask your mother if you can give this?'
>
> Sangam replied, 'It was made for me; I have no need to ask my mother. Please accept my *kheer* in your bowl.' The monk raised his alms bowl and Sangam poured all the *kheer* into it. Sangam considered himself to be very lucky because the great monk would help him achieve emancipation. The *muni* left and Sangam's mother soon returned home. As she entered her house, she saw her son licking an empty dish. She felt sadness in her heart. Sangam had eaten so much *kheer* but remained hungry! She felt that she was not providing enough for him and that the boy was starving. Sangam did not say anything to his mother about giving all the *kheer* to the monk. After a short while, Sangam fell ill. He tried to cry out to his mother but could not utter a single word. Within moments he died, and was reborn the only son of a wealthy merchant.[15/16]

The story of 'Sangam and the Muni' is paradigmatic in that it depicts the ideal relationship between householders and ascetics as an encounter of *personnages* (Mauss, 1987) or ideal roles. It represents a coming together of ideals: an unknown Jain ascetic arrives unannounced at the house of a pious individual and takes only 'surplus' food. The householder eagerly gives and is profoundly grateful for the *muni*'s acceptance of alms. Of course, within the contemporary Terapanthi community, it is rare that a householder and an ascetic would meet as strangers and accidentally. More often than not, they meet as individuals who know at least something about the other's background and family. And often enough, they meet as 'one-time' relations.[17] Nevertheless, in the *bhiksha* rite, they come together as householder and ascetic, as *'personnages.'* The *bhiksha* ritual creates their categories by delineating their identities.

In his book *Riches and Renunciation*, James Laidlaw discusses Jainism's otherworldly values, which, in their concern with the state of the individual soul or self, transcend the social. Drawing on Marcel Mauss' theories of the person, he discusses Jain cosmology in terms of both a '*moi*-oriented' and '*personne*-oriented' moral system. He writes that 'A *moi* theory is one which conceives the individuality of the human being in a cosmic (physical and/or spiritual) as opposed to social context; a conception of the individual as a spiritual and moral agent rather than as the subject of a political or social order'(1995: 16). Laidlaw writes that Jain thinkers have formulated their cosmology in this way, conceiving of the individual soul as 'alone in an impersonal cosmic system of cause and effect, and burdened with the consequences of its former actions' (17). But he argues that Jainism is comprehensible only if it is also understood as a '*personne*-oriented' moral system, of which the *bhiksha* ritual serves as a prime illustration. Mauss was interested in tracing the origins of the modern self from early, tribal roles (*personnes*) to the individual in modern society. He believed that for most of human history, individuals were not distinguishable from their social roles. Interestingly, the *bhiksha* ritual – through which Jain '*moi* universality' is established – is achieved through social roles or personnages. In the ideal *bhiksha* interaction, individuality is concealed within the idealized roles of householder and ascetic. It is largely a stylized and scripted piece of drama through which the roles of the householder and ascetic are created: the two come together and 'haggle' over alms and over identities.

Bhiksha and the Jain Ideal of Renunciation

In his book *The Jains*, Paul Dundas writes, '[T]here is one basic and essential institution which brings ascetics and laity together and at the same time defines their radically different positions in the world: religious giving' (1992: 150). Religious giving in general, and *bhiksha* in particular, stands at the centre of Jainism because it establishes the Jain ideal of renunciation.

Because *shravaks* and ascetics are well-established and definable groups, we tend to treat them as representatives of distinct ontological realms. We consider the laity and ascetics as separate groups, representing separate realms that come together during certain interactions, most quintessentially in the act of *bhiksha*: like billiard balls, they briefly impact before shooting off in separate directions. But I suggest it is *bhiksha* that creates the two groups as much as it represents a point of contact. Out of a homogeneous whole, division is created and the *laukik* (worldly) and the *lokottar* (transcendent) come into existence.

Transactions between renouncers and householders constitute Jainism by rejecting society. Only by renouncing the world can Jain transcendent values be established. In Jain cosmology, the 'spiritual' is revealed through the rejection of the 'worldly,' which clouds and contaminates it. All interactions with the laity provide an opportunity to delineate and demarcate the two, but it is the rite of *bhiksha*, above all others, that serves to demonstrate the renunciatory worldview on a daily basis. *Bhiksha* is the quintessential denial of exchange; it is an act that distinguishes the worldly from the spiritual in order that the worldly may be renounced.

The ascetic and the *shravak* are defined and distinguished in the *bhiksha* ritual by their contrasting approaches to spirituality, namely through 'generosity' and 'restraint.' The 'worldly' and the 'spiritual' are an outcome of an essential rupture created by the juxtaposition of the competing orientations: the 'generous' householder and the 'restrained' ascetic. The roles and performances are foreordained, fixed, and necessarily contradictory. Although both householder and ascetic are ultimately seekers of liberation, their methods – stemming from their positions either 'inside' or 'outside' the world – are contrary. The ascetic is counselled to take only 'surplus' food – a small quantity so as not to deprive the householder or cause her to make a sacrifice. But, as the Sangam story reveals, the householder – to be generous – must make an offering that *is* a sacrifice. Within the act of alms-giving, therefore, we find the coexistence of conflicting demands: the householder is compelled to give whereas the ascetic is obliged to resist. Success depends on the realization of ideal roles – that is, the degree to which generosity is displayed by the householder and the degree to which the ascetic resists this generosity. But as in any bargaining transaction, there can be no absolute 'winner': restraint is established within a context of generosity; and generosity is established within a context of restraint. The success of the ascetic ideal requires that a certain balance be struck between the ostensibly 'competing' positions. In the absence of this 'competition' of orientations, *bhiksha* becomes an undisguised form of social exchange instead of an act of worldly renunciation and is dispossessed of its raison d'être:

> Stated crudely, the ascetics carry the spiritual burden of the community *in return* for which they receive maintenance by the laity. Ascetics own no possessions and are prevented by the tenet of *ahimsa* from performing many tasks necessary to sustain life; they cannot cook, construct shelters, light lamps or use electricity, earn or carry money, or drink unboiled water, to name but a few restrictions. Furthermore, as enlightenment is attained through austerities and meditation, ascetics have neither the time nor the inclination to pursue such mundane tasks. (Banks, 1986: 449; italics added)

In the absence of a framework of spiritual haggling between the generous householder and restrained ascetic, the interaction appears as lay material support of the ascetics 'in return' for spiritual guidance and an opportunity to earn *punya*. But it is precisely this 'exchange' or 'return' that is vehemently denied by the ascetics (Flügel, 1995–6: 126). And it is the denial itself that establishes *bhiksha* as an act of renunciation instead of as a social act. *Bhiksha* appears as a social act and a form of interdependence only to the extent that we divorce it from its underlying soteriology. Any attempt to understand the Jain lay–ascetic relationship in terms of the socioeconomic mechanisms that underlie it would (inverting Marxist logic) obfuscate its religious ideals.[18] Exchange or reciprocity would involve the ascetic in worldliness, implicate her in violence, and thereby undermine the Jain claim that escape through renunciation is possible. It would threaten Jain society, founded as it is on the very idea of renunciation (Banks, 1986; Folkert, 1987). When *bhiksha* is ideally executed, it is meant to be an inversion of exchange, a rejection of social bonds, and an act of world renunciation.

Laidlaw describes the *bhiksha* rite as 'the exchange which constitutes and reproduces the Jain religion' (1995: 300). He writes:

The exchange between renouncers and lay people differs from the 'give and take' of society at large. The highest kind of gift is that which renouncers (or Tirthankaras) give to the laity, and the next highest, the best that householders can do, is gifts from them to renouncers. (300)

Nonreciprocal unilateral giving is antithetical to the give and take of normal social relations in that it repudiates fellowship and thereby undermines future interaction. Instead it affirms a different set of non-communal values, namely individualistic, other worldly ones. Within the Jain context (on the ideological level), the denial of exchange champions an elusive and intangible good: the accumulation of spiritual merit in opposition to social merit. If the gift takes on even the slightest sense of an obligation for return, it is no longer *bhiksha*. With reciprocity comes attachment, the primary evil leading to rebirth. Jonathan Parry summarizes the ideological function of *bhiksha* when he writes, 'The reciprocated gift belongs to the profane world; the unreciprocated gift belongs to a quest for salvation *from* it' (1986: 462).

Parry considers the Indian 'unreciprocated' gift to be a challenge to Mauss' theory of gift exchange and an exception to the anthropological norm. Whereas Mauss argued that gifts contain some part of the spiritual essence of the donor, which constrains the recipient to make a return and thereby creates spiritual bonds, Parry counters:

In the Hindu context this notion that the gift contains the person is associated with the idea that the gift is a kind of sacrifice ... There is no question, then, of the gift being a loan or pledge. It is alienated in an absolute way, and the very definition of the gift is that it involves the complete extinction of the donor's proprietary rights in favour of the recipient ... The gift does return to the donor, but it does so as the fruits of karma ... The return is deferred (in all likelihood to another existence); its mechanism has become entirely impersonal, and the recipient is merely a 'vessel' (patra) or conduit for the flow of merit and is himself in no way constrained by the gift or bound to the donor. (1986: 461)

And he states:

Whether we emphasize the impersonality of the return, or the ideology which denies that a 'true' gift is made 'with desire' for any kind of reward, it seems clear that we are dealing with a transactional theory quite unlike

Mauss' Melanesian, Polynesian and American examples. The Hindu 'law of
the gift' does not create society by instituting that constant give-and-take
which Malinowski described for the Trobriands. (462)

Instead, *bhiksha* creates the renunciatory ideal through the *denial* of
give and take; what Folkert describes as an 'anti-social religious ideal'
(1993b: 180). It is only because gift exchange *normally* leads to the development of social bonds that renunciation is established through its
denial. As much as reciprocity constitutes the material basis of society
through the formation of necessary alliances (cf. Mauss, Malinowski,
Lévi-Strauss), the denial of exchange constitutes the ideological basis of
Jainism. As Parry writes,

> While Mauss originally introduced this notion of 'spirit' to explain the
> inalienability of the object and the necessity of making a return, what it in
> fact explains in this context is why the gift *must* be alienated, should never
> return, and should endlessly be handed on. (1986: 461)

The institutional denial of exchange is tantamount to a repudiation
of this-worldly values and of the building blocks of society itself. Strenski's argument about the orientation of the Theravada Buddhist *sangha*
[religious order] applies equally well to the Jains. He claims that

> civilization or society has never for Buddhists been an end in itself; it is
> itself to be transcended, and that transcendence is nowhere better symbol-
> ized than in primary *Nibbana*[19]-questing activity of the *sangha*. (1983: 476)

Religious giving (*dana*) in general, and *bhiksha* in particular, is denied
as a form of reciprocity because it is an inversion of all normative social
exchange where there exists a donor and a recipient, and where
exchange establishes social bonds between the two parties. In theory,
the householder and ascetic meet 'by chance'; it is the householder who
urges the ascetic to accept alms, offers more than is accepted, and is
delighted to have given. The interaction benefits the giver more than it
does the recipient. Jaini writes:

> [I]mportant benefits result from the widespread practice of sharing one's
> food with others. This activity ... is called *atithi-samvibhaga*, sharing with
> guests. The terms *atithi* literally means 'no date'; such a 'guest,' therefore,

is one who arrives without invitation, who is simply passing by the door in search of alms. In Indian society only those who are brahmacarins (celibate students) or who have renounced the world altogether are allowed to beg food. A normal householder must never do so; his position is to give, not take. In those cases where extreme poverty drives ordinary people into a beggar's role despite this cultural restriction, it is understood that alms will be offered them only out of compassion on the part of the donor; no great spiritual merit accrues to such charity, since householders are not considered 'worthy recipients.' Presenting alms to an ascetic, on the other hand, is thought to bring one closer to salvation. (1990: 218)

And, unlike normal gift giving, it is the giver (not the recipient) who is in a subordinate position. As Laidlaw notes, 'supatra-dan [dan given to ascetics; bhiksha] is the only form of gift in the classification which is always given by definition to a superior. So the recipient is not demeaned in receipt' (1995: 316). The ascetic is neither demeaned nor obligated as in normal gift exchange. Instead she acts as a vessel through which 'give and take' come to pass. The giver (of alms) is also the taker (of merit), and no bonds are (in theory) forged. Both ascetic and householder seek moral excellence; each pursues spiritual progression through their particular methods (generosity/restraint) – stemming from their respective orientations to the world. Therefore, although the shravak and ascetic act out opposite sides of the laukik/lokottar divide, they are united in the bhiksha rite in esteeming other-worldly values.

The householder is worthy to give and the ascetic worthy to receive because both are joined in the pursuit of 'spiritual' rewards alone – in opposition to 'worldly' ones. However, it is not always easy to distinguish between the rhetorically persuasive realms of the 'spiritual' and the 'worldly'; and indeed, householders often blend the two together. We see, for example, that the 'physical' or 'worldly' is assumed to be a reflection of spirituality in Jainism. One's position in society (both caste and class) is said to derive from one's gotra or 'status-determining' karma; and one's physical appearance results from nama or 'body-determining' karma. Thus, karma plays a central role in many aspects of life that are considered to be 'worldly.' We recall that Sangam, as a result of the punya he earned from his spirituality (demonstrated by his generosity to the monk), was reborn in a wealthy and privileged family. Audrey Cantlie, in an essay on Assamese Hindus, writes:

The western model of physical and mental as separate interacting systems is foreign to the holistic view of man taken by the Assamese. Thus physical beauty indicates a mental state in that it is a manifestation of moral character, and all the Assamese saints, following Krishna, are credited with outstanding beauty of appearance and athletic prowess. (1981: 43)

Likewise, the Jain Tirthankaras are invariably depicted as strong, intelligent and beautiful – as are senior ascetics in the order. Guru Dev's paleness, large ears, and sloping shoulders were considered to be signs of spiritual greatness by both the lay and ascetic Terapanthi community. This indexical relationship between body and soul makes the rhetorically and ontologically sharp distinction between the 'spiritual' and the 'worldly' difficult to distinguish in practice. Furthermore, because the present era is one of decline (we are now living in the cycle of *Kaliyuga*[20] – a time of degeneration and instability), *moksa* is not possible; therefore the most that an ascetic and householder can hope for is that their accumulated *punya* (merit) will translate into a good rebirth. Whether this is a spiritual or worldly boon is contestable.[21] Nevertheless both householder and ascetic assume the proper execution of *bhiksha* will progress them along their spiritual paths until that time when they can attain *moksa*.

When properly performed, *bhiksha* is an embodiment and dramatization of difference. By defining and delineating the ascetic and the householder, it creates the essential division in Jainism between the *laukik* and the *lokottar*. The institution of *bhiksha* therefore creates the different positions in the world as much as it defines them, and it divides lay and ascetic as much as it brings them together. *Bhiksha* is as much a cause of the boundary distinction as it is a consequence. Thus, to the extent that the *bhiksha* ritual is ideally executed, it acts as a great divider, separating the worldly from the transcendent.

When the ideal roles are not properly enacted, distinctions between the two groups become harder to detect, and the worldly and the spiritual become dangerously fused. If strong, *bhiksha* stands as a great fortification between two realms, but if it is weak it acts as an open portal, leading to assimilation or to 'domestication' (Carrithers, 1979).

Bhiksha is the paradigmatic relationship for all other interactions between lay and ascetic. Where normal social interaction leads to interdependence, *bhiksha* leaves ascetic autarky and the renunciatory ideal intact. It is those interactions between individuals defined as 'not-exchange' – these denials of interdependence – which negate normal social bonds and authenticate the renunciatory ideal. But within it exist the seeds of its own destruction because, as Jonathan Parry writes, 'the gift threatens to cement the two together in a dangerous interdependence' (1986: 461). Ostensibly it brings the worldly and the spiritual together under a common spiritual motive, but it nevertheless results in the juxtaposition of the competing needs for generosity and restraint. If one party is more 'successful,' and equilibrium does not ensue, the public act of renunciation is foiled. This is why *bhiksha* is codified and ritualized; it is a coming together of *personnages* rather than of individuals. Behaviour is highly stereotyped and theatrical, leaving little room for individual variation or deviation. If a householder is too generous, or not generous enough, or if an ascetic is too restrained, or – more likely – not restrained enough, the relationship at the centre of Jainism is imperilled.

The Threat of Assimilation

Michael Carrithers suggests that the barrier separating lay and ascetic communities is inherently unstable and its eventual disintegration is inescapable. Writing on the history of the Theravada Buddhist monastic order, he observes:

> There is a gradual, unconscious, apparently inevitable, and in these senses natural tendency for the Sangha to become domesticated, so that the monks are no longer truly homeless, either in fact or metaphorically. (1979: 296)

Paul Dundas, likewise, notes the historical 'laicization' of Jain monasticism (see Cort, 1991b, on the historical and cultural development of Jain ascetic orders). The original mandate (shared with Hindu renunciants) prohibiting ascetics from remaining more than one night in a village and five in a town, was eased, and with time replaced by a myriad set of rules which focused instead on how ascetics should comport themselves while in householders' dwellings (1992: 150).[22] Dundas writes:

> In more recent times, lay–ascetic relations have altered somewhat compared to the old textual prescriptions. For example, monks, rather than

travelling from place to place in self-sufficient small groups, are today usually accompanied by lay followers who form an almost triumphal procession and see to their needs en route in a variety of ways. (1992: 150)

According to Carrithers, reform and domestication mark the ebb and flow of monastic life:

A simplified picture of the history of the Theravada Sangha is as follows. The order of ascetics, separated from the world, gradually evolves towards the equilibrium state, the domesticated Sangha. Once this is reached, reformers may then arise from within the ranks, and though the majority of the Sangha remain domesticated, there appear groups, necessarily small because necessarily self-referring, of reform monks. As these settle and grow, they evolve towards domestication, and though associated in name with reform, come to entertain in fact the opinions of village literary specialists.[23] Within these overgrown domesticated erstwhile reform groups there then appear further reformers ... and the process continues. (1979: 297)

'Laicization' and reform similarly mark the pattern of Jain monasticism. Within ascetic communities, fission occurs due to a perceived move towards 'the worldly'; discontent manifests itself as a revolt against domestication. The Terapanthi sect itself came into being this way. The story of its origin recounts a revolt against domestication and a move towards purity and reform. Bhikshu, its founder, broke with his *sangha* because of what he perceived to be its corruption. He believed his contemporary ascetics were leading such undisciplined lives that there was hardly a distinction between them and the householders.

The Birth of the Terapanthis

The source of schisms within Jainism has always been over the issue of what constitutes the 'true' ascetic path. From the earliest-known historical records, the ascetic ideal has been differently interpreted and its imperatives differently applied (Cort, 1991b).

In addition to the Svetambar/Digambar division, which encompasses all Jain communities, there are numerous sects and subsects within each branch, making the Jains one of the most fragmented religious communities in India (Banks, 1986). This fragmentation – which is always concerned with questions about the 'authentic' ascetic path – is evidence of the tradition's vigour, and challenges the once common view that Jain history is a monolithic and static body of doctrine. It was conflict over correct ascetic practice within the Murtipujak Svetambars that led in the fifteenth century to the emergence of the non-idolatrous Sthanakvasi order, and similarly, in the eighteenth century inspired a group of ascetics to break away from the Sthanakvasis to form the Terapanth.[24] The Terapanthi Svetambar are an offshoot of the Sthanakvasi Svetambar Jains. They emerged as a distinct sect under the leadership of Acharya Bhikshu in 1760. The non-idolatrous tradition from which the Terapanthis and Sthanakvasis have their roots is that of the Lonka Gacch of the fifteenth century. Peter Flügel provides the historical background of the tradition:

> This tradition emerged in 1451 as an anti-*yati* [property-owning ascetic] movement amongst the Murtipujak-laity in Muslim-ruled Ahmedabad, led by the Rajasthani-Osval court jeweller and copyist of Jain manuscripts, Lonka Sah (ca. 1415–1489). Lonka noticed a widening discrepancy between precept and practice among contemporary ascetics because he did not find any references to idol-worship nor to sedentary monasticism in the oldest textual tradition. With the help of the Jain minister L.B. Bhansali from Patan he then started a revivalist ascetic tradition on his own in 1471 under circumvention of monastic rules of linear succession. Although Lonka never initiated himself, it was he who drafted a set of organizational principles for the new Lonka Gacch in form of 69 maxims (*Lonka Sahki Hundi*). These rules played a paradigmatic role for all subsequent iconoclastic Svetambar movements. They explicitly rejected idolatry and sedentary monasticism, and stressed the ultimate authority of 31 of the ca. 45 scriptures of the Svetambar 'canon' (*agam*), and the importance of ascetic wandering (*vihar*) for the maintenance of a propertiless (*aparigrah*) monastic order into which 'only *banias* [merchants] should be initiated.' (1995–6: 122)

Flügel continues:

> Some years later, after Lonk was murdered by the followers of a rival sect, the Lonka Gacch split into factions and the cycle of reform and routinization started again. In protest against the renewed lax behaviour (*sithilacar*) of the ascetics and the re-emergence of temple-worship the *munis* Lavji and Dharmsinhji split off the Gujarati Lonkagacch in 1644 in Surat and founded the Dhundhiya (seekers) sect, which then divided itself into 22

schools (*baistola*) and later became known as the Sthanakvasi (hall dwellers) tradition. For similar reasons *muni* Bhiksu (1726–1803) and four
sadhus broke away from the Sthanakvasi *acarya* Rughanath in 1760 in Bagri
(Marvar) and founded the Terapanth *gan* four months later in Kelva
through a collective rite of self-initiation (*bhav di ksa*). (123)

Bhikshu was critical of what he considered to be the 'worldliness' of
his contemporary ascetics. He considered the boundaries between the
shravak (householder) and ascetic to be dangerously blurred and so he
sought to sharply delineate them. His most notable doctrinal innovations are the rigid distinction he made between the *laukik* (the
'worldly') and the *lokottar* (the 'transcendent'), and his exclusively 'soul-
centric' (as opposed to sociocentric) interpretation of *ahimsa*. To Bhikshu, *ahimsa* is strictly an ethic of noninterference and a method of disconnecting or separating oneself from worldly existence.

Today the Terapanth community numbers approximately 500,000
and remains overwhelmingly associated with the Rajasthani Bisa Osval
bania caste (among the ascetics, only a handful did not belong to this
caste). Over generations, many have migrated out of Rajasthan to
wealthier states but have remained connected through a strong religio-
socio-economic network.[25] The lay and ascetic communities are tightly
integrated under the spiritual leadership of a single leader (presently
Acharya Mahaprajna) and his ascetic disciples.

As the Terapanthi ascetics tell it, Bhikshu (or Bhikanji – the Marwari
version of his name) was initiated as a Sthanakvasi monk into the order
of Guru Sri Raghunathji in 1751. Because of his intelligence, charisma,
and loyalty, Bhikshu soon became Raghunathji's favourite disciple. Several years later, the householders of Rajnagar, a far-off village, grew so
frustrated with the lax conduct of the ascetics that they unanimously
decided not to honour or offer alms to them until the situation
improved. Raghunathji decided to send his most intelligent disciple to
quell the householders' concerns and convince them to resume paying
homage to the ascetics. So Bhikshu was sent to the village of Rajnagar
for *chaturmas* (the four-month rainy season retreat). When he arrived,
he was disturbed to find that his fellow monks were, in fact, lax, igno-
rant of the scriptures, and deeply involved in worldly affairs. Bhikshu
met with the householders and, after hearing their complaints, decided
they were right. But he said nothing because he deeply admired his
guru and did not want to oppose him. However, his internal angst was
more than he could bear and, that first night in Rajnagar, he fell

deathly ill. He knew that if he did not uphold the truth, he would die. He then became resolved to study the scriptures and discover for himself the 'distinction between right and wrong,' and his illness suddenly disappeared. The next day he asked the householders to be patient, explaining to them that he intended to devote his entire *chaturmas* to finding the solution to their concerns though a study of the scriptures. At the end of the *chaturmas* he told the householders that their complaints were justified: that the ascetics were indeed violating Lord Mahavira's ideal. But again he asked that they be patient. He was convinced that once he presented his findings to Raghunathji, everything would be resolved. At the end of *chaturmas*, he, along with the other Sthanakvasi monks, left Rajnagar. But unbeknown to Bhikshu, two monks had left ahead of the group in order to reach Raghunathji first to tell him what Bhikshu was up to. When Bhikshu finally arrived, he found Raghunathji hostile towards him. Nevertheless, he pleaded his case, urging his guru to return to a purer form of ascetic practice. Paul Dundas writes:

> Bhikshu railed against Sthanakvasi ascetics living permanently in lodging houses built especially for them, taking food from the same families every day and compelling lay people to take initiation from them exclusively. (1992: 218)

For two years Bhikshu debated and pleaded, but Raghunathji had no interest in reforming the order and persisted in his lax ways. Dundas describes the controversy:

> In one of the anecdotes recorded about Bhikshu's early career, Raghunathji is depicted as arguing that, since the time in which they lived was the fifth spoke of the wheel, the corrupt age, everything was inevitably in a state of decline and that as a consequence anyone who could maintain fully correct ascetic behaviour for as little as an hour would become an omniscient *kevalin*. Bhikshu mockingly retorted that if that was the way to achieve the goal, he would sit and hold his breath for that period. For Bhikshu, the Jain path could involve nothing less than total commitment. As he is reported to have told Raghunathji, he had taken ascetic initiation to do something about the state of his soul. (1992: 219)

In 1759 Bhikshu felt he had no choice but to act, so in the town of Bagari[26] he and twelve other monks broke with the order. Present-day

Terapanthis maintain that Bhikshu had no desire to start a new sect; he simply wanted to reestablish the truth. Raghunathji was outraged and quickly spread rumours among the community that the thirteen monks were troublemakers and should be avoided. The householders ostracized Bhikshu and his disciples because, though dissatisfied with current practices, they deeply respected Raghunathji. So the breakaway group was immediately faced with serious obstacles. It had nowhere to stay and no food or drink, as no householders were willing to offer accommodation or *bhiksha*. They fasted and during the night stayed in cremation grounds.

One day they were performing their religious duties in a small shop stall when a minister of the state and a local poet passed by. Surprised to see them there instead of in their own lodgings, the minister asked, 'Why are you at this place?' Bhikshu explained that he and the monks considered the owning of *sthanaks* (lodgings) to be a violation of the true ascetic path because it involved possession. Instead they considered any place as appropriate for religious duties. The minister was impressed and asked, 'How many ascetics follow this viewpoint?' They answered '*Terah*' ('Thirteen'). The poet said aloud, '*Terahpanth*' ('The path of thirteen'). Bhikshu, upon hearing this, raised his head to the sky and, making a play on the appellation, declared, 'Lord, we have accepted *Tera Panth*' ('Thy Path'). Later, they added another auspicious interpretation of the name: they were representatives of the path of thirteen principles: five *mahavratas*, five *samitis*, and three *guptis*.[27] In 1760 Bhikshu initiated himself into the Terapanthi order, started a campaign for purity of conduct, and wrote a constitution (*maryada patr*) that established a single *acharya* as the absolute leader of the order.[28] As the story goes, the Terapanthi sect grew slowly but was eventually victorious, and the number of lay and ascetic followers steadily increased.

Confines of the *Lokottar*

One of the most interesting aspects of the Terapanthi 'origin story' is the prominent role it accords householders in the push to reform. More typically, if ascetics acknowledge a threat of domestication in their order, they generally see the source of the problem as external to themselves. Many Jain stories depict 'unfavourable' lay–ascetic transactions, and the problems are almost exclusively presented as originating among householders, who are blamed for being either irreligious and stingy, or overly demanding of ascetics. The scriptures, too, see the greatest threat coming from householders. Paul Dundas writes,

> One important text describing normative ascetic behaviour points out the potential danger of the relationship with lay people by describing the monk as a deer and the layman as a hunter (NBh 1649: *curni* comm.). (1992: 149)

Therefore, unlike the Hindu narrative literature in which there is an abundance of stories warning of corrupt ascetics – what Kirin Narayan calls 'an enduring cultural theme' in Hindu storytelling (1989: 144) – there are few such stories in the Jain corpus.[29] This is likely a reflection of the singular importance of the renunciatory ideal in Jainism. Folkert writes that in the Jain tradition one does not find *sadhus* being treated as 'the objects of suspicion and occasional outright hostility' (1993c: 183), as they occasionally are in the Hindu tradition. He explains, 'Because Jain teachings as a whole are critical of the standard values of engagement in social and economic life, one would not expect to see the ascetic viewed in such ambivalent fashion as is true for Hindu culture as a whole' (183). The Terapanthi's own origin story is a conspicuous deviation from this norm. In an inversion of the normal logic, householders are presented as defenders of the tradition, and it is the ascetics who are chastised for their worldly ways. Of course, this single inversion of the more typical 'infallible ascetic' theme undoubtedly had rhetorical purposes for a reform movement eager to distinguish itself from its predecessors and to establish its own ascetic credentials among a lay community.

Acharya Bhikshu was determined to establish an order in which the *laukik* and the *lokottar* would be clearly delineated, and in which the lay and ascetic realms would never overlap, making 'domestication' an impossibility. Holmstrom describes the Terapanthi's doctrine as follows:

> The Terapanth was an offshoot of the Sthanakavasis from 1760 AD, and much stricter. One of their basic principles is a very strict division between religious action and social action. Two ways of expressing this are: the terms *dharm*, taken in the sense of 'religion,' as opposed to *adharm*, not 'irreligion' in the sense of going against religious tenets, but simply not to do with religion; or the terms *adhyatmik dharm*, 'duty' as benefiting one's

soul, *atman,* as opposed to *laukik dharm,* one's social duty, e.g., supporting one's parents or offering hospitality to one's guests. Both are important, but only if recognized as essentially separate. (1988: 13)

This 'worldly–transcendent' division is central to the Terapanthi's understanding of Jainism (Flügel, 1995–6), and from very early on in my stay it was important to the ascetics that I understand it. On many occasions, they would concoct hypothetical scenarios and then quiz me to see if I knew the difference between social and religious duty. Samani Urmilla, the nun with whom I quickly established a friendship, listed by rote Bhikshu's twenty principles of *dharma* (gloss as religion or eternal truths):[30]

1   *Dharma* is *tyag* (restraint), not *bhog* (enjoyment of pleasure).
2   *Dharma* is in compassion, not in violence.
3   *Dharma* is that which is permitted by Lord Mahavira, not what he prohibited.
4   *Dharma* is in efforts to change the heart, not in force or bribery.
5   *Dharma* cannot be bought, it is priceless.
6   For *dharma,* one life cannot be taken to save another.
7   *Dharma* and *adharma* cannot be mixed.
8   A 'right' end can only be achieved by 'right' means.
9   It is a form of attachment (*adharma*) to yearn for another being to live long.
10 It is a form of aversion (*adharma*) to want others to die early.
11 To leave a home where the activities are not good is *dharma.*
12 When a being dies is not violence.
13 When a being lives is not compassion.
14 To kill is violence.
15 Not to kill is compassion.
16 To save a large being by taking a small one is not *dharma.*
17 Worldly duty and spiritual religion are different.
18 Necessary violence is still violence (except for ascetics).[31]
19 The spiritual religion of ascetics and householders is one and the same.
20 Nonviolence and compassion are one and the same.

After rattling off the list at great speed, Urmilla then sought to explain what these points mean to the Terapanthi community in practical terms:

Laukik dharma is related to the world, and *lokottar dharma* is related to *moksa*. Only those acts concerned with *moksa* are true religion. If one is in society, one must perform one's duties, such as helping each other, feeding each other. Monks and nuns are strictly within the realm of *lokottar dharma,* so they cannot involve themselves in worldly activities. For a householder to do anything for a nun or monk is *lokottar dharma* because the ascetics have renounced the whole world.

For householders, therefore, only those acts deemed as purely spiritual acts, principally religious giving to the ascetics (and most quintessentially *bhiksha*), are of religious (*lokattar*) worth. For a renouncer, no involvement in worldly existence is permissible. In its purest form, observance of this doctrine means that an ascetic can not only not physically help others, she cannot even advise the laity to do so.

If there is one story that the ascetics feel encapsulates their doctrine, it is 'The Merchant and His Son.' This is a popular tale recounted by ascetics to householders of all ages because of its simplicity. I present its summarized version: 'One day a merchant had errands to run so he decided to leave his son in charge of his shop, which sold butter and tobacco. The father instructed the boy on how to serve the goods to customers, and then left. The boy was anxious to please his father, and came up with an idea. He saw that the containers for the butter and tobacco were only half-full, and since the cost of the products was identical, he thought he could save space by mixing the two together into one. When the father returned he was aghast – in front of him was a pot full of buttery tobacco! Now no one would buy either. The substances, useful when separate, were no longer of any use, and were even harmful when confused and mixed together.' (See Holmstrom, 1988: 13, for a slightly different version.)

Thus the Terapanthis stress that although a householder has social duties to perform, they do not constitute 'religion' or 'spirituality' because some form of violence is inherent in their performance. Samani Urmilla asked rhetorically, 'How can I tell a householder to build a hospital when such an act would involve digging the earth and killing so many living beings?' But she added that householders 'should' fulfil their worldly duties; and if they don't want to, they should become renunciants.[32]

The Terapanthi's narrow interpretation of what constitutes the 'transcendent' (*lokottar*) has led to ridicule and criticism from other Jain communities. Padmanabh Jaini (1990) provides an example:

[T]he attempt by a renegade Sthanakavasi monk called Bhikhanji (eighteenth century) to establish a sect based on the doctrine of total non-assistance to any living being (except mendicants) was greeted by protest from nearly all members of the community. It is said that Bhikhanji could initially gather no more than twelve disciples; the sect he founded, therefore became known as the Terapantha, which means 'the path of thirteen.' (1990: 313–14)

Jaini elaborates:

Bhikhanji's theory was that saving the life of a dog, [for example] makes one responsible for the violence committed by that dog in the future and thus should be avoided. He also claimed that 'helpful' behaviour almost always involved some interest in the result, hence brought an increase in karmic attachments. Bhikhanji here exploits the doctrinal split inherent in any community that preaches the ideals of total renunciation and moksa, on the one hand, and the value of compassionate and charitable behaviour (leading to heaven) on the other. Pushed to a purely logical extreme, the canonical teachings might well be thought to justify the Terapanthi interpretation. Even so, such interpretation violates the spirit of anekantavada and has been considered a form of ekanta by most Jainas.[33] Since its inception, therefore, the Terapanthi sect has lived in virtual isolation from the larger Jaina community. (314, f.n.)

In the course of his research, Laidlaw recorded the following comments about the Terapanthi:

Once when I was asking a Khartar Gacch friend about *dan*, he brought up the Terapanth doctrine: 'They say that *patra* must be *supatra*. Acharya Tulsi's people, that's what they say. If I give to a poor man, he may do some bad thing and they say the sin will come to me. They say it is not *dharma* to give to the poor. Of course it is good to give to someone who is worthy, and it is best to give to *sadhu-sadhvis*. But how much do they need? And if I see a beggar in the street and I feel something, it is my duty (*kartavya*) to give. And how can I know what is in his heart? It is not my duty to ask, "What will he buy?" or "What will he do?" It is my duty to help, because I feel compassion (*karuna bhav*). Didn't Mahavir Swami feel compassion for everyone? And we should do what we can.' (1995: 300–1)

The comments of Laidlaw's friend reflect common, if not stereotypical, misunderstandings of the Terapanthi and are therefore worth considering. Contrary to common assumptions, no Terapanthi would disagree with the idea that a householder has a 'duty to give.' However, an ascetic would maintain that such an act is not *dharma* – but not for the reasons the Khartar Gacch friend assumes. Contemporary Terapanthis do not claim that one is responsible for the ill thoughts or actions committed by, for example, a beggar after helping him. It is only the repercussions of the immediate act itself that are of concern. An example that Samani Urmilla gave me to distinguish between the two was this: Suppose a man is sick and his wife gives him medicine hoping to help him. By chance, the man is allergic to the medicine and dies. In this case, the woman is responsible for violence. If, however, the man got better from the medicine and at some later date commited murder or told a lie, she would not be responsible.

Giving food to a beggar is *adharma*, not because of what the beggar might do in the future but because it involves violence [preparing of food] and it encourages nonrestraint. Violence and nonrestraint are never *dharma*. According to the Terapanthi, giving food is only considered *dharma* when the recipient is an ascetic because – in a reversal of the beggar predicament – here such an act supports and champions a life of restraint.

Muniji, the elderly monk with whom I met most evenings, told me many times that whether or not householders follow the religious advice he gives them has no karmic effect on him. While he hopes that they become more spiritual, if they persist in their worldly ways, he is not responsible. In fact, he still succeeds in burning away karmic matter (*nirjara*) for having preached the 'Right Faith.'[34] Indeed, Muniji insisted that the ascetics' involvement with the lay community in general (daily sermons, individual consultations, etc.) is performed because it is spiritually beneficial for the ascetics, whether the laity follow their teachings or not. During the year in which I was Muniji's 'disciple,' he was incredibly gentle and kind, and always had endless patience. But when I would try to thank him for his special kindness, he would become serious and inform me that his primary motive for instructing me was that it was a helpful part of his own *sadhana* (religious practice). This view seeks to clearly delineate the spiritual from the worldly and to deny that ascetic instruction is given 'in return' for lay material support.[35]

According to the Terapanthi, *dharma* is that which leads to 'effecting a positive change of heart.' The Terapanthi assert that the common Jain practice of purchasing an animal at a market to prevent it from being butchered is not a religious act because it does nothing to encourage the butcher to abandon his violent practice. Laidlaw quotes Acharya Tulsi on this issue and on the Terapanthi understanding of mercy (*daya*):

> Mercy can only be done when the opponent's heart is changed. When we save someone by force, or by some wrong means, or by tempting, then we do not consider it spiritual (*adhyatmik*) mercy. It can be from a worldly point of view (*laukik drishtikon*), but not from the spiritual. Suppose we save a rat by beating the cat who is chasing him, that is not pure *daya*. Suppose some person is killing some creature and we give him money, that is not pure *daya*. Until the heart of the killer is changed, it cannot be considered pure *daya*. Changing a violent man to a non-violent man – that is *daya*. (1995: 164)

Furthermore, lay Terapanthis do coordinate and organize many charitable projects. The Terapanthi have an active Women's Organization (Terapanthi Mahila Mandal) that is very involved in social work projects (e.g., it coordinates eye clinics for poor families, educational projects and camps, to name but a few). And the Jain Vishva Bharati Institute is open to all students free of charge. However, as Laidlaw noted, what does distinguish the Terapanthi from other communities is its conspicuous absence of animal shelters, and this is likely to stem from its doctrinal peculiarity. Even a few Terapanthi ascetics accepted that perhaps the Terapanthi distinction between worldly and spiritual duty has been wrongly interpreted by householders to mean they should not involve themselves in such activities. But they insist that householders should perform such social duties, even though they do not lead to good karma.[36] It is reasonable to assume that householders, believing no good karma will be gained through such efforts, might abandon them altogether. Whether the lay community believes their philanthropic works are only 'socially good' and do not lead to the accumulation of merit is hard to know. When I spoke with members of the Terapanthi Mahila Mandal, the majority believed – through a creative interpretation of their doctrine – that their efforts would benefit them karmically. As one woman explained, 'Perhaps the acts themselves are not *dharma*, but the compassion that drives them is, and this surely leads to *punya*.' And I knew of at least one *saman* who interpreted philanthropic acts in the same way.[37]

Today, despite these often painstaking efforts to separate the worldly from the spiritual, the unqualified *interdependence* between the laity and ascetics is one of the most conspicuous aspects of Terapanthi religious life – as it is a feature of monastic life more generally. It is 'conspicuous' because it clashes so sharply with the Terapanthi ideal. The divergence from the ideal of Lord Mahavira is rationalized, in part, by the fact that we are presently living in an era of decline, which makes the rigours of heroic asceticism impossible.[38] But generally speaking, laxity is not acknowledged and, in fact, most householders and ascetics spend a considerable amount of time talking about the hardships of the ascetic path. Despite rhetoric to the contrary, however, interdependence and mutual accommodation are a salient feature of monastic life.

Like Janus, the Roman god of doorways, *bhiksha* has two clearly distinguished aspects. It is both a menace (in that it juxtaposes competing interests), and a creative force (in that the juxtaposition is necessary to delineate the two realms in the first place). Ivan Strenski, in his study of Buddhism, considers the unavoidable interaction between householders and ascetics (whether defined as exchange or not) as the root cause of domestication.[39] In particular, ritual giving to the *sangha*[40] is at the centre of both the creation of the renunicatory ideal and its erosion. He writes, 'The problem of how domestication came about is, then, the problem of how Buddhist society was formed in the process of ritual giving' (1983: 470). He continues:

[R]egular patterns of social relationships grow along with regular patterns of giving ... [and] it is not so much that the material nature of monastic residences made them the agents of domestication as it was their status as gifts which in turn called forth certain social obligations. (470)

And,

Perhaps the first thing one comes to appreciate is how treacherous exchange can be for a social formation of renouncer ascetics such as the *sangha*. If no qualification were placed upon the exchange between *sangha* and laity, the *sangha* would soon become laicized. A *sangha* which exchanged food given it for food it preferred would ipso facto have taken the first plunge into merchandising; in the south Asian context, it would simply be another *jati* (caste) among others ... On the other hand, without exchange between *sangha* and laity, the *sangha* would either have to become economically (and in all other ways) self-sufficient, or would simply cease to exist ... If the alternatives of unqualified exchange and no exchange lead to dead-ends, then perhaps we can understand why and how the laity and *sangha* entered into relations of qualified exchange. (1983: 472)

In his essay 'On the Moral Perils of Exchange,' Parry talks about the similar danger of obligation facing the Hindu Brahmin priest in his acceptance of *dana*:

> The ideal Brahman should as nearly as possible approximate his life-style and behaviour to that of the world-renouncer, but the problem with *dana* is that the priest's acceptance of it irretrievably compromises this ideal of ascetic autonomy and inextricably enmeshes him in the material and social order. It is the Brahman's ascetic transcendence of the world which qualifies him as a 'worthy vessel' for the gifts of the pious; but the paradox is that his receipt of such gifts inevitably endangers this very transcendence. (1989: 74)

Interestingly, Parry considers the nonreciprocated *bhiksha* given to an ascetic to be of a completely different order, and not to pose a danger at all. He claims that *bhiksha*

> in no way entails the kind of moral difficulties associated with *dana*. The crucial point here, I suggest, is that such prestations are given to the renouncer, with whom no relationship is possible since he is outside the social world. (1989: 77)

I would counter, however, by arguing that the renouncer is 'outside the social world' only to the extent that she and the householder collude to deny *bhiksha* as a form of exchange. If an ascetic were to appear overly eager in accepting alms – thereby violating the demeanour of detachment – or if a householder were a reluctant giver, forcing the ascetic to solicit alms, the ascetic ideal would be weakened. The ideal relationship between the two should not be assumed, since it must be reestablished in each transaction. *Bhiksha* is the litmus test of healthy lay–ascetic relations. When it serves as an interaction between *personnages* it is a creative force maintaining householders and ascetics as two distinctive, even to some degree opposing, domains. But when roles are poorly performed, it is the first step towards domestication. Therefore the relationship between the state of the *sangh* and the state of the rite of *bhiksha* is intimate. The latter is a microcosm of the former. The constant tug of war between the *shravak* and the ascetic, and between the worldly and the spiritual, is at the centre of Jain religious life.

The Drama of *Bhiksha*

The months passed and *bhiksha* became a common and predicable daily rite for me. Many mornings when the ascetics would arrive at the guest-house, I would join the encircling devotees and follow them into Bapu's kitchen. There, along with the others, I would try to have a turn at making a generous offering of rice, *roti*, or *kheer.* And although almost all the nuns and monks were familiar to me, and some I knew as friends, we would meet as *personnages.* We did not greet each other by name, or talk of our mutual concerns as we normally did. Instead, we came together as representatives of the 'worldly' and the 'spiritual.' *Bhiksha* is the drama through which the roles of householder and the ascetic are re-created daily, and through it we embodied ideals and demonstrated our worthiness as moral beings. Although to some extent householders and ascetics are always embodiments of the 'worldly' and the 'spiritual,' the categories themselves are more negotiable outside of the *bhiksha* ritual. Variability, versatility, and dynamic identities are more characteristic of private lay–ascetic encounters. For example, on those mornings when I joined the *sadhvis* on their vigorous jaunts around and about the town of Ladnun in search of *bhiksha,* we juggled with our roles, putting on and taking off our *bhiksha* masks. Our identities were as limber as our steps, as we wove our way through the narrow village streets, darting in and out of homes for alms.

Joining the *sadhvis* on their *bhiksha* rounds meant an early start to the day: at 4 a.m. I would leave my room quietly, so as not to awaken Bapu. He would be stretched out on his *charpoy* immediately in front of the door to my room. He and the other workers at the residence had no rooms of their own, and would invariably set up their *charpoys* in some corridor to protect themselves from the chill of the night. His day began at about 5:30 a.m., and on these mornings I envied him the extra ninety minutes of sleep. He always looked so warm, wrapped and secure in a large woollen blanket. Yet it wouldn't be long before he would be awo-ken by a holler from the guesthouse superintendent, gasping for his morning cup of *chai.* And Bapu would make many pots of sweet tea before his day would be done. I, too, would later come asking for my cup. Whenever I went on *bhiksha* rounds with the *sadhvis,* I returned to the monastery too late for breakfast and would rely on Bapu's *chai* to sustain me. However, whenever I tagged along with the *samanis* on their swifter rounds, I would be back in plenty of time for breakfast at 7:30 a.m.

The lives of *sadhvis* and *munis* are considered to be much more rigorous than those of *samanis/samans,* in part because of the rules governing their *bhiksha* collections. Unlike 'full' ascetics, the latter accept from householders food that has been specifically prepared for them.[41] It often seemed as though the *sadhvis'* days were organized around alms collection – first at sunrise, then again before noon, and finally in the late afternoon. It takes time to collect the alms, since like 'grazing cows,'[42] they take just a small amount from a large number of houses so as not to burden any one householder unnecessarily. They then return to their residence, often a thirty-minute walk, divide the food among their group of six or seven, eat, and clean up. From start to finish, the procedure can take a good two hours and is a thrice-daily occurrence. The *samanis,* by contrast, unencumbered by the rule of seeking alms at homes unannounced, are free to collect all their alms at the same place, if they so wish. In practice, lists are prepared in advance by the Niyojika (head *samani*) designating the places where each group of *samanis* will collect alms for the upcoming week. When they are in Ladnun they mainly collect from the Jain Vishva Bharati's 'institutional' setups: the meditation centre, the guesthouse, the kitchen for workers, and so on. Each week the groups are rotated, to prevent the formation of attachments between the lay servers and ascetics. The collection usually does not exceed twenty minutes, so the *samanis* can be finished eating their morning meals by 7:30 a.m. – a time when the *sadhvis* are typically still on their *bhiksha* rounds.

The 'semi-ascetic' or *saman* category was established to enable a group of 'ascetics' greater freedom to proselytize. The traditional restrictions on ascetics in the areas of travel, toilet, and alms collection were considered by Guru Dev to be obstacles to the spread of Jainism, and especially to his Anuvrat Movement, both within India and outside. There were six initiates into the semi-nun (*samani*) order in 1980, and by 1996 there were eighty-one. Four semi-monks (*samans*) were initiated in 1986 and it was this same group that still comprised the order in 1996.[43]

Standing on the terrace of the guesthouse at 4 a.m. and looking out across the stretch of sand leading to the *Gautam Shalla* (the *samanis'* residence), I could feel only stillness – a calm that easily lures one back to slumber. Crossing the cold sand to the *samanis'* residence – no more than 100 metres away – I held out hope that the desert's night air would invigorate me. The stars, showing no signs of weakening, would be high and mighty in the sky. The ascetics insist that this tranquil hour is the most sublime for meditation, when the rhythms of the universe are at their most harmonious and most peaceful.

In the predawn hours, the *samanis* would be gathered together in a single room, each sitting in a lotus position, their eyes shut. An exposed yellow light bulb, burning the whole night, jutted out from high on the wall.[44] It radiated a dreary, sleepy, yellow hue across the room, and made the faces of the nuns appear harsh as they quietly recited their prayers. Muted beneath their *muhpattis* , their voices seemed to come from far away. I would sit and listen to the deep hum until the gloomy yellow of the room became washed in white light with the beginnings of sunrise. When the light becomes sufficient to read the lines of their fingerprints, they begin *pratilekhna* – the practice of examining their belongings for insects before changing into their daytime saris. After this, they leave the monastery grounds to head to the nuns' residence for *darshan* from Sadhvi Kanak Prabha and the other *sadhvis*. From there, with the *sadhvis*, they return to the monastery for *guru darshan*. It is the one time of day when all the ascetics (and many householders) converge in the assembly hall to receive Guru Dev's and Acharyasri's blessing.

Sadhvis, like all ascetics, take turns collecting alms for their group, and today it was Sadhvis Malatiji and Bhavitaji's duty. Sadhvi Malati (not her real name) had been to America when she was a *samani* and learned to speak English very well. She now loved to practise. She was extraordinarily busy, most of her time being taken up by a new project with Acharyasri to produce an English-language dictionary of Jain philosophy. I would meet her daily to work on this project. In the presence of Acharyasri we focused on the task at hand and never talked of anything beyond it. We found the best time to talk of other matters was on the *bhiksha* rounds. On this morning I caught up with her and Sadhvi Bhavita immediately after arriving at the nuns' residence with the *samanis*. Together we walked back to the assembly hall for *guru darshan*,[45] and then headed off on our rounds.

Even though the night had given way, the village was still covered in a great sleepy shadow, and the bite of the night air lingered. Only when the morning sun began to break through the darkness did I feel myself waking up. The village animals – the cows, dogs, and horses – were still nowhere to be seen, and many of the villagers had not yet emerged from their homes. We were well bundled up, snug in our shawls as we walked briskly down the narrow village paths in search of *bhiksha*.

Sadhvi Malatiji is one of the more ambitious nuns in the order, and has many ideas on how she can use her ability in English to promote Jainism. She had been sent to travel outside India in the hope that she and the others could strengthen the religious commitments of the (assumed to be) spiritually beleaguered Terapanthi Jain families in England and the United States.[46] To many in the Terapanthi community, with its base in rural Rajasthan, 'the West' symbolizes amorality and corruption. The *samanis* and *samans* are often described in ways reminiscent of the literature of Christian missionaries – as pioneers bringing light to an area of darkness. Sadhvi Malatiji had great plans to write books on Jainism in English and was eager to have me help her. We talked about working together on various projects – children's books, vegetarian cookbooks – all in the hope of reaching an English-speaking audience. Though often engrossed in our own conversation, we kept up a fast pace, with Sadhvi Bhavita never more than a stride ahead of us. We walked and talked as companions – as individuals with particular and mutual interests. But as soon as we stepped into the home of an entreating householder, we stepped into our *personnages*. The shared interests that had bound us as we walked together were trivialized before the differences created, highlighted, and juxtaposed in the *bhiksha* rite.

The *sadhvis* entered the cement courtyard ahead of me and stood momentarily at its centre, waiting for an invitation to proceed deeper into the house. Decoratively painted arches leading into small rooms surrounded us, and the sun, which was now asserting itself in the sky, shone down into the courtyard through the exposed roof. Soon a middle-aged and heavy-set woman appeared at one of the doors. Her body was slightly bent over in a posture of humility and, with hands joined, she urged the *maharajas* to enter. Without hesitation, the nuns headed into the main room of the house, and I followed behind them. It was clear that this was a home they had frequented many times before. Two young girls approached and, with their hands joined, moved over to touch the *sadhvis'* feet. A sleepy-looking man in his thirties joined the group, followed by a woman of about the same age – perhaps his wife – and then another man and a young boy. An elderly woman, whom I had seen stretched out in bed in a tiny dark room as we entered, now slowly approached the *sadhvis*. All bowed as they came closer, repeating '*Matthayena Vandami*,'[47] and the women touched the feet of the *sadhvis*. If the family was surprised to see a foreigner in their home, they didn't show it. It would have been the height of rudeness to inquire about me at such a 'spiritual moment.' The *sadhvis* stood at the tiny kitchen entrance and busied themselves with their task at hand, paying little attention to the humbling efforts of the devotees. Slowly the *sadhvis* placed the stacked *patras*, still in their *jholi*, on the ground before them. The *jholi* keeps the *patras* secure when the ascetics walk. They carefully untied it, uncovering the alms bowls. Sadhvi Malatiji had four *patras* stacked one on top of the other, each fated to carry a particular type of food: milk, rice, *kheer*, tea, sweets, and so forth. The *patras* are made by the nuns themselves out of coconut shells, and some are remarkably beautiful.[48]

Stotras (stanzas) from the scriptures are painted in minute letters along the sides of the bowls, and most bowls include a sign of some sort by the nun who did the work. The family gathered around the pots and pans filled with food, hands still joined. The drama was about to begin.

The woman who had invited us in was now squatting on the floor beside her stove, in front of her preparations. With a ladle, she dug deeply into the rice porridge and leaned over to pour. With one hand, Sadhvi Malatiji held her *patra* towards the woman, while with the other hand she indicated restraint. But the woman poured quickly, and scooped for some more. Soon Sadhvi Malatiji was saying '*Bas*' ('Enough'), but because the bowl had not yet been withdrawn, the woman kept filling it.

When all her family members had given generously, the woman gestured for me to make an offering. With appreciation, I approached. Sadhvi Malatiji kept her eyes on her *patra*. She stood still, her posture perfectly straight. I found myself bending slightly, paying homage with my posture along with the other humble devotees. A stack of warm and crispy *pappadum* sat in a deep aluminum dish and I reached over, managing to get hold of a goodly number. Sadhvi Malatiji frowned and clicked her tongue in disapproval, but the *patra* was not withdrawn. As I placed them in her bowl she exclaimed '*Bas! Bas!*' pulling the *patra* out of my reach. 'So little?' I heard myself asking aloud, just as a generous householder ought to. Quickly the *sadhvis* placed the bowls one on top of the other, pulled the *jholi* over them, and created a knot to form a handle. We were off. Stepping out of the house, Sadhvi Malatiji and I stepped out of the scripted roles and we took up our talk where we had left off.

Soon we would be at the next home, where again our 'likenesses' would give way to our differences, and where we would stand facing each other, rather than side by side. Above all else, the ritual of *bhiksha* is a confrontation of difference, and we each would play our parts. But for the moment, as we strode shoulder to shoulder through the sleepy town, enjoying each other's company, we could forget just how important our differences were.

4
The Making of an Ascetic:
The Construction of Difference

Wrapped in an oversized shawl, I shuffled through the stretch of sand that separates my room from the assembly hall. Ahead was the blurred outline of women sweepers, barely visible in a dense cloud of sand lingering in the air around them. Throughout the day they would battle the Rajasthani desert with twig brooms as weapons, striking and flattening the mounds of sand, spreading them upwards and outwards. And for a short while, the beaten sand was easier to walk on.

The ascetics only rarely cross the sand, for fear of crushing the swarming ants, preferring the longer walk along the paved path encircling the monastery grounds. But really the ants are too big to be accidentally crushed, and many times, in the short but slow walk to the hall, it was my step that was halted when our paths crossed. I would watch with curiosity as these bulbous black critters, bureaucratic and officious, marched through the tiny spoors left by the sweepers' brooms. The area immediately around the hall is nearly devoid of ants because the sand is packed tightly after years of sustaining the weight of thousands of devotees. I slipped off my *chappals* and stepped barefoot onto the cold marble of the open-air assembly hall. Today, for once, I was early.

The hall was empty except for some sweepers clearing the floor of the ubiquitous sand with their long brooms. A handful of elderly women sat silently in prayer. But it would not be tranquil for long. Signs of the coming excitement were everywhere: a banner covering the back wall announced the occasion of the Terapanthi *diksa* (initiation), and a pile of technical equipment, microphones, speakers, and video cameras stood neatly organized around the stage. The elderly women wearing the *muhpatti* fingered their *mala* beads, marking their prayers. They come here most mornings to spend much of their day listening to sermons, talking with their favourite ascetics, or lost in private prayer. Today they would be joined by several hundred others in the 'celebration of renunciation' – the public affirmation of worldly negation and individual asceticism (see Goonasekera's [1986: 136–43] account of a Terapanthi *diksa*; see also Shântâ, 1985: 343–64).

Renunciation establishes Jain identity negatively, vis-à-vis the external world – that is, Jain moral identity is defined in terms of what it is *not*. The ascetics, by embodying the negation, are symbols (and creators) of the distinction between the worldly (*laukik*) and the transcendent (*lokottar*), of Jain reality itself. The ascetics are at once the purest expression of the worldly–spiritual ontology, and also the main foot soldiers in its construction and maintenance. *Diksa* is more than an initiation of an individual into the ascetic order; it is the idealization and dramatization of Jain reality, *through negation*. As Michael Lambek demonstrates in his analysis of taboo among Malagasy speakers in Mayotte, 'structure can be located in negation, prohibition and restriction' (1992: 253). His recognition that '[t]he observance of a taboo is a kind of continuous performative act in the sense that it brings into being and maintains – embodies – a particular moral state' (253) is applicable to the Jain understanding of the world, in which the renunciation (or negation) of 'worldly existence' is the only true moral path.

Diksa lays bare the two primary forces of Jain reality: *jiva* (soul) and its negation *ajiva* (non-soul), and allows us to see how these opposed essences are constructed and affirmed. Through *diksa*, Jain ontology is objectified, embodied, and shored up in pageant. The ascetics symbolize and embody the inversion of worldly existence – they are purity within pollution, order within chaos. *Diksa* is the formal acknowledgment and observance of difference. It is the intensified celebration of boundary demarcation, an enthusiastic and explicit observance of differentiation that otherwise forms an implicit part of Jain day-to-day existence. *Diksa* is the culmination of a long process of constructed demarcation and distinction that begins with the girl's first musings about becoming a *sadhvi* (nun). Because *diksa* is the publicly recognized crossing over of the boundaries between householder and ascetic, it makes explicit, by summoning into relief form, precisely what the boundaries consist of. On this day, three young women would publicly make that crossing. In so doing they would show that the 'rupture' between the *laukik* and *lokottar* is real, and that although the span between the two realms is great, with effort it is attainable.

The ideological demarcation between the *laukik* and the *lokottar* is at the centre of the Jain worldview. It is critical to an understanding of the rhetorical devices used in the process of banishing the 'worldly,' and of the central role the ascetics play in constituting Jain reality. As I argued in chapter 2, human distinctiveness and dignity are established in Jainism through ethical behaviour, not through any claim to being a privileged possessor of an essential, exclusive characteristic (such as having a soul or a monopoly on reason). Human uniqueness depends above all on the *construction of difference*. Humans are superior only to the extent that they can demonstrate difference from worldly existence around them and partake of the *lokottar*. Human difference in Jainism is neither intrinsic nor necessary – it must be displayed, expressed, illustrated and so forth, and it is the ascetic, above all others, who best exemplifies *difference*. Demolishing homogeneity and constituting difference is at the heart of Jain ontology, and it is the ascetics, by embodying worldly negation, who are the trailblazers.

Each morning before the sun has risen, the ascetics and householders assemble in the open-air hall in the centre of the monastery to start their day with communal prayer. It is a spacious hall and well suited to Rajasthan's climate and is the axis around which the ascetic community revolves. Except for narrow support beams, it is completely open on three sides, and serves as an airy refuge from the cruel sun and hot blowing sands in the summer months. Even now, in the winter, it is warmed by the morning sun and is a shelter from the cool desert winds. Pre-dawn sermons are moved indoors in the winter, into the largest room of the monks' residence. But by mid-morning, with the sun high in the sky, it becomes warm enough to sit in the open assembly hall, as hundreds would today, for the *diksa*.

The hall is surrounded everywhere by sand, interrupted only by other buildings and parched shrubs. The top end of the hall is connected to the monks' residence – a large, whitewashed, terraced two-storey building that is home to all 165 monks while they are in Ladnun. At the opposite end, a narrow canopy providing shelter stretches over a walkway from the hall to the *samanis*' residence. The *samans*, due to their small numbers (just four in 1996), do not have their own building, and are housed in a small section of a workers' residence about fifty metres from the hall. This area constitutes the main centre of action in the monastery, where on a daily basis all ascetics converge and where devotees come to pay their respects to 'their' *maharajas*. The remainder of the monastery consists of the 'worldly' administrative buildings, residences for the workers, an educational institute, and a library – and it is to this surrounding area, as well as the town outside, that ascetics venture three times daily to collect alms.

The *sadhvis* have two residences outside the monastery grounds, about a ten-minute walk nearer the town. The first building along the road is where the majority of the *sadhvis* reside when in Ladnun. It is a grand L-shaped building, located at an intersection of two main paths in the town, safeguarded behind high walls and an immense solid gate. Like the monks' residence, it is a busy place with devotees coming and going all day long, except during the lunch hours when entrances to the nuns' small rooms are blocked by two *rajoharan,* criss-crossed like swords at the entrance.

The second residence is a much older building, a little farther up the main road leading into the marketplace. Unlike all other ascetics' residences, it is the permanent home for very elderly and very sick nuns. Ascetics are ostensibly homeless nomads, wandering from village to village all year round except for the four months of the rainy season (*chaturmas*), when continuance of their nomadic lives would result in too much violence. During the rainy season, the abundance of life is overwhelming: plants and insects and rain (itself considered to be alive and sentient) are everywhere, making it impossible to avoid causing them injury. But even at the end of the *chaturmas,* when the ascetics resume their wanderings, the old and infirm remain at the residence and depend on a few younger *sadhvis* (appointed by Guru Dev) to collect alms for them, wash their saris, and sometimes even say *pratikraman*[1] on their behalf.

Turning east from the *sadhvis'* residences is a path that leads in the direction of the Parmarthik Shikshan Sanstha (PSS) – the boarding school for aspiring nuns. The girls are called *upasika* and *mumukshu* sisters. *Upasika* ('worshipper') is the name given a girl during her first year at the institute. After the introductory year, if she still wants to pursue the ascetic path, and if the superiors consider her eligible, she will move on to the next stage, that of a *mumukshu* ('one who is desirous of emancipation'). She will remain at this stage anywhere from six months to over ten years, depending on her rate of spiritual development, before finally being given permission to take *diksa,* or initiation, into the ascetic order.

The *sadhvis, samanis,* and 'sisters' make their way to the assembly hall several times a day: for early morning prayers, for mid-morning sermons, and then afternoon meetings. And they come for important events or lectures, provided they occur during the day, since by sunset they must be gone. Nuns and monks are forbidden to meet together after dark. (The *upasika* and *mumukshu* sisters, because they are still 'householders,' are allowed to remain at night.) Most of my days would be spent making the rounds from the assembly hall to the monks' residence, back through the assembly hall to the *samanis'* residence, then into the village to meet the *sadhvis*, and finally to the PSS to see the *mumukshus* and *upasikas* before returning to the assembly hall in the evening. Every morning I would come to the assembly hall to hear part of Guru Dev's sermon on the virtues of a religious life. I would take a shortcut from my room along the southern grounds of the monastery and enter the hall from the right. This was the 'men's section,' so with *chappals* in hand I would cross the hall to join the *mumukshus, samanis,* and lay women on the left. There were always a couple of hundred people in attendance on any given day. The atmosphere was relaxed, but not informal. Children, for instance, were expected to sit still, if not listen attentively, and no one got up to leave without bowing the requisite three times in the direction of the ascetics.

Sermons were almost always in progress by the time I arrived. I would usually end up sitting with some of the women before leaving to meet Muni Dulharaji. Dulharaji (or just 'Muniji') is a gentle, elderly monk with enormous dark eyes that droop slightly under bushy brows, which give his face a perpetually mournful look. Because of the *muhpatti*, which, like a huge white bandanna, blots out half the ascetic's face, the eyes above it take on exaggerated importance. Muniji's eyes are strong and steady, and not without irony. Perhaps his age and experience have softened him, allowing room for humour not readily found among the younger, more earnest ascetics. Muniji took time out of his translation work to see me during the mid-morning sermons and again in the evening. As a rule, a monk can never be alone with a member of the opposite sex. Another monk must always be present. And the same rule applies for the nuns. Muniji told me that Guru Dev had made an exception in our case, because my time in Ladnun was relatively limited and, more importantly, because of his age – a factor Muniji himself found comical. No such exception was made for my meetings with the younger monks. Muniji told me that *brahmacarya* (celibacy) is a difficult vow for the monks because of their constant contact with women householders. It is a sin even to have to an erotic dream – requiring special penance – let alone to think of such things in a wakeful state.

In all my time in Ladnun, I never heard a *sadhvi, samani,* or *mumukshu* use her vow of celibacy rhetorically to gain prestige and admiration. For the nuns, sexual continence is not a quality that they can put forward in order to gain personal status and honour. Indeed, it is a striking difference between the nuns and monks' strategies of ascetic self-affirmation. Given the Jain cultural context, in which female sexuality is considered threatening and in need of control (Reynell, 1985: 176), it is not surprising that nuns should choose to depict themselves as without desire. It is not uncommon for monks to speak of their ascetic steadfastness in the face of worldly (sexual) temptation in order to demonstrate their spirituality, as Muniji did. But given the fact that, in the ascetic literature, women are typically portrayed as symbols of attachment, lust, and temptation, this is not a viable method for nuns to demonstrate their ascetic credentials. We find Mahavir himself asserting:

> The greatest temptation in the world is women ... Men forsooth say, 'These are the vessels of happiness,' but this leads them to pain, delusion, to death, to hell, to birth as hell-beings or brute beings. (cited in Nevaskar, 1971: 159)

For the nuns, the vow of celibacy is treated as categorical and unconditional as are the vows of ahimsa (nonviolence), satya (truth), and acchoria (nonstealing).[2] These first three of the five mahavratas ('great vows') adopted at the time of initiation have no rhetorical power for the ascetics vis-à-vis the lay community because their violation is unthinkable, and because the identity of both the laity and ascetics is rooted in their observance. Indeed, Muni Jineshkumar defines a shravak as 'one who follows ahimsa, satya, and acchoria' (1990: 22). The real difference between the lay and the ascetic community lies in the observance of the vows of celibacy and nonpossession. Married life and possessions are not 'evils' in and of themselves the way himsa (violence), asatya (nontruth), and acchoria (stealing) are considered to be. Rather, they are vigorously pursued and praised by the householders without censure from the ascetic community. Only the elite and the enlightened are considered capable of renouncing married life and possessions, and for these reasons these vows (especially aparigrha, 'nonpossession') have considerable rhetorical power to create boundaries and to demonstrate difference between householders and ascetics, between the laukik and lokottar. In fact, the preparation for ascetic life and its fulfilment in the diksa ceremony reveals that within a wealthy business community, no other factor demonstrates spiritual progress as much as the renunciation of wealth.

Unlike the majority of monks, Muni Dulharaji had been married long ago, and had a daughter.[3] A year after his marriage, he and his wife travelled to Rajasthan to receive a blessing from Guru Dev (formerly, Acharya Tulsi),[4] as is common among Jain newlyweds. Something magical happened to him at that encounter. Seemingly out of the blue, he was struck by the righteousness of the ascetic path and wanted to renounce on the spot. But his wife was already pregnant and so he could not join the order immediately. Nevertheless he told her his wishes and she too shared his worldly disenchantment 'because she was a very pious woman.' She accepted that they lead a 'restrained life' (i.e., without sexual relations), and so they lived as 'brother and sister' until she died suddenly a few years later. After her death, he joined the order. He insisted that he was the 'last person anyone would have thought would become a monk,' implying that he was once very attached to worldly pleasures, but that sometimes 'enlightenment strikes out of seemingly nowhere.' His parents reared his daughter, and now his granddaughter is a *sadhvi* in the Terapanthi order. Muniji also has permission to instruct her without having another ascetic in attendance – another exception to the rule that reveals the continued importance of family relations, in spite of the order's great efforts to deny them. Today Muniji and I decided to forego our meeting and attend the *diksa* instead. Of course it was not a matter of choice. A *diksa* is one of the most important events for both the ascetic order and the Jain lay community, and no one would intentionally miss it.

I stood and watched the hall being transformed from a place of solitude into a lively scene of pomp and splendour. I had wanted to arrive early to secure a good place from which to observe the ceremony. Thousands of devotees had descended on Ladnun from all over India, from as far as Calcutta to the east and from Ahmedabad, Bombay, and Bangalore to the south. Although the Terapanthi community has its roots in Rajasthan, the past few generations have witnessed a large migration of the business community out of the poor desert state to settle in major business centres in India, and overseas.

Over the past several days, the monastery had been transformed from a sanctuary – deserted except for the wandering ascetics – into a bustling pilgrimage site with all its attendant commercialism. Around the monastery gates, stalls had been set up to sell books and paraphernalia (posters, photos, pens, music cassettes), all bearing images of the ascetic leaders – in particular that of Guru Dev, but also Acharya Sri, Sadhvi Pramukha Kanak Prabhaji, and the young monk Yuvacharya Munditmuni, who was widely assumed to be the future Acharya of the order. Rhythmic, repetitive *bhajans* (devotional songs) filled the air, competing with recordings of Guru Dev's sermons blasting from mini-speakers attached to the makeshift stalls. A canteen was opened for the occasion and was doing a brisk business selling Indian fast food (e.g., *utapams*) and the cola drink 'Thums Up' to the newcomers.

Large buses carrying devotees had been arriving all week. They lumbered through the village, moving at a snail's pace along the narrow and uneven paths, forcing the passersby and horses and carts to move dangerously close to the open drains that lined them. The arrival of the first buses looked decidedly odd in Ladnun, but in just a few days the festival atmosphere had transformed the monastery into a bustling market centre where their appearance no longer seemed incongruous. Another three tour buses arrived earlier this morning, carrying hundreds more devotees. So now, seven buses stood idle inside the gates of the monastery.

No one, except for the manual labourers employed at the monastery (mostly *Harijans*[5] from a neighbouring village, responsible for the general upkeep of the grounds), seemed harassed by the noise and ballyhoo. But since the bigger the celebration, the more meaningful its negation, the hullabaloo had been steadily increasing over the past few days. There was, however, considerable consternation among the families that had arrived this morning. It hadn't occurred to them that they would have difficulty in finding accommodation after their long trek, but upon arrival they were told that all living quarters were full within the grounds of the monastery and that they would have to make arrangements for themselves in the town. For many, that prospect was disheartening. Except for the few elegant homes belonging to mainly absentee Jains now living in India's big cities or abroad, Ladnun is a poor town with no urban amenities.

I laid my carry-bag to the side of a support beam, and arranged my shawl to serve as a seat. In all my time in Ladnun, I never got around to getting my own 'darshan mat' – a small, square piece of cloth that women devotees carry with them to sit on during *darshan*. I would usually just sit down on sand or marble, but my cavalier conduct was considered peculiar behaviour to those around me, and was almost always commented on. Women carrying extra mats for their children, who, in turn, preferred to stand or use their mother's mat, would insist that I use their extra one so as not to ruin my clothes on the sand.

I could see two emaciated and mangy dogs curled up like snails under the shade of a tree. Each night stray dogs dig small dens in the sand as beds to sleep in, only to be scared away by one of the workers, either with a stone or with a yell. After months of perseverance I befriended a timid, scraggly black dog with offers of biscuits. I called him 'Kalu.' He would join me on my walks around the monastery and the village, but always shied away from the grounds around the assembly hall, where most of the workers would be found. Indian dogs may be terrified of people, but they are vicious with each other. The monastery grounds had long been divided up among the rival gangs of dogs, who fero ciously guarded their turf from 'outsiders.' One morning, after having my breakfast at the meditation centre at the far end of the monastery, I saw one of the sick dogs that was ravaged by mange. Every day, as I would approach with some scrap of food, he would pull himself up off the sand, the open sores on his hairless and cracked grey skin festering, and begin to dance around me expectantly. But this morning he was so engrossed with something that he didn't see me, devouring some piece of food, I imagined. When I approached him, I could see he was eating the front leg of another dog – a black dog – who must have wandered onto alien turf and been killed by a pack of hungry dogs. I was tormented that it might be Kalu. To the nuns, this was a lesson on the evils of attachment. My dear friend Samani Urmilla Prajna asked sardonically 'And if it is not "your Kalu," then what? Would that make you feel better?' I admitted that it would make some difference but that I would have been disturbed no matter what. And like all the nuns, she reminded me that saving a life should not be one's goal, since death is inevitable. 'What is the point of saving one, when you cannot save it forever, and what is the point of saving one when you cannot save all?' she asked. Terapanthi Jains sharply demarcate between social and spiritual action in a way that makes them distinct among the other Jain orders. Only religious guidance that leads to 'a positive change of heart' is truly spiritual and earns good karma. They argue that while acts of charity (feeding, clothing, healing, etc.) are social duties, they cannot be considered religious or spiritual acts.

Of the three *diksarthis* (those about to take initiation), I knew only one fairly well, Mumukshu Jyoti. Unlike the other two, who were in their early twenties, she must have been in her mid-thirties. She had been a *mumukshu* for eleven years and had seen many girls come and move on to the *samani* life before her. Neither she nor any of the other *mumukshu* sisters ever suggested to me why she was so tardy, but for one reason or another the authorities had reservations about her ability to cope with

the ascetic life. I had my suspicions that the trouble lay in her inno-
cence. She was a plain, overtly friendly, and almost childlike woman.
Most problematic of all, I suggest, was her incapability of projecting an
attitude of worldly indifference (*vairagya*) essential to the life of an
ascetic. Shântâ describes this demeanour as follows:

> Voilà un mot très souvent utilisé par les sâdhvî dans leurs conversations,
> instructions, écrits, biographies. Il exprime le fondement de leur vie avec
> ses implications et ses conséquences. Vairagya a un aspect très négatif et un
> aspect très positif. Aspect négatif: *vairâgya* est l'indifférence foncière envers
> tous les plaisirs de la vie, les honneurs, l'argent, le bien-être, les liens fami-
> liaux, ceux de l'amitié ... Aspect positif: ce dépouillement de toute posses-
> sion, de toute attache, de tout ce qui est la vie de ce monde – vie qui,
> suivant la doctrine, est un enlisement dans la matière – conduit à l'unique
> nécessaire: la connaissance et la réalisation de l'âtman. (1985: 343)

And:

> Une *vairâginî* est une candidate admise à partager la vie des sâdhvî; ces
> dernières l'appellent par son nom, mais elle a déjà quitté ce monde, elle
> est entrée dans un état encore intermédiaire, certes, mais orienté vers un
> engagement définitif, elle a tout laissé pour écouter, apprendre, s'initier, se
> préparer. (347)

Mumukshu Jyoti's behaviour did not suggest a 'departure from the
world.' She smiled constantly, and would show deference to all the 'sisters' around her, even her juniors in rank. The Terapanthi order
observes a very strict and well-defined set of hierarchy rules. The
'youngest' (most recent initiate) must show deference to all above her
in a variety of ways (perform most chores, touch the feet of her superiors as a sign of respect, etc.). When the hierarchy is not observed as
such, difficulty arises. For example, during the early weeks of my stay, I
would greet the *samanis* no differently than anyone else – with hands
joined in 'namaste.' But I soon learned that this was entirely unacceptable behaviour for a householder like myself.[6] So when Mumukshu Jyoti
would touch the feet of the *upasika*, it was seen to disturb the natural
order of things, and certainly it made the *upasika* uncomfortable. Nevertheless, in public she was quiet and retiring, always keeping to the back
of the group, more in keeping with the ideal of worldly detachment
(*vairagya*) than her giddiness at the PSS. Whatever her shortcomings,

the authorities must have felt they didn't warrant her being held back indefinitely, and now the day she had anxiously awaited for so long had finally arrived.

The morning was growing warmer. The crowd was getting larger, filling the front section of the hall. The front twenty feet or so on the left side is reserved for the *samanis, mumukshus,* and *upasikas,* and a low wooden banister marks the area beyond, where the householders can sit. I could see that some women were 'reserving' a good seat by placing their *darshan* mats as close to the banister as they could and then wandering off to talk with other women. As I sat and waited in my 'seat' some distance back, I knew that Mumukshu Jyoti and the two other young women were spending their last 'private' moments with their families in their respective villages, not far away. Really, however, there was very little that was private or personal about the activities of the past few weeks of intensified family contact. A month previously, the three chosen by Guru Dev for initiation returned to their homes to be 'daughters' for the final time. The weeks in between the announcement and the *diksa* are a magical and exhausting time for the *diksarthis*. They return home as veritable *maharanis* and indeed are treated as royalty during the interim. Presents are lavished on them, usually in the form of luxurious saris and jewellery, and they are fed enormous quantities of delicious foods – the idea being that they will never again have the opportunity to indulge in such things. The same reasoning motivates many families to take their daughters (or sons) on trips to see some of India's famous historical sites. Mount Abu, home to the magnificent Jain Dilwara temples of the eleventh century, is a common pilgrimage for the *diksarthi*. And because it is considered a great privilege to spend time in the company of the *diksarthi*, she will be invited to visit many, many homes for an honorary meal. It is a period marked by the intensification of all things worldly (reduced in reality to eating and gift giving), of which the *diksa* ceremony is its subdued culmination. The real drama occurs 'behind the scenes' in the home villages, and the climax (the *diksa*) is not intensification, but a negation of all that preceded it. The *samanis*, having already gone through this worldly rite of passage, insist that the whole experience is overwhelming and exhausting:

My parents and my aunts and uncles all bought me saris. It was ludicrous. I could only wear them once, and then give them up. So my aunts now wear them. They fed me so much food. Really it was exhausting! Every day I would be brought to meet my relatives, always in a new sari. They too would have gifts for me, and so much food! I would want to burst. Then I would have to get dressed up in another fancy sari, and go visiting again. I wasn't interested in any of this. I did this for my family. Why would I be interested in such things? (Samani Prasandji)

'Worldly existence,' which the young *diksarthi* is preparing to renounce forever, is objectified and mainly reduced to clothes, jewellery, and rich foods. Since she cannot effectively opt out of the world, the world must be made manageable and *renounceable*. Many times the ascetics would inquire about my 'worldliness' through questions of possession and restraint: How many clothes do you own at your home? (my limited attire in Ladnun being seen as a sign of spirituality), How many shoes do you have? How many books? How big is your house? How many rooms do you have? How many items of food do you eat each day? and so forth. 'Worldliness' is circumscribed, reified, and transformed into discrete things to be catalogued. Like an inversion of C.B. MacPherson's (1962) notion of the 'possessive individual,' the ascetics acquire identity through a *lack of* possessions. But possessions are central all the same. The monks and nuns were quick to tell me that almost all their members come from well-to-do families. This point was meant to be evidence of their genuine spirituality. Renunciation is meaningful only within a context of abundance, and a life of detachment can be best observed in a vicinity of wealth. As Muniji once asked me rhetorically: If one is poor, what can he possibly renounce?

I witnessed a few instances of pre-*diksa* 'celebrations' when I was invited to the home where one of the *diksarthi* was visiting. In a state of uninterrupted excitement, bodies would flit from humbling to jostling in an effort to offer respect, food, and gifts to the young ascetic-to-be. The beautifully decorated *diksarthi* embodies contradiction. She enters a home like an ornamented doll, with paint, powder, and jewels, but she remains detached from her 'external' self. Her body represents all that she seeks to reject.

I gained a fuller understanding of the scope and importance of the festivities from the photo albums and videos that circulate widely among family members – or, more precisely, from the tremendous interest the *mumukshu* sisters and householders take in these recorded memories. On one occasion, Samani Sharda Prajna and I watched the video of her *diksa* together. It had been held in Delhi in 1994, when Guru Dev was spending his *chaturmas* there. It was a truly a tremendous affair to observe: the lavishly dressed *diksarthis* sit in ornamented, horse-pulled chariots, moving behind bedecked elephants and camels in an enormous procession spanning many streets in downtown Delhi. A large percussion band marches ahead, and thousands of spectators line the streets as far back as the eye can see. The drummers play with increasing speed, and young marchers enthusiastically wave banners announcing the *diksa* to the world. Trucks with loud speakers blast music, and floats carrying life-size cardboard figures of Guru Dev and Acharya Sri make their way down the busy streets. On other floats, young people dressed in elaborate costumes enact scenes from the lives of the *Jinas,*[7] while hundreds of members of the Terapanthi Mahila Mandal (Women's Organization), all dressed in identical orange and red saris, march behind in unison. Jain school children in their navy uniforms sing songs and wave banners, while great numbers of men, all dressed in white *khadi pajamaz,* follow behind singly joyously. Near the back of the procession, the *upasikas* and *mumukshus* in their *kavatchan* (tunics) move slowly, quietly singing devotional songs. The *samanis,* carrying alms bowls for later collections, walk behind in total silence, forbidden to celebrate in the worldly aspects of the *diksa.* The video leaves off as the procession slowly makes its way through the northern part of the city, ending at the Terapanthi Jain meditation centre (the Adhyatma Sadhana Kendra), where Guru Dev and Acharya Sri are staying along with the other *munis.* The video then resumes in a room at the meditation centre, where the *mumukshu* sisters merrily fuss about a table of sweets and other foods in preparation for the *diksarthis'* arrival. It would be their first chance to meet their former 'sisters' since Guru Dev chose them for initiation well over a month before. The video captures the *diksarthi* Mumukshu Sharda entering the lively room: on seeing the exuberant 'sisters' she allows herself a smile only to have a sweet put unexpectedly into her mouth. As the other *diksarthis* follow behind her, the 'sisters' set upon them in a feeding frenzy, until the *diksarthis* gain some control and begin to stuff the *mumukshus'* faces with goodies as well. A few householders also participate in the celebration, handing the *diksarthis* gifts of framed pictures of Guru Dev and Acharya Sri, which they accept and then put aside for good. The gifts are symbolic, and represent the final intra-worldly exchange the young women will ever be allowed to participate in. After initiation, all exchange between the ascetic and lay community is strictly forbidden, and the cross-boundary transactions that do occur (e.g., *bhiksha*) are translated into a language that does not include exchange (see chapter 3). For the remainder of the day, the *diksarthis* are on display before the lay community, listening to songs and speeches by family members and community, and making their own speeches about their decision to renounce the world. The public celebrations continue late into the evening, and then during the night. The *diksarthis'* female friends and family relations sit up singing *bhajans* (devotional songs) in her honour.

It is an extravagant procession, financed in part by the *diksarthis'* families (close to the cost of a middle-class dowry) and by the Terapanthi community. They re-create the archetypal renunciation scene common to many of the Jain Tirthankaras as well the Buddha – but with an important difference. Whereas the celebrated renunciants were moved to renounce by the contradictions they saw in their lives of abundance, today the Jain community re-creates those contradictions so as to make the renunciation meaningful. The 22nd Tirthankara Neminath, for example, decided to renounce after realizing that his marriage would be the cause of so much violence; and the Buddha's decision was prompted by his first exposure to human misery. The modern-day community re-creates the opulence so as to make renunciation a momentous and purposeful event. Babb's description of the display of wealth at periodic Murtipujaka (idol-worshipping) Jain rites of worship is insightful:

> The ceremonies supported by this cascade of wealth are typically sumptuous, lavish occasions – full of color and suggestions of the abundant wealth of the supporters. They seem to have little to do with liberation from the world's bondage.
>
> And yet here is the paradox. If we peel away the opulence and glitter from these occasions we discover that liberation is there, right at their heart. At the centre of all the spending, the celebration, the display, the stir, is the figure of the Tirthankara. He represents everything that the celebration is apparently not, for he is, above all else, an ascetic. His asceticism, moreover, has gained him liberation from the very world of flowing wealth of which the rite seems so much a part. Liberation and the asceticism that leads to liberation are thus finally the central values, despite the context of opulence. Wealth is not worshipped; wealth is *used* to worship the wealthless. (1996: 26)

The morning hours before the *diksa* are the *diksarthis'* last as 'householders,' and they are spent with their individual families. Over the period of my stay in Ladnun, I was shown innumerable family photos and several home videos of these 'private,' emotionally charged scenes.

In the last hours with her family, the young woman has her last-ever bath and then is bejewelled in gold and dressed in the most beautiful of saris by her family, usually in the *mangalik* (auspicious) colours of red and gold. As in a pre-wedding celebration, henna patterns are drawn on her hands and on the soles of her feet, and a saffron *tikka* marked on her forehead. (In previous times, before the present Acharya, the young woman would also wear the head-dress of Rajasthani married women. Young male *diksarthis* still continue with this practice and wear the large and elaborate men's marriage head-dress during the ceremonies.)

There is typically a large crowd of family, relatives, and neighbours present, singing *bhajans* when the *diksarthis'* long, dark tresses are released from their braids and let to tumble splendidly down her back. Her mother first combs out and then washes her hair for a final time in *mangalik* curds. Lastly, in a rarefied atmosphere of intensifying *bhajans* and whimpers from family members, and before an expectant audience, the barber shaves off all her hair with a long blade (save for a small tuft that will be ceremoniously plucked out at the *diksa*). As her long locks of hair fall to the ground around her, her family weeps. The grey shadow of her shaven scalp appears improper and even a little disturbing atop her decorated body. Her relatives then draw a *swastik* in red on top of her shaven head with the edge of a coin. It is a terribly difficult time for the family as they prepare to relinquish all ties to her, and tears flow freely. But the *diksarthi* at the centre of all the attention remains steadfastly resolute. Her determination is greatly admired and praised, but in reality it is a dubious praise, for if she were to falter and display any emotion, it would be catastrophic. My thoughts returned to Mumukshu Jyoti, in her home village about a 100 kilometres away. Surely by now she had passed through this rite. I wondered if she had managed not to smile or weep.

'*Apka nam kya hai?*' '*Apka nam kya hai?*' A group of excited children had gathered around me, demanding to know my name, but before I could answer, they darted off giggling to where their mothers were sitting. The hall was now full, but it was not yet overrun. As the adults sat in prayer or talked among themselves, smartly dressed children played about freely, mainly sticking to their respective side of the hall. Little girls, many with Western-style smocks and ribbons in their well-groomed hair, ran around the support beams at the back of the hall, and on the right side, the boys did the same.

Many youngsters, caught up in the exceptional event, insist that they too want to become ascetics. And it is no wonder why: the *diksa* is so spectacular an event that it cannot but leave an impression. Even so, it is merely the culmination of a long phase during which the young ascetic-aspirant enjoys an elevated moral status (see Reynell, 1985: 248–54). I met many young girls who, while visiting Guru Dev with their family, would tell me that they too wanted to be *sadhvis*. Parents do not always react happily to these statements from their daughters. Often they try to dissuade their daughters and sons from pursuing the ascetic path, and in so doing, they display the cultural norm of the worldly and attached family that is expected of them. The gap between the worldly and the spiritual is always presented as great and insurmountable, and the drama between the two is played out continuously. But from the moment the young person convinces her family that her intention to become an ascetic is genuine, she becomes a distinguished member of her family, gaining almost celebrity status. Her special standing only intensifies with her stay at the PSS boarding school, where each year she becomes more and more 'ascetic-like.'

The girls self-consciously strive to be 'different from householders' in bodily comportment. They try to be more careful in the way they walk, sit, talk, eat, and so forth. They straightforwardly assert that the cultivation of difference is one of their goals, and many times I was asked whether the distinctions were as obvious to me as they appeared to them. Establishing difference is, of course, their principal means of demontrating nonviolence and spirituality. The first-year girls – the *upasikas* – are allowed the greatest number of possessions (e.g., five saris) and greater lenience (e.g., they can wash their hair up to twice a week). With each year, the girls try to make do with increasingly less, and thereby come to see the distance between themselves and house-holders as great. This distance is perceived, in large part, through the contrast between the relatively 'indulgent' life of the householders and their own. *Mumukshu* sisters come to see 'worldliness' in the relatively narrow terms of 'possessions,' because it is in relation to the practices of their own community that they come to judge their own lives.

That 'worldliness' is viewed by ascetics primarily through a narrow discourse of 'possessions and indulgence' is a function of the affluent community – both the source of prosperity and its rejection. Because all Jains esteem the ascetic ideal, and try to incorporate ascetic values into their lives, the nuns and monks – who fully embody the ideal – are seen as outstanding and courageous, as representatives of the community's elite. Affluence (or more precisely, its manifestation in possessions) and householders' limited efforts at 'restraint' provide a readily available gauge against which to map their own lives of total self-denial. Although violence, lust, greed, and so on, are the worst forms of 'worldliness,' and lead to the greatest and most dense forms of bad karma, they are not used rhetorically in the constitution of the ascetic self. The relationship with 'the renounced' – if it is to have any rhetorical power – is complex and must allow for a degree of manoeuvrability not possible with more serious forms of 'worldliness.' In addition, these 'gross vices' are not used rhetorically because of their distance from the community's day-to-day life, and significantly, because they are *universally* condemned. Renouncing violence, lust, and greed may reflect righteousness, but it does not reflect extraordinary restraint or enlightenment – the domain of the ascetics. For the ascetics to assert and maintain a moral monopoly, they must be seen to renounce what others cannot.

Although lay Jains clearly do not devote themselves entirely to renunciatory goals, ascetic values and practices are the measure against which they distinguish themselves from non-Jains (Babb, 1990, Banks 1992; Dundas, 1992: chap. 7; Jaini, 1979: chap. 6; Reynell, 1985, 1987). Ascetic values are at the core of their identity, defining who they are and permeating their daily lives. Babb writes:

> Jains say that once the seeds of righteousness have been planted, progress is always possible, no matter what the ups and downs in the meantime. An Ahmedabad friend once told me that if you possess right belief (*samyaktva*) for as little time as a grain of rice can be balanced on the tip of the horn of a cow, you will obtain liberation sooner or later. Therefore, even if one has little immediate interest in the ultimate goal of liberation or little sense of its personal gainability – which is in fact true of many ordinary Jains – one can still believe that one is on the right road if one has been touched by Jain teachings and if one has the necessary 'capability' (*bhavyatva*). (1996: 36)

Jain lay codes of conduct allow individuals to practise as much renunciation as they are capable of – as is clear from the set of fourteen principles (*chauda nyem*) which a person is encouraged to follow every day:

1 To restrict the use of green vegetables and fruit.
2 To limit the amount of *dhal*, rice, *chappatis*, and sweets eaten.
3 To abstain from meat, liquor, butter, and honey and to abstain from one of the following daily: *ghee*, milk, curd, sugar.
4 To limit the number of slippers or shoes worn.

5 To limit the number of clothes worn to eleven items a day.
6 To limit the number of *pan* and *supra* eaten.
7 To limit the number of fragrances enjoyed to fifteen a day.[8]
8 To limit the number of vehicles used to two a day.
9 To limit the number of chairs, sofas, and beds used in a day.
10 To limit the ornaments and cosmetics used per day.
11 To limit sexual intercourse.
12 To limit the distance travelled in one day.
13 To limit water used while bathing.
14 To limit the overall quantity of eatables and drink consumed within
   a day. (Reynell, 1987: 21)

The degree to which lay Jains incorporate ascetic practices into their
lives is a reflection of their moral status, and is tied to family honour.
This is especially true for women. Female religiosity takes the form of
ascetic practices (especially fasting), whereas male religiosity is more
often expressed through *dana*, the giving of donations (Reynell, 1985).
What is most striking about the *chauda nyem* – more than the self-
imposed restrictions – is the prosperous context that evidently gives it
meaning. To the poor, this list would not only be meaningless, it would
be absurd. But this is precisely the point: voluntary poverty requires a
context of affluence in order to be consequential; renunciation is not
for 'the have-nots.' We recall Muniji's observation: 'If one is poor, what
can he possibly renounce?' In this context, Muniji told me the story of
the beggar and the ascetic:

A notorious beggar in the neighbourhood was not successful at obtaining
food. Every day he would go to many homes, but the women would rarely
give him anything. One day he saw a monk approaching one of the homes
he often went to and, to his amazement, he saw that the woman of the
house was eager to feed him. He was equally amazed to observe the monk's
bizarre behaviour: he refused most of the things she offered, and of those
he accepted, he took only the tiniest quantity. The beggar had an idea. He
thought that if he disguised himself as a monk, he too would be fortunate.
So the next day he went to the same home dressed in white robes. At first
the woman was happy to offer him food, but she soon realized he was an
impostor when he eagerly accepted all she offered. His greedy, gluttonous
behaviour betrayed him.

To Muniji, this story demonstrated the differences between ascetics and beggars: whereas the ascetic is disciplined and motivated by restraint, the beggar is unrestrained and driven by desire. Clearly, restraint is the most cherished of virtues, but it requires a garden of temptation to burgeon, and to be acknowledged.

Swiftly the hall filled. The crowd became tremendous and its intensity was palpable. Men, women, and children of all ages were entering in large numbers now and settling down as close to the stage as they could. Dozens of pairs of *chappals* that had been neatly placed against the support beams of the hall were quickly disappearing beneath the onslaught. Invariably, a few pairs would be lost in the scramble afterwards. The high ceiling fans, which provide some respite from the afternoon sun, had not yet been switched on, and pigeons, who make homes for themselves in the high wood planks, seemed to know it. They frolicked carelessly about them, resting like daredevils on the immense blades. I wondered if they ever get cut down during the daily religious services, and how the community, overtly anxious as it is about even the smallest signs of violence, would react to a mangled bird in their midst.

The *mumukshu* sisters could be seen entering from the eastern gate of the monastery. The start of the ceremony could not be too far off now. Like the ascetics, they moved quickly and kept their eyes focused on the path before them. As is the rule, all were silent as they walked toward the assembly. Today they would be on their very best behaviour, for the audience observing them was large, and likely filled with members of their own family. Other than the actual *diksarthis* and their families, the *mumukshus* were without doubt the most excited by the day's events, and, as if conforming to their role as novices, most would openly admit to being thrilled. The ascetics, as a rule, would not. The *mumukshus* had been talking of little else for the past weeks, anxiously awaiting the ceremony's arrival. Today three more 'sisters' would be honoured and they could revel in the ceremonies knowing that their day would soon come. Characteristic of the *mumukshus* is their single-minded focus on attaining *diksa*. Their years at the PSS are spent in anticipation and preparation for the day they will be allowed to take initiation, and for many it is difficult to even imagine beyond it.

As the group approached, their faces were visible and I could see that quick bashful smiles were passing between each other. For many of the girls, the overt and exaggerated attention they receive from householders is unwanted and even embarrassing. They have not yet come to see themselves as the symbols of purity and representatives of the human ideal that the community projects onto them. But in time they would (see Reynell, 1985: 248–50). Indeed, acceptance of this role, embodying it and mastering its particular demeanour, is a prerequisite for the ascetic life. Most of the 'sisters' made no eye contact with the householders, retaining a detached facial expression as they entered the hall before the hundreds of gathering devotees. The difference between the girls' comportment was almost always a function of years spent at the PSS boarding school. The longer their stay, the better they performed their expected roles. Although I never heard it put so directly, it is highly unlikely a girl would ever be given permission to take *diksa* until she had mastered and embodied the outward guise of the detached ascetic (*vairagini*). (Publicly, even Mumukshu Jyoti was proficient in this demeanour.) In addition to learning basic prayers and scriptures, the aspirants learn to behave in a very specific way, reflecting the ascetic cultural norms of restraint. Above all, they learn to see themselves as different from the householders. Many *samanis* – though experts at projecting a demeanour of worldly detachment (*vairagya*) – find the post-*diksa* period an especially awkward time because they are immediately treated as 'maharajas' by the householders, who accept the crossing over of the boundary from householder to ascetic as complete (see Babb, 1996: 62). I would watch as women and men of all ages approached recently initiated *samanis*, looking for advice for their worldly problems, seemingly indifferent to their novice status. The expression on the *samanis'* faces would betray intense discomfort, as they would look around to the more seasoned *samanis* for assistance.

The sixteen *upasiksas* (candidates in their first year) entered the gates directly behind the fifty-three *mumukshus*, and were only barely distinguishable from the householders who accompanied them. However much they dislike it, they resemble the worldly householders more than any other in the ascetic community. Although all are eager to immerse themselves in ascetic life immediately, the pace at which they do so is fixed. The operating logic is that the ascetic life is very trying and so radically different from worldly life that the girls should be eased into it gently. In the first year the *upasikas* must wear flower-patterned saris when they are at the PSS. They dislike their 'pretty' uniforms, since their prettiness identifies them with the worldly life of pleasures that they are so eager to renounce publicly. The visual, aesthetic element of the ascetic life cannot be underestimated: the bare feet and identical uniform of white robes are taken as indexes of spirituality both for the lay community and within the ascetic community itself. In addition, the aesthetic factor plays an enormous role in the recruitment of girls and boys, many of whom yearn less to lead a life of meditation than to belong to the charismatic and powerful group of ascetics (see Reynell, 1985: 249–52).

When the *upasikas* go on their daily visits to the monastery and to the nuns' residence, they wear the same simple white saris with thick, colourful trim (usually they opt for a deep blue or purple band) as the *mumukshus* wear. But even here, their difference is marked: their saris are tucked in on the right and draped counterclockwise, distinguishing them from the *mumukshus*, who secure their saris under their left arm and drape them clockwise over their faces. And, more conspicuously, the *upasikas* do not wear the *kavatchan* (tunic). To an outsider the differences between the two groups seem minor, but they are important to the girls themselves. The construction of difference is important in itself: the further the girls progress into their ascetic career, the greater the distance between them and the householders should be. The distinction between the worldly and the spiritual is never categorical; instead it is mapped according to the constructed 'worldly.' It is negotiable with, and contingent upon, the worldly. In fact, the changes from one stage to another in the ascetic hierarchy are not so great as the outward signs would suggest. Instead, the outward signs are the main differences between the *upasikas* and *mumukshus*. But difference is the important factor, the 'truth' that must be demonstrated and observed. *Meaning lies in difference because difference is meaning.* It is not evocative of anything other than itself. Difference is indicative of division, of contrast, and this is precisely what is constructed through the rhetorical discourse of asceticism, which supports an ontology that distinguishes two realities: that of *jiv* and *ajiv*, the *lokottar* and the *laukik*.

As the 'sisters' approached, I could see Mumukshu Promika – one of the girls I was closest to at the PSS – near the back of the group. Her long hair had been meticulously secured under the hood of her tunic, and she was carrying with her a small book, probably of prayers. I always enjoyed Promika's happy company. Forever bubbling over with energy, she would jounce about her chair delighting in our talk about *mumukshu* life. The first time I met her, she had been fasting for four days, only taking boiled water, but her energy and enthusiasm were strong even then. Whenever she would become enthused about something (which was very often indeed), she would punctuate her sentences with spirited hand gestures, and then laugh at her own vivaciousness. Strands of long, braided hair, hastily tucked beneath the 'hood' of her sari, would fall before her eyes, and her thin fingers would scramble to secure them again. During our very first encounter, Promika confidently announced that she would be one of the initiates at the next *diksa* (today's event). Although the decision about which girls would renounce had not yet been made, she was confident because her family, who were visiting at the time, had specially requested Guru Dev to consider their daughter for early initiation. I remember being surprised at her self-assuredness, but her confidence was as much a strategy as it was wishful thinking. Many of the girls assert that they will soon take *diksa* as a way of demonstrating their strong desire to renounce the world as well as their preparedness to do so.

When the novices first arrive at the PSS, all are eager to prove their ascetic credentials, and fasting is the quintessential method – not just for the 'sisters' but for the lay community and the ascetics themselves. (This is truer for lay women than men, just as it is far more common among nuns than monks. I will return to this in chapter 7, 'Devotion and Divinity.' See also Reynell, 1985, 1987.) Asking about the motivation for a fast will always result in an answer about getting rid of karma. But these acts must be seen within the context of the ascetic ideal where such self-imposed deprivations and concomitant stoicism are a powerful form of currency. When I asked Promika if she felt any hunger, she just laughed saying, 'No! Of course not!' Hunger would have represented attachment and weakness, and could never be admitted – perhaps not even to herself – and certainly never to an outsider! She was already known among the 'sisters' and the ascetics as a 'champion' faster. And this, she felt, would be evidence of her maturity for ascetic life. But almost in the same breath as her assertion of ascetic fitness, she added that everything depended on 'His Holiness'; only Guru Dev would know when she was really ready to renounce. This tension between independence and dependence runs throughout every aspect of the ascetic life, and will be discussed in Part Three of the book.

Over the months, I had grown quite fond of Promika and marvelled at her unflagging good humour. We had been meeting at the school several times a week since I first arrived, usually in the afternoon. I would always come early, when the girls were still in class, and make my way to the reading room. Automatically, I would open the old wooden shutters of the one small window to allow a little natural sunlight to pierce the darkness. The sunlight would throw into relief the long bookshelf that stretches the length of the back wall, and above which hangs a large black and white portrait of an early administrator of the PSS. In front of the bookcase is a long reading table with old newspapers strewn on it.

The walls are covered with artwork done by the girls themselves, and, perhaps not surprisingly, the subjects of the works all concern one aspect or another of the ascetic life. Many are paintings of Guru Dev, or of Acharya Bhikshu, the founder of the Terapanthi order, or of a famous scene from the life of Lord Mahavira. I was struck by one large piece – part painting, part collage – that hangs high on the wall. It is a depiction of Jain reality from the point of view of these young women. It presents an upward trajectory of five possible states of human existence – beginning with the lowliest: at the bottom corner on the far right is the female householder shown in a colourful sari standing over a low cooker. A little farther over to the left and higher up on the canvas comes a *mumukshu* sister, dressed in a pink and white stripped sari and looking upwards. About midway up the painting is a *samani*, followed by a sadhvi, represented by an actual picture of Sadhvi Kanak Prabha, the head nun of the order. Finally at the top centre of the painting is an image of an emancipated 'male' *Jina*,[9] sitting cross-legged, eyes closed in deep meditation and a halo around his head.

Promika, like most of the 'sisters' at the PSS, was in continual contact with the direction her life should take. As soon as she would see me in the reading room, she would rush off to bring me a glass of water or a cup of sweet *chai*. One day, when I asked her the already hackneyed question I had been asking the ascetics, 'Why have you chosen this life?' she surprised me. I had been used to speaking with the *samanis, sadhvis,* and *munis*, whose different tales invariably centred on disillusionment with worldly life (with marriage, violence, possessions, childbearing etc.), but instead of providing a negative response (negative in the sense of being a rejection of the world that led them to the order), Promika gave an unselfconsciously affirmative reason: the tunics. 'I love the *kavatchan!* I saw the girls in their white *kavatchan* and I wanted to wear one too. They look so-o-o lovely!' She laughed when she spoke, and said that since arriving, she found so many other things to interest her, but that the tunic had been the beacon. The *mumukshus* provided a wide range of answers to the question and, for all but a handful (of the 53 sisters), their answers involved the aesthetic element of asceticism as well as a communal aspect of belonging to a special group or clique.

There is little doubt that the notions of heroism and nobility associated with asceticism are also of central importance in inspiring young women to renounce, as Carrithers (1983) hypothesizes. Carrithers argues that motivation to renounce the world finds its origin in the cultural valorization of asceticism (1983: 8–15). Following Carrithers, Reynell claims that Jain society's positive evaluation of asceticism is a key motivation for its young women. She writes:

> What is important here is the allure of a noble ideal in terms of the circum-
> scribed role held by Jain women. I suggest that this ideal is particularly
> attractive to young women for two reasons. Firstly, the avenues of public
> prestige are largely closed to women, and secondly, the status and prestige
> which a married woman does accrue, comes after many years of marriage.
> (1985: 249)

Although the allure of power and prestige undoubtedly informs many young women's desire to renounce the world, it is clearly not a motivation that they themselves would put forward.

The PSS was born out of the desire to allow young girls who wanted to be initiated into the order of nuns first to undergo a preparatory train-ing for full-fledged monastic life. The aspirants should be 'exposed to austerities' in stages and provided with opportunities to understand Jainism. It was founded in 1948 with only twenty girls, and amidst great controversy. Many within the community saw it as a break with tradition and as a scandalous suggestion to have their daughters living in a board-ing school, without family supervision. The only criterion of admission was, and is, that the aspirant should 'display a positive evidence of her desire to attain to the state of final emancipation from worldly bondage' (Bhatnagar, 1985: 82). Although the school was designed with the goal of providing training and education for girls, a few boys also attend day classes when they are not at the monastery. Training for young men and women is considerably different because of the relatively small number of male candidates 'desirous of emancipation.' They typically have much shorter training periods, usually gaining entrance into the monkhood within a year. The practical consequence of these arrange-ments is that young women are far more prepared for ascetic life than are young men at the time of *diksa*. Yet, I would argue that this has the ironic effect of undermining the glory of female asceticism, of down-playing its extraordinary nature. Renunciation is paradigmatically a bold and courageous act; it is an occasion of high drama in which all ties with social life are ostensibly severed. Although the *diksa* ceremony itself attempts to recreate this drama, the fact that women go through a long-term training program where they essentially 'learn' to renounce under-mines the impact of renunciation at the public level. The drama of the young male renunciant is more true to the ideal. Even though the Terapanthi ascetics are today far removed from the original ideal of isolated mendicant wandering, and are instead very much 'public persons' (Babb, 1996: 52), women's symbolic separation from society is somewhat equivocal (I look at this in detail in chapter 8). In addition to spending years at the PSS, after initiation, the vast majority of the girls first become *samanis* (the semi-nun status) for a number of years before finally becoming *sadhivs*. Although a parallel category – *samans* – exists for boys, only those with exceptional oratory powers and knowledge of some English are selected for it.

Across the sand where the dogs had been sleeping, the *samanis* could be seen filing out of their residence. Two by two, they moved quickly and purposefully, with long strides[10] and serious faces. Their walk distinguishes them as ascetics in the calm of village India. They act, look, and feel important because they *are* important. They constitute Jain reality by embodying its principle of worldly negation. Without the ascetics actualizing the renunciatory logic, there would be no examples of the distinction between the worldly and the spiritual, only endless expressions of the *jiv/ajiv* combination in the absence of a pathfinder. The ascetics are important because they create the very reality that in turn determines their lives, and their demeanour conveys this sense of self.

The Terapanthi Jains, unlike all other Jain communities, are a proselytizing order, and it was in this spirit that Guru Dev created the *saman/samani* order in 1980. His goal was the spreading of Jain teachings throughout the world. Unlike full ascetics, the *samans* and *samanis* are allowed to travel by any means of transportation available and to accept food that has been specifically prepared for them. Whereas the lives of the *sadhvis* and *munis* are considered completely nonviolent, the 'allowances' implicate the *samans* and *samanis* in some degree of violence. After a number of years, they take '*muni diksa*,' as it is called for both nuns and monks. The *saman/samani* stage is not considered permanent; instead, like the *upasika* and *mumukshu* stage, it is yet another step in the life of spiritual advancement. Interestingly, many *samanis* do not yearn to move on to the next *sadhvi* stage, and this sharply distinguishes them from the *upasika* and *mumukshu* sisters, who dream of moving 'upward.' *Samanis* almost never talk about the change, except when pressed. They typically declare that 'It is my ultimate goal of course.' In confidence, a few have told me that they never wanted to become *sadhvis,* because at that level, all their time would be taken up with *bhiksha, panchami* (toilet), *vihar* (pilgrimage), and making the *rajoharan* (whiskbrooms) and *patra* (alms bowls)[11] and mending robes, both for themselves and the monks. They lamented that they would have little time for their education and, ironically, their *sadhana* (spiritual practice)!

In a moment's time they would be in the hall, and I would be expected to sit with them. I was happy with where I was, on the periphery, because nothing was hidden from my view. Not only would I be able to see the *diksa* ceremony on the stage ahead, but I would also see the reactions of the householders, *upasikas*, *mumukshus*, and *samanis* on the floor around me. I was most curious about the *mumukshus* since it was, after all, the day in which their 'sisters' cross the boundary in the rite of passage from householder to ascetic, once and for all.

The seating arrangement in the hall reflects the ascetic hierarchy: On the stage with Guru Dev and Acharya Sri sit the ascetics – *sadhvis* to the right and *munis* to the left. Occasionally, a few very prominent lay persons (men) share the stage with the *munis*. On the left side of the floor, directly beneath the stage, sit the *samanis* (the *samans*, because of their low numbers, sit among the *munis*). Behind the *samanis* sit the *mumukshus* and *upasikas*, and behind them are the women householders. On the right side of the hall, separated by an aisle, sit the male householders; the more prominent, the closer to the stage. The placement of the *mumukshus* and *upasikas* reflects their liminal status: as a buffer between the ascetics (in front of them) and the householders (behind them), it symbolically represents their ambivalent status as neither ascetic nor householder.

I would be expected to sit with the *samanis* because I spent practically all my time with them since my arrival. The *mumukshus* had initially been much easier to befriend, but it was among the *samanis* where I learned the most and formed my closest friendships. The *mumukshu* sisters had been easier to approach and to form friendships with because of their 'in-the-world-status.' I was able to meet with them as relative equals, whereas I was required to show deference before the *samanis*. Although 'attachments' in the abstract were shunned, our meetings did not constitute an attachment or a threat to *mumukshus* the way it did for *samanis*. They spoke freely about their families (with whom they continued to spend several months of the year), whereas the *samanis* only spoke grudgingly of theirs. In general, the *mumukshus* had no reservation in expressing their excitement about their lives and tended to provide positive reasons for renunciation, whereas the *samanis* provided negative ones (e.g., disenchantment with the world). Although the *mumukshus* were warm, they resembled a group of highly motivated teenagers studying for their final exams – in this case, for *diksa*. Few had

begun to imagine what kind of lives they would lead after becoming
samanis, other than saying 'It is up to my guru.' The simplicity and uni-
dimensionality of their lives ends with *diksa*, when a single goal no
longer looms large before them.

Not shifting from my seat, I watched as the *samanis* entered the hall.
Many were carrying things to busy themselves with during the ceremony
(books, saris to mend, scriptures to memorize, etc.). For the *samanis*,
the impending *diksa* was not a topic of great interest. They had seen so
many and, of course, had experienced their own (of which they liked to
talk). I watched as they stood, knelt, bowed, and stood again doing *vandana* (paying homage) to their gurus. They did so with such poise,
effortlessly moving up and down, before settling into a more settled
cross-legged position. The elegance of their movements was only slightly
lessened by their worn and weathered feet peeping out below their saris.
Like rusty old hubcaps, ugly calluses cover their anklebones, from years
of sitting cross-legged and barefoot on hard surfaces. Probably more
than any other part of their bodies, their feet suffer the brunt of their
ascetic lives. Burned by the sun in the summer and chilled in the winter,
they become the symbols of hardship and worldly abandon, and almost
signify group membership! When I would sit with the *samanis* in the
early evenings[12] of winter, I would watch them put ointment[13] on the
cracks of their torn feet and then bandage them with scraps of old sari
cloth for the night. I would be shown their wounds, and my 'abhor-
rence' was the appropriate response from which they then could demonstrate ascetic stoicism: 'It is nothing.'

Finally, the monks could be seen emerging from their quarters. The
ceremony was about to begin. A small group stood at the threshold
between their quarters and the stage, allowing Guru Dev and Acharya
Sri to come out and take their places on the elevated dais. A young, thin
monk with a surprisingly full coif of hair, supported Guru Dev by holding his arm and moved him toward his seat. The youngest and most
recent initiate, just eleven years old, followed directly behind them, and
waited for Guru Dev to take his seat before sitting down at his feet. The
youngest monks usually sit in a half circle around the leaders, reflecting
the intimate relationship that exists between them. Quickly, the lay followers rose to their feet and held their joined hands high in the *namaste*
position. They began to pay homage: in a standing position, they moved
their joined hands in three circles high in the air in the direction of the
ascetics, then knelt and touched their foreheads on the floor. They
would repeat this two more times. It was a difficult ritual for the very eld-

erly or the overweight, and occasionally such devotees would perform the act of humility and respect without standing up. Their hands joined, they would do three circumambulations in the air while on their knees, and then lower their heads for a few seconds, mimicking the prostrations. This they would do three times before settling into a more comfortable cross-legged position. Among idol-worshipping Jains (i.e., most other Jain orders other than Sthanakvasi Svetambars), the devotees circumambulate three times around an idol of a Tirthankara. But since the Terapanthis forbid idol worship, householders symbolically circumambulate around the living ascetic instead.*

As the lay devotees moved up and down like broken waves, the *sadhvis* were arriving from the left, from behind the stage wall. The greatness of their numbers was impressive; at least half (approximately 250) of the entire population of all the Terapanthi nuns were in Ladnun for the ceremony. The mass of flowing white gowns, moving in pairs briskly and assuredly, ushered in a sense of immediacy and solemnity to the charged atmosphere. On the other side of the stage, the stout and sweet-faced monk Subritmuni was actively involved in directing the 'traffic' away from the ascetics, urging the lay followers to settle down and keep back. Whether it was an assigned task or of his own doing, I don't know, but he often assumed the role of a 'bouncer' during the morning sermons, making sure the lay followers did not throng Guru Dev and Acharya Sri. He was one of the few ascetics who could not or would not conform to the (public) demeanour of worldly detachment (*vairagya*).[14]

My friendships with the nuns and monks had required considerable time to develop, but with a few of the extroverts, like Subritmuni, friendship was almost immediate. And – especially in the first few months of my stay – I was grateful for these people's amiable departure from the norm. Perhaps it is a matter of projecting backwards, but everything about Subritmuni suggested worldliness: he was a great joker and he delighted in testing my Hindi and my knowledge of the names of the monks. Our simple conversations would always be interspersed with laughter. His large head, topped with prematurely white stubble, would shoot back to allow a boisterous and contagious laugh to burst forward, only barely restrained by his *muhpatti*, and his rotund belly would peer out from his robe, jolly and delighted to be entertained. He was also a performer, loving to sing a song to whoever would listen. Often, as I

*Interestingly, in other Jain traditions, this would be considered impious practice. See Cort (1989).

would be leaving the monks' residence after seeing Muni Dulharaji, Subritmuni would wave me over to the marble veranda. Other monks would be sitting near him, usually studying or meditating, but Subritmuni always appeared too restless for such stilled activity. After testing my knowledge of the names of the accompanying monks, he would begin to sing. The first time it happened, I was surprised at his unconventional behaviour, and at a loss about how to react. Most monks are ill at ease or, at best, reserved with women. Rules about the interaction between the monks and women are detailed, rigid, and reproachful. Not only can a monk not be alone in a room with a woman, he must wait thirty minutes before sitting on a spot where she has been sitting – for it to cool down – lest her 'sexual energy' remain and tempt him; if an exchange of some item has to be made between a woman and a monk, it must be passed along the ground between them, never allowing their hands to be simultaneously on it, again lest temptation arise. A monk or nun cannot touch an infant of the opposite sex, and the ascetics are even forbidden to dwell in shelters where animals may be, because the sound or sight of copulating animals may bring forth corrupt ideas.

The rules about guarding celibacy are identical for the nuns' relations with men, although the nuns many times told me they believe that temptation is a much greater challenge for the monks than for them. The rules are laid out in detail in Acharya Bhikshu's work *Shil ki Nau Bar* (The Body's Nine Fences). It is one of the most important scriptures for the ascetics, and required learning for those seeking renunciation. The language of the scripture presupposes male asceticism and female temptation, and this presumed antagonism forms an extremely common theme in Jain storytelling.[15] Because suspicion underlies relations between the ascetics and members of the opposite sex, I was surprised by Subritmuni's unorthodox familiarity. I found myself flustered: beguiled by sweet and smooth sounds, my mind raced to make sense of my encounter with the charming monk. Had I understood the words – presumably about the falsehood and deception of worldly pleasures – I may have been less bewitched. Nevertheless, I only began to enjoy the 'show' when a group of elderly women, moved to tears by lyrics I could not follow, joined me. I came to cherish Subritmuni's unconventional ways. He seemed such an unlikely monk – very much preoccupied with the here and now – and gregarious and affable with everyone. I always had the impression that if it were not for the *muhpatti*, he would be laughing or singing all the time. Except today. *Diksa* was far too momentous an event to make light of, even for Subritmuni.

Loud sobs suddenly pierced the buzz of the energetic crowd. Everyone turned around to see a group of sorrowful family members, several crying, moving quickly along the sand leading up to the assembly hall. A young woman in the centre of the group seemed to be leading the way and dictating the brisk pace. Her face was sombre, and her head, covered by her sari, was slightly lowered as she hastily moved forward. As she got closer, we could see she was wearing a fancy red sari with gold embroidery and garlands of flowers around her neck. Bracelets dangled from her wrists, and her hands, with rings on almost every finger, were beautifully decorated with *mendhi* (henna). To a non-Jain, she looked as though she were on her wedding day. But on closer look, one could see that her head had already been shaved, save for the few strands to be plucked out during the ceremony. Her body now served as a site, a 'theatre,' through which the conflict between the spiritual and the worldly was enacted. Her transitory body, decorated with finery, was a symbol of worldliness, but her face displayed her 'true self'; she was a *vairagini*: cool, detached, and indifferent to her bodily decoration, as well as to her anguished family. Just like a *Kevalin* surrounded by worldly delights, her mind remains detached (see Babb, 1996: 31). To show emotion now would be inconceivable; it would be an enormous calamity. In order for her to have been chosen for *diksa*, all her superiors (*samanis, sadhvis, munis*, lay teachers, etc.) must have been convinced that she fully appropriated the role of an ascetic, characterized above all else by an outlook of dispassion and withdrawal (*vairagya*) (see Shântâ, 1985). The young woman's mother kept her sad eyes on the ground before her. Her sloped and anguished brows distorted her face, making her look like an old woman. She held one hand over her mouth and the other firmly on her daughter's arm – for the last time. She would never be permitted to publicly express affection for her daughter again. The finality of the circumstance was heightened, and indeed was more fiction than fact, since parents do continue to pay visits to their daughters. Now another sobbing crowd was quickly approaching. Within just moments, the weeping quieted, and the *diksarthis* were all on stage before us.

Niyojikaji ('leader')[16] caught my eye, and with just a tilt of her head, beckoned me to come sit with her. After hours of sitting at the periphery of the hall, I finally moved to take my place among the *samanis*, a place of privilege because our seats were, in effect, front row centre. The ceremony would be in perfect view, but all the activity of the *mumukshus* and householders would be lost to me. There was a tremendous buzz in the air, though the faces of the *sadhvis* and *munis* did not betray it. With cultivated indifference, even distractedness, they averted their eyes from the immense and excited crowd.

Sitting with the *samanis*, I felt like a smudge on a white canvas; a blotch of muted colours among angels in white. But I was by now a familiar presence. Urmilla Prajna, my closest friend, was two rows over from me, and was busy reviewing her Prakrit language text, a course she teaches to the *mumukshus* at the PSS. She is a very bright woman in her late thirties, and an excellent and patient teacher of Jainism. She told me that on one occasion several years earlier, when the *samanis* were spending their *chaturmas* in Bombay, she had the opportunity to meet with a professor of Prakrit from the University of Bombay over a period of several months. On the last day of her study before returning to Ladnun, he told her that if she was not a nun, she could have had a brilliant academic career. It was a story she told me more than once, revealing perhaps a degree of ambivalence with her ascetic life. Perhaps unwittingly, the Terapanthi order's attention to education and support for degrees of higher education may unwittingly nourish aspirations among the *samanis* that extend beyond the limits of the ascetic boundaries. The Terapanthis pride themselves for their educated order, but it is the *samanis* above all other groups who receive the greatest number of years of formal education. The *samans*, the male order of semi-monks, are a tiny group in huge demand by the lay community. The Terapanthi lay communities throughout India compete among each other to have a group of monks spend *chaturmas* with them (Flügel, 1995–6). It is a boon and an honour to have an ascetic present to teach and bless the community, and this is especially true if it is a male ascetic. But because the monks (and nuns) travel only by foot, a community may never get this opportunity. With the creation of the *saman* order, which allows the monks to travel by any means available, lay devotees saw an opportunity. Innumerable requests are made of the four *samans*, and as a result they often spend just a week at any one destination before moving on. *Samanis* are also sent all over India and abroad, but they are not as high in demand, resulting in about half of the group of eighty-one remaining in Ladnun year-round to study. Because of the relaxed rules for the *samanis*, their daily routines are less centred on 'self-maintenance' (alms collecting, toilet) than they are for the *sadhvis* and *munis*, and they have considerably more time for study. Indeed, during my stay, the majority of the *samanis* in Ladnun were pursuing master's degrees, and a few were even pursuing doctorates at the Jain Vishva Bharati Institute (JVBI).

The JVBI is another brainchild of Guru Dev. Founded in 1970 to promote Jain studies, the institute was built on grounds of the Jain Vishva Bharati, a regional headquarters of the Terapanthi lay community. It is open to all students free of charge, irrespective of their religious background. But the way in which it is organized clearly reveals its raison d'être is to serve the ascetic community. For example, classes begin late, only after morning alms collection, and break again for sermons and afternoon alms collection. And the *samanis* can interrupt their study indefinitely for their travels. Interestingly, degrees remain very important 'possessions' for the *samanis*, and they are generally intensely proud of their academic credentials. For the vast majority of these young women, a university education would have been an impossibility outside the order, and now they can boast a master's degree after two years of study. In addition to their interest in pursuing higher degrees, most of the *samanis* spend an average of six to seven years at the PSS before taking *diksa*, and during that time many receive a BA degree through a correspondence course with Jaipur University. They study languages (Hindi, Sanskrit, Prakrit, and English) and philosophy. The consequence of this structuring of ascetic life is that the bulk of learned ascetics of this generation are now nuns. This could have serious consequences for an order that in every other way remains resolutely male-dominated. The relationship that the ascetics have with formal education is interesting and ambivalent. Guru Dev often praised his order for their education, and the *samanis* are obviously proud of their achievements. Most of the *samanis*' female relatives outside the order marry young and have little opportunity for advanced learning. One *samani* told me that her main reason for becoming a nun was so that she could continue her education (see also Reynell, 1985: 248–52). Nevertheless, pride in scholarly achievements has its limits within an order that, above all else, most values knowledge derived through introspection or at the feet of the enlightened guru.

Samani Urmilla Prajna[17] is one of the most gifted teachers of Prakrit at the monastery, and intends to write her own book on Prakrit grammar. Because of the constraints on monk–nun interaction, she is passing her knowledge on exclusively to other nuns and *mumukshus*. I watched her as she poured over an old Prakrit language textbook, shaking her head in frustration at its deficiency, seemingly oblivious to the high drama of *diksa* around her.

Samani Savita Prajna is another close friend. Today she looked lost in thought, perhaps penning another poem in her mind. She was a prolific writer, having filled dozens of notebooks with short stories and mournful poetry. Ascetic life could do nothing to tarnish her beauty. The bridge of her nose is high and haughty, and her cheekbones so prominent they cause her eyes to angle slightly upwards. Physical individuality is difficult for the ascetics, who wear identical uniforms and who are taught to walk, sit, and eat alike. But her face, cloaked beneath the *samani* uniform, was anything but ordinary. As if demanding recognition of its beauty, it defied homogeneity, and mocked the official ascetic pretext to bodily neglect. She told me that she could have married well because of her looks, but that now at thirty-seven, her looks were fading. In fact she once was engaged to be married to a 'very beautiful and very rich' man, but several months before the wedding she decided she didn't want to go through with it, and joined the PSS instead. In reality, her good looks are a form of currency in the order as well. She is frequently chosen to represent the order at conferences in Calcutta and Bombay, and she has travelled abroad in the same capacity. In a conversation with Muniji, he once explained why she was chosen over another *samani* to go overseas, saying 'Her appearance would give a better impression.'[18]

Directly behind the *samanis* sat the *upasikas* wrapped in warm shawls over their simple saris, and the *mumukshu* sisters in their smart tunics. I saw my cheerful *mumukshu* friend, Promika, sitting proudly, holding her white handkerchief before her moving lips, as she recited a blessing. In her crisp white *kavatchan*, she was in her element. She looked excited, but I wondered if she felt any disappointment at not being among the *diksarthis* today. Promika had a ways to go yet. She had not yet mastered the required skill of projecting an air of perpetual introspection, nor had she yet reinterpreted her past in terms of a narrative of disenchantment – as her candid attachment to her *kavatchan* patently demonstrated. Memory or experience is always sifted though a narrative, ordered through an organizing principle that confers significance upon it from a vantage point of the present. Over a period of years at the PSS, the girls 'learn to remember' and reinterpret their past in accordance with a narrative of ascetic detachment. Motives are rephrased and funnelled into disdain for worldly existence. As a publication on the PSS puts it, 'The inmates of the PSS have to pass through a series of experiments aimed at bringing about a radical change in their attitudes towards life' (Bhatnagar, 1985: 82).

Perhaps Promika's attitude towards life remained too cheerful to be considered for this year's *diksa*. At eighteen years old, she would have been younger than the average *diksarthi*, but certainly not the youngest. This year already, one girl of fourteen became a *sadhvi* directly, skipping not only the PSS but the *samani* stage altogether. There were varying views on why this happened, from the 'official' version that the girl was especially enlightened and had wanted to renounce since she was five, to the very 'unofficial' and somewhat cynical view (held by some household-ers and at least one *samani*) that since her family are big donors, it was a way of honouring her family. But most of those I asked said that it would be impossible and even presumptuous for them to claim to know the rea-son, but that it 'must be right' since it was Guru Dev's own decision.

Guru Dev held his face close to the large microphone placed before his platform, and his laborious breathing could be heard throughout the entire monastery. The use of microphones by the ascetics was one of the many controversial changes Guru Dev had initiated during his time as leader of the Terapanthi. His intention – to enable the greatest num-ber of devotees to hear sermons – was highly controversial because microphones require electricity, and therefore violence is an inherent part of their use. Although it was a concession to the importance of the lay community and to the socially significant role the ascetics play, it was distilled through a discourse of liberation-centric morality: the ascetics insist that their primary goal is the liberate their own souls, not to enlighten the masses, but that since preaching leads to the elimination of karma, it is therefore beneficial to everyone. To state otherwise would implicate them in worldly life. Many times Muniji began our daily tuto-rial by reminding me of this. This issue of violence was resolved the same way it is with the ascetics' 'use' of electric light bulbs: since they themselves do not turn the electricity on and off – and would never be associated with its use if it were not for the householders – they incur no bad karma.

The amplified wheezing continued, and we all sat in anticipation of the start of the ceremony. Over the past few years, Guru Dev's health had deteriorated, and he was now seriously asthmatic. Sometimes, in the middle of a sermon, he would begin to lose his breath and a younger monk would rush forward with a large inhaler, holding it steady to Guru Dev's mouth as he worked to regain his calm. Today his large dark eyes were fixed on the immense and eager crowd before him. His breathing stilled the buzz of the people until at last he summoned his voice and he began to chant the *Namaskar Mantra*. Without a second's hesitation, sev-eral hundred devotees harmoniously joined in and the huge assembly hall resounded with the tuneful prayer:

Namo Arihantanam
Namo Siddhanam
Namo Ayariyanam
Namo Uvajjhayanam
Namo loe savva sahunam
Eso Panch namukkaro
Savva pava panasano
Mungalruha savvasim
Padhaman havai mangalam[19]

Even before the vibrations of the soothing mantra had faded, the first speaker was making his way up the steps of the stage. It promised to be a long ceremony. The president of the Jain Vishva Bharati Institute, the chancellor, the vice-chancellor (all householders, of course), and prominent community members each took his turn to praise the order, the ascetics, the ascetic ideal, and the three *diksarthis*. It was well into the second hour before members of the ascetic community spoke, and the murmurs and fidgeting among the audience were evidence of their restlessness. Throughout, the *diksarthis* remained motionless to the side of the stage, kneeling and with their heads lowered. Niyojikaji listened, seemingly intently, to all that was being said, occasionally adding her own commentary on events for me. The prominent monks and nuns spoke of the uselessness of worldly activities and encouraged the devotees to reflect upon renunciation as the one and only true spiritual path. Finally it was the turn of the leaders of the Terapanthi order to speak: Sadhvi Kanak Prabha, the head nun in charge of over 500 *sadhvis* and *samanis*, made a short speech on the righteousness of the ascetic path. This was followed by a lengthy talk by Acharya Sri – liberally peppered with anecdotes and stories – until at last the microphone was placed before Guru Dev once again.

The audience became silent. Guru Dev wasted no time, and quickly turned to address the *diksarthis*, calling upon Mumukshu Jyoti to stand up. It was hard to see her face, since the hood of her sari was pulled forward, and she held her joined hands high. Her family in the audience was also asked to stand. Guru Dev spoke loudly and with intensity, but his voice was full of warmth when he told them that this young woman to his right will no longer belong to them at the close of the ceremony; she will then belong to the order. He asked them if they fully accept this. The family members stood rather sheepishly among the enormous but stilled crowd of onlookers; some smiled weakly, others looked rather upset, but one by one they agreed. The *diksarthi* bowed to Guru Dev before kneeling again, and the next young woman and her family were called until all three candidates had received parental permission, as is required by the order (written permission had been given earlier). At this point, the three *diksarthis* disappeared behind the stage (where they were joined by a few of their female relatives) and returned about fifteen minutes later in their white *samani* robes.

Each *diksarthi* was then called upon to make a brief speech stating her reasons for wanting to take *diksa* (each a variant of the other about their disenchantment with worldly existence), and then together they stood with heads bowed in homage, as Guru Dev recited the initiating *slokas,* taken from the *Avasyak (Pratikraman) Sutra.* The mantras call upon the candidate to give up 'sinful, worldly activities.' Through the act of bowing, each demonstrates her consent and thereby becomes an ascetic. She is believed to immediately advance from the fifth into the sixth *gunasthana* or 'spiritual stage.' (There are fourteen such stages of spiritual development; see Appendix 1. See also Jaini [1979] for a detailed explanation of the *gunasthanas.*)

The atmosphere is joyous, and the hushed audience is animated again. Guru Dev swings his arms about, joking among the ascetics, who beam back at him. Then he addresses the three young women for a final time: still using the prefix '*mumukshu*' ('one who is desirious of emancipation'), he calls on each to individually stand before him while he bestows upon them new names. Interestingly, the Terapanthi (and the Sthanakvasi) ascetics retain their householder names or a variant thereof (see Cort, 1991b: 664). Thus *Mumukshu* Jyoti became *Samani* Jyoti.[20]

Finally, the three walk across the stage, a distinct moment in the rite of passage, and the climax of the *diksa.* One by one they bow before the Sadhvi Promukha, presenting their bald heads. She plucks the single tuft of hair (an act called *kesha locha*), the last sign of worldliness to be symbolically and literally uprooted. Each young nun then bows and pays homage to all the nuns and monks before her. At last, the rite is over, and she sits down 'on her own, individual, spatially separate mat amongst the ranks of the *sadhvis*' (Holmstrom, 1988: 21). Goonasekera describes the *diksa*'s conclusion:

[They] reject all that which caused their suffering: the household and everything associated with it ... [T]hey renounce their free will, their social selves, their individualities, in total surrender to the Acharya. They surrender themselves to a superparent, a father who represents omniscience, omnibenevolence, and pure love. By this act of negation of the society in their conscious awareness they renounce the world and their selves and acquire an alternate society which they believe to be the very opposite of the household and acquire a new parent whom they believe to be superior to their social and biological parents; acquire new siblings who are believed to be superior to their social and biological siblings; and acquire selves which are believed to be superior to their pre-monastic social selves. (1986: 142)

Within the next few weeks, Samani Jyoti and the two other initiates will undergo a second *diksa,* called the *bari diksa* (great initiation), at which time they will accept the *Mahavratas* (great vows) of Jain monasticism: *Ahimsa* (nonviolence); *Satya* (Truth); *Acchoria* (nonstealing); *Aparigraha* (nonpossession); and *Brahmacarya* (celibacy) (Cort,1991b). It will be a smaller event, and will take place before an audience of ascetics alone. It does not receive a fraction of the attention that the public *diksa* does, neither from the householders nor from *mumukshus* or ascetics. This may be because, among an audience of near-equivalents, difference is harder to strategically and rhetorically employ; here righteousness of the ascetic path cannot make use of the explicit rejection of worldliness. And in the absence of difference, the possibilities for objectification and dramatization are gone.

Jyoti's formal renunciation of society, its rules and values entails the acceptance of another type of society, with a different set of rules and values. And ironically, renunciation will bring with it a reduction, not increase, in autonomy. Each day, from the time she wakes until she sleeps, her life will now be structured according to ascetic discipline. Cort writes, 'Following initiation, the course of the mendicant's life is determined by the daily obligatory rites of the mendicant, and the requirements and requests of the laity with whom the mendicant interacts' (1991b: 654). The daily obligatory rites, called the *Avasyakas*, form the core of ascetic ritual (for a detailed account, see Dundas, 1992: 146–9; Shântâ, 1985: 243–58). They are:

1 *Samayika* (equanimity)[21]
2 *Chaturvimsatistava* (praise of the twenty-four *Tirthankaras*)
3 *Vandana* (homage to the teacher)
4 *Pratikramana* (repentance of faults and negligence, performed twice daily)

5   *Kayotsarga* (abandonment of the body)
6   *Pratyakhyana* (the promise to abstain from a variety of transgressions for a fixed time)

Shântâ describes the daily rites as 'les premiers pas dans la voie,' and outlines their significance for the *sadhvis*:

> Leur observance régulière est déjà le signe d'un début de cheminement sur la voie droite; et pour les ascètes elle est le signe d'un engagement définitif: en effet, l'acte majeur, durant la diksa, est le vœu de sâmâyika pour la vie, vœu renouvelé deux fois par jour. Le sâmâyika est à la fois un état de vie et l'âvasyaka primordial. (1985: 243)

And:

> Le mot âvasyaka signife: nécessarie, obligatoire, indispensable, inévitable, ce à quoi on ne peut se soustraire. Il s'agit ici d'observances spirituelles qui sont une obligation pour tous les jaina parce quèlles constituent l'actualisation, la pratique dans la vie quotidienne, des aspects essentiels de la doctrine. La première étape vers la purification étant la non-soumission aux passions, les sages ont considéré la signification d'âvasyaka dans cette perspective: celui qui n'est pas sous la domination (*vasya*) des sens est *a-vasya*, ferme, il ne cède pas aux convoitises et impulsions, et ses actes sont âvasyaka, ceux de quelqu'un qui se contrôle. (244)

I watched Samani Jyoti Prajna leave with the *sadhvis*, and I wondered how she would adjust to her new life. Although she was well prepared, having spent many years at the PSS, and had family members already in the order, the initial transition must be difficult. The immediate and singular focus of her life over the past many years (*diksa*) and especially over the past few weeks, was finally realized. Now the goal of attaining the state of *avasya* will become the logic, and determine the rhythm, of her daily life. She had made the crossing and now there was no turning back.

5
Death, Demons, and Desire

It was nearly 8 p.m. Young Mudit Muni with his tiny physique and colossal voice moved swiftly through the rooms of the monks', calling all to prayer. Being the most recent *muni* initiate of just a few months, and because of his tender age of twelve, he is given such special privileges. His tiny stature makes him appear even younger than his years, yet his oratory powers are exceptional. He is frequently called upon to make a speech in front of the lay community, who delight in watching and listening to this pint-size marvel. Last year, when a group of *sadhvis* were in Maharashtra, Mudit Muni and his mother attended their lecture in the village. He was immediately impressed by the confidence of the *sadhvis* and by the respect they received in the community. The topic of the nuns' lecture was 'fearlessness.' They told the audience that fear, like all forms of human suffering (*duhkha*), is born of desire; that fearlessness comes from worldly detachment. He heard that only the weak are prey to fears and that those who attach no importance to the body are afraid of nothing. The nuns quoted the words of the great Lord Mahavir: 'Once I had the longing to live and was afraid of death. I desired comforts and feared pain. I pined for fame and feared being criticized. I was greedy for gains and feared losses. But I don't have cravings for life anymore, so why should I then be afraid of death? Only those who have a longing for life fear death.'

The *sadhvis* told their audience a story from Lord Mahavir's twelve years of 'afflictions' – a time during which he endured the wrath of innumerable demons, evil humans, and ferocious animals, and yet he never lost his equanimity. The story impressed little Mudit greatly:

One day during his wanderings, Lord Mahavir arrived near a small village on the banks of river *Vegvati*. Outside the village on a small hill stood a temple surrounded by scattered heaps of bones and skeletons. Considering it to be an appropriate place for his practices, Mahavir sought permission from the villagers. They informed him that this forlorn village was once a prosperous town. But the ferocious lance-wielding demon, Shulpani Yaksha, who dances and laughs on heaps of bones, had turned it into an *Asthikgram* – the village of bones. The temple in which Mahavir sought to perform his practices was guarded by the demon. If anyone dared to stay, they never came out alive. The villagers tried to dissuade Mahavir from staying in the temple, but he was determined to root out fear and sow the seeds of courage.

That evening he meditated within the temple. When darkness descended, the air filled with eerie sounds. Shulpani the Demon appeared in the courtyard and started making fearful trumpeting noises. He was surprised to see a human being standing fearlessly in meditation. He produced a thunderous roar that shook the thick walls of the temple, but Lord Mahavir still did not move, nor did he show any change in his serene bearing. The demon lost his temper and began his horrifying atrocities. A mad elephant suddenly appeared and goaded Mahavir with its pointed tusks. It lifted him by its trunk and tossed him about. When this had no effect, a horrible ghost appeared and attacked Mahavir with its fangs and claws. Next appeared a black serpent that attacked with its large venomous fangs and toxic breath. Finally it caused extreme damage in seven delicate spots of Mahavir's body (eyes, ears, nose, head, teeth, nails, and back). But Mahavir had an endless capacity to tolerate pain. Even this extreme torture failed to disturb his composure.

Drained of all his demonic energy, Shulpani became apprehensive. He feared that he was facing a divine power much stronger than his own and that he was nearing his own demise. All of a sudden, Shulpani felt a divine spiritual light illuminate his inner self. Slowly his anger subsided, fear dissolved, and a feeling of goodwill took over. He touched Mahavir's feet and with repentance begged his pardon.

After the *sadhvis'* talk, Mudit approached them alone: he wanted to know if there were any monks in the order. The *sadhvis* were buoyed by his interest and told him that they could see that he was one of the special few who could meet the ascetic challenge. They told him that only those who are great, strong, and fearless should consider pursuing the ascetic path, and that he should not waste his life in worldliness (see Carrithers, 1983, for a discussion of the socially perceived grandeur of asceticism). Much to his mother's shock, Mudit decided on the spot to become a monk. The *sadhvis* spoke to his mother about the futility of trying to deter him because once a soul has been awakened, it will never slumber again. Within a matter of weeks his parents were in touch with the nuns (who were by this time several villages away) and made arrangements for their son to visit Guru Dev in Ladnun. On the day of his arrival in Ladnun, Mudit dressed himself in a white *kurta pyjama* and sat near the monks listening to Guru Dev's morning sermon. Just weeks earlier he had been moved by the nuns' assertion that the ascetic path is for the strong and fearless, and Mudit took it to heart. Suddenly, at the end of Guru Dev's talk, Mudit jumped to his feet (though he still only reached a few inches above the seated *munis*) and, in front of an large audience of ascetics and householders that included his own parents, he delivered a speech worthy of a *Tirthankara*. He had been awakened, he declared boldly, and now begged Guru Dev to allow him to renounce. Guru Dev began to chuckle – perhaps remembering a similar declaration he himself made when he was just eleven years old – but didn't respond. The audience was rapturous: greatness was in Mudit's future. The next day Guru Dev advised that he should spend several months living among the ascetics and to then make a decision. Within four months Mudit took initiation as a *muni*. Still something of a star phenomenon at the monastery, Mudit Muni all but swaggered in his new ascetic robes. He held his head high as he called the monks to prayer and, without even having to bend forward, his hand-held *rajoharon* swept the floor as he moved forward.

The sun would soon be down; there was no time to dawdle. '*Matthayena Vandami*,'[1] I said as I bowed deeply before Muni Dulharaji. Young Mudit Muni's voice could be heard trailing off in the distance. Everywhere there was immediate activity as the monks stopped what they were doing to move towards the assembly hall, and householders rushed to be on time for the final gathering of the day. As always, the call to prayer signalled the end of Muniji's and my meeting. I gathered up my notebooks and – since there was nothing I could do – tried not to notice his difficulty in standing. His badly arthritic knees make it difficult for him to move after sitting for a long time. Soon two younger monks would arrive to help him up and accompany him to the hall.

The monastery would soon be engulfed in darkness, and a calm would descend upon its inhabitants. The night was really the only time when the all-important symbolic distinction between the ascetics and the *shravaks* was actually *spatially* true: the householders would reluctantly separate themselves from the ascetics and retreat to their 'worldly' homes, leaving the ascetics alone. The ascetics would then be free of the bejewelled and bedecked devotees; free from the sweet smell of their perfumes and oils; free from their offerings, their tales of 'worldly' transgressions and their adoration. But *shravaks* are not the only representatives of 'the worldly' nor the only threats to the ascetics' resolve, even if they are the most tangible and common forms of temptation.[2] When these perils of the daytime disappear with the setting of the sun, new dangers lie lurking in the shadows of the night, as the story of Lord Mahavir forewarned. The ascetics must always be vigilant.

The *pratikraman*[3] prayers, broadcast by loudspeaker, would accompany me on my short walk from the monks' residence to Gautam Shalla (the *samanis*' residence). The broadcast allowed the *samanis* to sing in perfect unison with the monks, though a couple of hundred metres away. Usually they would wait in silence until they heard the monks' lead, and then join the refrain. The monastery would be filled with prayer, dominated by the beautiful and rich voice of a single monk who stood at the microphone. Only inside the sandy courtyard of the *samanis*' compound itself could I distinguish their voices from the male chorus. The *samanis* would sit on the veranda in two perfect rows of three across and ten or more deep, facing each other. Niyojikaji would sit in the middle and lead the group in prayer. Every night for months, I would join them at the back of the large group, chanting the melodious mantra with them. Sitting among the nuns, my eyes shut, and the a cappella rhythms resonating throughout the open courtyard, I could forget about myself as an outsider and share in the beauty of their experience. But on this night, when I entered their compound, the marble veranda that extends around the courtyard was deserted and cold; and I was met only by silence.

Where were the *samanis*? And why hadn't I been told of their departure? I worried as I stood alone in the open courtyard, the sun vanishing behind the monastery's western gate. The sounds of the monks' prayers could be heard, but, in the absence of the *samanis*, I had no desire to join in. I felt frustrated by the break in the routine. Every night, immediately after the prayers, there would be a buzz of activity and laughter in the dark. The *samanis* would call out and say, 'Oh it is so dark tonight!' or 'Only the stars light up the room.' Theirs was almost a chicane observance of the rule that they should never cause violence or have it caused on their behalf. It would be impossible for them to simply ask me to switch the light on, since that would directly implicate them in

Sadhvis in Ladnun, 1996.

Map of Rajasthan.

Samavasaran. The gathering of devotees around the Jina. From *Illustrated Bhaktamar Stotra*, ed. Shrichand Surana 'Saras'. With kind permission from Diwakar Prakashan Publishers.

Guru Dev in fore, with Acharyasri and several munis on their vihar (pilgrimage). They are followed by lay devotees. Munis are carrying patras (alms bowls) in jholis (slings) and rajoharan (whiskbrooms). (Bhatnagar, 1985; with permission from JVB)

Acharyasri Mahaprajna receiving bhiksha from shravaks. (Bhatnagar, 1985; with permission from JVB)

Devotional card of Acharya Bhikshu declaring 'He Prabho! Yaha Tera Panth' (O lord, this is your path). (Source unknown)

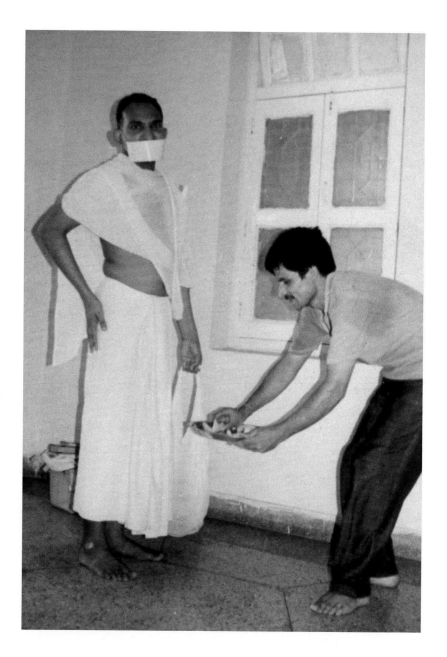

Muni receiving bhiksha.

Sweeper woman. (Drawing by the author)

Women's section of assembly hall. (Bhatnagar; with permission from JVB)

'First ever Samani initiation' from booklet *Saman Diksa*. (JVB)

'Cosmic Man' depicting Jain cosmos. Circle represents our universe where human beings are born. Infernal beings reside in the upper hells and in the in-between areas around our universe. (Los Angeles County Museum of Art)

Kirn asks for permission to perform santara. (*Satyug Ki Yaden* by Mumukshu Santa, 1992; with permission from JVB)

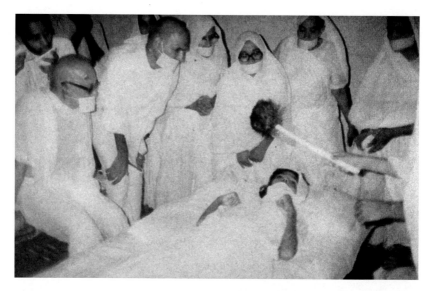

Kirin takes Diksa. (*Satyug Ki Yaden* by Mumukshu Santa, 1992; with permission from JVB)

Mumukshus carrying Kirin's body in funerary celebration. (*Satyug ki Yaden*; with permission from JVB)

Mumukshu sisters awaiting pre-diksa ceremony. (Bhatnagar, 1985; with permission from JVB)

आचार्य श्री महाप्रज्ञ   गणाधिपति श्री तुलसी

Examples of devotional items: wallet-size photo of Guru Dev, pens bearing images of gurus, and a cassette of gurus' recordings.

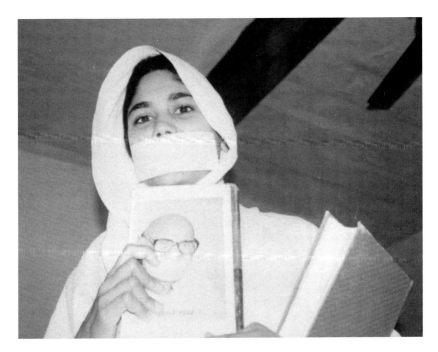

Samaniji with photo of her guru, Acharyasri.

Samanis singing devotional songs. (Bhatnagar, 1985; with permission from JVB)

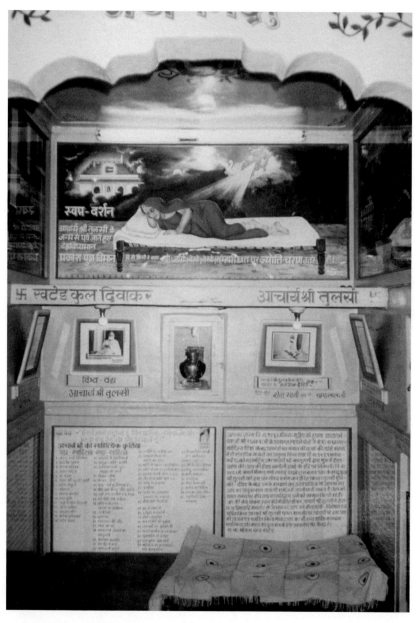

Mural of auspicious dreams of Guru Dev's mother, above bed where Guru Dev
Tulsi was born 20 October 1914.

Mural of Baby Tulsi.

Niyojikaji with mother, younger sister, sister-in-law, and her children.

the violence of killing innumerable 'fire-bodied'[4] beings, so they had
fun within their limits. Once I, or the keeper, turned on the lights, the
samanis would retire to their respective rooms to read, study, or meditate. Then Urmilla and I would set ourselves up at the back of her room
under the window and away from the three other samanis sharing the
room, and spend the next few hours in conversation. We would talk late
into the night, long after the other samanis had stretched out their cardboard pieces and gone to sleep. To shield their eyes from the exposed
light bulb, they would pull the sheets over their faces, and tuck them in
under their heads. If it were not for the occasional snores, they could be
mistaken for body bags. Unfortunately, since it was also my 'job' to turn
off the lights I had turned on, the time of my departure was always
clocked, and Urmilla would occasionally be chided for keeping such
late hours.

The residence was deserted, but I wasn't eager to return to my room.
The generator was down again and the power had been off since morn
ing. I decided to stay here, where the generator almost never fails, and
do some reading. I opened the door to Urmilla's room, flicked on the
light and was relieved to see that her tiny wooden table was loaded with
books. At least this meant that she hadn't been sent off to some village
or city for a lecture tour, as I had feared. The samanis never know from
one day to the next where they might be staying. If Guru Dev wanted a
Terapanthi representative at an event, anywhere in India, the samanis
would be sent. And indeed, in 1996, about half of the 81 samanis, at any
one time, were dispersed throughout India and overseas. Although
many appear to enjoy the indeterminacy and spontaneity of their lives,
saying that they 'have no stress' and 'don't have to think,' most prefer to
stay put. Indeed, the majority of the samanis in Ladnun are either teaching or studying, and this provides them with some deterrent to the
nomadic life.

Suddenly, out of the silence, I heard the sound of footsteps coming
from the stairwell at the end of the hall. I assumed it to be the night
watchman, though without his thunderous stride. But instead it was
Urmilla who appeared, and before I could even say my respects (i.e., do
vandana), she rushed over to me and hastily said, 'Tonight we cannot
meet.'

Although I had anticipated this, I looked at her and waited for an
explanation, but she seemed rather uncomfortable.

'What is it?' I asked. 'Where is everyone?'

'The samanis are at Rishabdwar [the sadhvis' residence]. Except me

and Samani Bhavitaprajna. We are with Samani Ashaprajna – upstairs.'
She was clearly frazzled.

'Is everything alright?'

She pressed her handkerchief against her face and looked around her.

'Why are *you* not at Rishabdwar? Are you not well?' I pressed, knowing that Urmilla's recent bout of malaria had seriously weakened her and prevented her from participating in many regular meetings.

'No, no,' she shook her head. Clearly I was off the mark. Then, after a moment of hesitation, she whispered '*Bhuts*' (malignant spirits).

The word startled me, and my face betrayed it. I just looked at her for more, but all she said as she hurriedly escorted me out of the room was, 'Everything will be okay. Tomorrow we will meet. Come tomorrow morning.' As we left the room, I switched the light off, and without another word, I could hear the sound of her bare feet moving along the floor down the dark hall.

The path from Gautam Shalla back to my room was dark, and the few and irregularly placed yellow light bulbs – fixed to low fences – caused the trees to cast giant shadows. I walked quickly, stalked by my own shadow. The gritty wind was agitated, blowing in circles and causing the sand to rise. The wind grew stronger, muffling the sound of my steps and silencing the world around me. Surely this was the hour of the *bhuts*, I thought. *Bhuts* are part of everyday life in India (Kakar, 1996: 57) but they are always feared. And although the ascetics typically dismiss them out of hand as unworthy of their attention, it is a feigned bravado. In reality, many are deeply troubled by their existence. Though they believe that through ascetic austerities (*tapas*) they can defeat *bhuts*, and that if they remain detached nothing can harm them, they also know that *bhuts* take these measures as challenges, and delight in tempting the ascetics.

The demons or 'demonic gods' are confined mainly to the middle and lower area of the *triloka* or 'three-world' cosmos. The cosmos is shaped like an egg timer, or like a giant human standing upright (sometimes called the 'cosmic person'). Gods reside in the upper section of the cosmos; humans, animals, and plants in the middle section, and infernal beings in the seven lands of the lower section (*Tattavartha Sutra*, 1994: 69). The demons have access to, and flit between, the middle world of human habitation and the top three hells of the lower world. The *Tattvartha Sutra* describes these beings as sadists who

find pleasure in devising torments for the infernal beings. They force them
to drink molten iron, embrace red-hot hammers, attack them with hatchets
and knives, sprinkle boiling oil on them, fry them in pans, bake them in
ovens, drown them in the hellish streams, crush them in grinders. (72)

In total there are fifteen types of demonic gods, with different predis-
positions and forms (e.g., some appear as deformed human beings;
others as giants, or as fiery or thundering spirits[5]),[6] They are born as
demons because of a deluded world-view and a predilection for wicked
acts in past lives that led them to perform misguided austerities and to
unwittingly expel beneficial karma (69). These demonic gods do not
know the misfortune that awaits them but take pride in their status, considering themselves the luckiest of all creatures (72). In his study of possession in popular Hinduism, Sudhir Kakar claims that *bhuts* are the
spirits of those who met with an untimely death. He writes:

> The *bhuta-preta* are said to exist in a halfway house between the human
> world and the world of ancestral sprits (*pitri-lok*). Until they have been
> judged, have paid their Karmic debts and are allowed into the world of
> ancestral spirits, the *bhuta-preta* continue to yearn for a human body which
> they can enter and contrive to make sick through their nefarious activity.
> (1996: 56)

I do not know if Jains share this view of *bhuts*, though in many of the
stories I heard, they did arise from someone who died suddenly and prematurely. In either case, it is in moments of quietness, or in the stillness
of the night, that the *bhuts* seize the opportunity to attack. While they
usually busy themselves with tormenting the infernal beings of the first
three hells, they also delight in terrifying human beings – especially
ascetics, who often provoke their ire with what the *bhuts* consider to be
their pretensions at godliness. But demons are important in monastic
life and for ascetic discourse for another reason: they present the ascetics
with an opportunity to prove their superior spiritual power, and thereby
reaffirm the proper order of things. Indeed, the celebrity status of a few
of the ascetics at the monastery developed as a direct result of their courage and strength in the face of demonic attacks. Withstanding an attack
or subduing a demon affirms and authenticates their ascetic spiritual
power. In a world in which the good life is associated with all that is *not-*
worldly, these passionate worldly beings serve a powerful rhetorical end.

As I approached, I could see that my residence was still without light. Electricity would certainly not be back until tomorrow. The dog Kalu was curled up snugly next to the entrance of the building, sleeping soundly and oblivious to the brewing sandstorm. The worker-boys had already laid out their *charpoys*, which partially blocked the door of my room, but were nowhere to be seen. The cots were light – and even with one of the boys stretched out on one, I could easily push it aside. The boys at my residence, most in their late teens, all had decent jobs: they were primarily responsible for maintaining the guest rooms built to accommodate the steady flow of devotees. Every room but mine saw a brisk turnover: devotees would come to make their pilgrimage, stay for a day or two, and then disappear for another year. The rooms were meant to inspire piety: simple wooden beds with no mattress, a wooden desk, and a 'W.C.' – a cement square with a wide drain, and a tap above it for all ablutions.

The spartan quarters meant the boys had a relatively easy job cleaning them – far easier than the jobs most workers had at the monastery. During cricket season, they would set up a radio on the front steps of the residence and blast it so loudly that it could be heard from whichever room they were in. No one ever complained – not their bosses, nor the devotees – because so important is the match that it simply cannot be broadcast too loudly. Cricket is the nation's great unifier. The boys at my residence were low-caste Hindus, as were all the workers at the monastery, most coming from the neighbouring *Harijan* village. 'Bapu' the cook, though from a low caste, was not an 'untouchable.' Daily, the food he prepared would be served to the devotee-guests, and offered to the ascetics as alms. He was a shy fellow with a dark, round face, bushy brows, and an allusion to a moustache. He was soon to be married, and there was considerable teasing leading up to the occasion. After a day's work, and after the excitement of the day's cricket match, the boys would sit cross-legged on their *charpoys*, joking about marriage and sex in their native Rajathani tongue.[7] Bapu's village was a day's trip away. After marriage he planned to keep his job at the monastery where he would work for periods of two months at a time, before taking a few days leave, as is the custom of the married workers.

I loathed entering my room when it was dark. The sound of the creepy-crawlies carrying on amidst my notebooks sent dread up my spine. My industrial-strength flashlight became my most cherished possession because with it I could restore order. With a beam of light, the bugs would disappear into the cracks and drains from which they came.

It was a ritual we would go through several times a week. My mind was unsettled: I had heard so much about *bhuts* and their impotence before the ascetics' *tapas* (spiritual power) since arriving, but I had not witnessed them myself, and I was eager to do so. The light from my flashlight danced on the wall, and the wind howled outside my room, and I tried to imagine the goings-on on the second floor of the Gautam Shalla. As I imagined Urmilla and the other *samanis* battling the demon, I realized that I was not baffled by the phenomenon. I felt I already had an idea of what was transpiring. My imaginings were not on *terra nova*; they were not without a blueprint. They played against a backdrop made familiar by innumerable tales of ascetics and demons. Demons are often central characters in Jaina storytelling, making their contemporary, 'real life' appearance if not commonplace, at least less than extraordinary. Kirin Narayan in her book *Storytellers, Saints, and Scoundrels* argues that narratives can be considered 'cognitive instruments' in that they are a means of making sense of the world (1989: 100). She writes: 'As the stories become incorporated into listeners' visions of the world, religious belief is bound up with the course of action the morals prescribe' (1989: 244). I knew that these worldly demons, no matter how tempting or terrible, could never defeat a dispassionate, detached ascetic. The actors and events may change, but the plot and the outcome do not. In fact, so similar were the stories in my mind that I found myself conflating stories about the ascetics that I knew with those of the *Tirthankaras*.

By turning off my flashlight I put an end to the shadow puppets. Most nights I would fall asleep reading and wake up hours later slumped over my book with the light still on. I switched it off and would never know about the nightlife in my room. And sure enough, this night it didn't take long before my room became animated with the sounds of my little roommates, but I wasn't bothered as I had enough to distract myself. Just last week Sadhiv Pannaji, the greatest demon-basher of the order, passed through Ladnun on her nomadic wanderings. Unfortunately, she was already off to a neighbouring village, and could be of no help tonight. Her whirlwind visit was of great excitement to the community. She is known to have tremendous spiritual power (*tapas*), and everyone – including many Hindu families – wanted to have her blessing. Her power was known because of her lifelong dealings with demons and, in later years, through her ability to perform miracles. The two abilities were connected: through years of performing penances, she had acquired so much *tapas* that her powers were now wondrous. She had the power of clairvoyance and the power to heal. Her austerities were equally extraordinary – she seemed to be forever on some type of fast. Indeed many nuns claimed she fasted for several months at a time – sipping only boiled water!

Early in her ascetic career Sadhvi Pannaji encountered a dangerous *bhut* that was determined to destroy her religious life. He tormented her over a period of seven years. Her courageous encounters with the demon – and her eventual appeasement of it – are well known among the Terapanthi community, and they are the source of her celebrated status as a *tapasvini* (spiritual expert). Her ordeals and triumphs are important because they reveal the paradigmatic response to *bhuts* (which, I argue, represent a form of worldly desire): namely that of unwavering courage and discipline. Her courage recalls that of the great ascetic heroes and presents an ideal for all ascetics.

It began during the first *chaturmas*, when she and a small group of nuns set themselves up in a building that turned out to be the home of a demon. A number of householders warned the nuns not to stay there, but since Guru Dev assigned the place, the nuns were determined to make a go of it. Soon after they moved in, the demon became enraged and threatened their lives if they didn't leave. The demon first appeared late at night as a woman. Sadhvi Pannaji was meditating close to midnight when she saw a woman coming upstairs towards her. She called out, 'Who are you? What are you doing here now?' The woman said nothing and stood staring at Pannaji and then she simply vanished before her eyes. Pannaji knew then that it was a *bhut* in disguise. Her devotees urged her to leave the building, but Pannaji replied, 'I don't think of anything beyond what my guru says. He says I must stay here and thus I will stay.' Her stubbornness enraged the demon, who then started to trouble other nuns as well. They tolerated everything, though many of the nuns were terrified and wished they could leave the building. Pannaji, as group leader, would hear none of it. The demon assumed different and terrifying forms, made blood-curdling sounds, and threatened them cruelly throughout the *chaturmas*, but Sadhvi Pannaji insisted on staying put.

At the end of the rainy season, when the nuns left the building and began their wanderings, the demon stopped his harassment against all except Pannaji. He forbade her to ever return to his building, but she knew that other *sadhvis* would likely be there again the following year – and she told him so. One night the demon appeared before her, presented her with a handful of eggs, and roared at her to break them (i.e., kill them).[8] Pannaji responded, 'I am a nun, I have renounced all violence – how can you ask me to do this?' Another day he put a hen in front of her and commanded her to 'Kill and eat it.' Each time she resisted, the demon would make graver threats. On other occasions, during their daily journeys by foot, the demon would appear beside her completely naked and refuse to leave her side. He would ridicule her with ribald language, promising to stop only when she obeyed him. To this she would reply, 'I have faith in my guru. I am not afraid of you.' When he would threaten to take her life, she would say, 'As long as I have life in my body, I will remain a *sadhvi*.'

The troubles continued for years but she never gave in. Finally one day, the *bhut,* appearing in human form, told Pannaji that he could not live where the nuns do, that their presence in his building caused him great pain. Sadhvi Pannaji explained that she wished him no harm, but that the building had been chosen by her guru and that is why she refused to leave. The *bhut* was impressed by her devotion, and asked only that the upstairs remain uninhabited for his use. Pannaji accepted his proposition, and eventually the trouble subsided. Pannaji, however, would endure hardships with *bhuts* throughout her ascetic career.

My own sleep that night was restless, filled with werewolves and vampires – idioms, I realized, of evil from my own culture, which, I would later learn, have little in common with *bhuts* of India. *Bhuts* represent desire incarnate, and battle stories between ascetics and *bhuts* serve as a discourse about good and evil – in the distinctly Jain terms of spirituality and worldliness. The stories of the dispassionate ascetic ever-victorious over worldly desire (represented as *bhut*) were inexhaustible and colourful, and always followed a set pattern: the passionate demon eventually either fled or was subdued; and detachment always won the day. I imagined the heroic *samanis* at Gautam Shalla (the *samanis'* residence) confronting the *bhuts,* defiantly mocking their worldly ways. The raw materials for another *tapasvini* are in the making, I imagined. But things were to turn out differently than I had expected.

Early that morning after the sun had risen, I returned to Gautam Shalla, where I found Urmilla alone in the room, at her desk. She looked especially tired but was calmer than the previous night. She scrambled to find her handkerchief to cover her mouth, and then told me that she had not slept at all.

'What happened?' I asked.

Though the compound was empty, she motioned for me to close the doors behind me. I did and then sat before her. Alone in the room, she leaned forward so we were just inches apart and, in a tiny whisper, told me that the previous night, near midnight, 'the *bhuts* "caught" Samani Asha.' By 'caught' she meant that the *bhuts* had taken possession of Asha.

This was new to me: in all the demon stories I had been told, I had never heard of a possession. Urmilla assured me they were uncommon – but I learned later that they are more concealed than uncommon. They are downplayed, trivialized, and deliberately omitted from popular discourse. Unlike demonic attacks, which affirm the spiritual/worldly, good/evil ontology, possession upsets it.[9] Possession is a language of surrender to the avatars of worldliness and as such it undermines ascetic claims to dominance and inverts the normal balance of power.

The previous day Asha had been alone on the roof in the middle of the afternoon meditating. When other *samanis* went upstairs, they called out to her, but she said nothing. Finally she started making a noise – 'mmmmmm' – and tossing her head about. When they tried to move her, she had become very heavy and six *samanis* were needed. Urmilla was beckoned and together they carried the incapacitated Asha downstairs, and placed her in a room on the second floor. The other *samanis* went to Rishabdwar (the *sadhvis*' residence) for *pratikraman* prayers and stayed the night. Urmilla and two other *samanis* remained with Asha. Later in the evening the two other *samanis* who had stayed behind retired to another room to sleep. They did not want to be in the same room with her at midnight – a very inauspicious time when demons abound. So Urmilla stayed alone with Asha. Sure enough, at about midnight, eerie voices came from beyond the closed doors. Samani Asha began to tremble and whimper. Suddenly, the doors swung open as if blasted with a gust of wind, and Asha began to sob. When Urmilla asked 'What is it?' Asha said that spirits were entering the room. Within moments, one entered her body. Soon Asha was transformed from a terrified *samani* into an aggressive *bhut*. Occasionally she roared, and then laughed, but the voice was deep and wicked and not her own. The fact that a body can be occupied – that the boundary of one's body is penetrable – was not contentious to Urmilla. What was scandalous, however, is that the body of an ascetic should be.

Urmilla made me promise that I would not mention it to any of my householder friends, or monks. Guru Dev would not be told, if it could be avoided. She was adamant that I not see Samani Asha, claiming that she feared I too could be 'caught.' In reality, I did not believe that this was the source of her apprehension, but I didn't press her. Possession is not only shameful to the victim, it also presents an awkward situation for the order. Of course the news would eventually leak, as it did in a matter of weeks, but every effort to contain it was made. The householders who assisted Urmilla in attending to Asha while she was incapacitated were her family members. And it was in her family's interest not to broadcast the event.

That afternoon the *samanis* returned from Rishabdwar. Many had hoped the situation would have resolved itself since their departure the day before and were visibly upset that it had not. Asha was still on the second floor, and many of the *samanis* were reluctant to go there. Arrangements were made for their books and 'mattresses' to be temporarily shifted downstairs to the first-floor rooms. Urmilla's room now housed an additional two *samanis*. Since she was among the very few *samanis* who were not afraid to go upstairs, I saw little of her over the next few days. However, I continued to meet with her each evening for a shortened period of time, after which she would join Asha upstairs.

The situation was tense, and, for many, my presence made things worse. The *samanis* were reluctant to talk to me about the possession – because they wanted to protect Asha, or because the situation was difficult to rationalize in terms of a world-view which held ascetic dispassion to be the greatest of all powers. Even among themselves, Asha's possession was increasingly presented as having 'something to do with' her karma from a past life. It appeared that because of its destabilizing potential, efforts to normalize possession were being made at her expense. Urmilla was beginning to speculate aloud that perhaps it was Asha's karma: 'It has happened to her before,' she told me soberly. Several months earlier when the ascetic community was in a nearby town, a small group of *samanis* were sharing a building with the monks during the afternoon hours. Asha, seemingly out of the blue, began screaming, crying, and thrashing herself about. Urmilla was among the *samanis* present at the time. They were alarmed because Guru Dev was in the same building and they didn't want him (or any of the monks) to know what was going on.[10] She and four other *samanis* carried the hollering Asha out of the building and over to the where the *sadhvis* were staying. Sadhvi Kanak Prabha squeezed the big toe on Asha's left foot, and an unmerciful roar came out of her: 'CHORDO' (Leave me alone!). It was not Asha. Sadhvi Kanak Prabha asked who it was and what it wanted. It revealed itself as a Harijan *bhut* who was angry because Asha had defecated on his home (in the fields) earlier in the day. The nuns apologized on her behalf and convinced him it had not been intentional. He accepted this and then disappeared, leaving Asha bewildered and exhausted.

Urmilla continued to remain with Asha on the second floor. And by the start of the third day, it seemed that no one was talking about anything other than *bhuts* – but almost exclusively in terms of demonic attack. The topic of possession was largely avoided, and if discussed, it was trivialized. Possession in and of itself is not so astounding, and everyone could tell me cases of its occurrence within the larger lay population. It is widely assumed that householders periodically succumb to demonic attacks by way of possession because they do not have the spiritual power to resist them. It is its appearance among the ascetic community that is most troubling.

In Possession of Self

I want to argue for an interpretation of Jain possession as a process, rather than as an impasse or condition. This might enable us to see the similarities it bears with certain mechanisms in Western culture and to thwart a reflex to exoticism. Possession by a *bhut* to a Jain ascetic means loss of control, but more importantly, I would argue, possession allows for the externalization of passion in a world where dispassion is an ideal. It means that the worldly passions expressed and experienced by the ascetic do not derive from her; instead they originate from an *external* source. Responsibility is shifted; the 'evil' of desire is distanced and the worldly is made alien. Asha, perhaps due to past life experiences, may be susceptible to possession, but she is not accountable for her 'worldly' behaviour. Her piety is not in question.

Possession results in the diversion or shifting of *agency* from the self to the alien other, and at least, on this level, all cultures have mechanisms through which this is achieved. Kakar, in his examination of female possession in India, treats it as a phenomenon of the 'hysterical personality.' 'Hysteria,' he writes,

> is uniquely a neurosis that takes on the coloring of a specific historical and cultural setting. 'Vapors,' fainting fits, inexplicable paralyses and convulsions in the Victorian era, the devil or a witch wrestling control of the body to use it for its own purposes in the Middle Ages, are some of the many costumes that the hysterical personality has worn in its time in the West. In fact, the hysterical personality is probably unique in aligning itself with what Krohn calls the prevailing 'myth of passivity' of its culture. I am the 'passive' vehicle of gods, or of the devil, of my twitchings, or my *bhutas*, which make me do these things, not my own desires. (1996: 75–7)

I would argue that in the sense of 'sanctioning' passivity or 'external-izing' agency, *possession* is to Jains what *emotion* (arising from our instinc-tual animal nature or 'Beast Within') is to modern Westerners. The Western commonsense view of emotions is that they are something that *happen to us*, that we are overwhelmed *by* them. Janice Boddy writes that spirit possession 'commonly refers to the hold exerted over a human being by external forces or entities more powerful than she' (1994: 407). Except that where passions are reified and then internalized as instincts in contemporary Western culture, they are more likely to be reified as objects (karmic matter or *bhuts*) in Jainism. Of course, the cor-relation only goes so far, but it may help to consider possession in Jain-ism as a social mechanism – as a symbolic form through which people perceive and experience themselves, and through which they preserve their moral status.

Emotions in Jainism result from the interaction between the soul and karma with the soul having exclusive agency not from the 'instinctual body' as we understand it in the modern West. The *samanis* often explained the scourge of passions in the following way: although the soul is the original agent, a dialectic exists between it and karmic matter. According to Jain philosophy, the phenomenon of the transformation of forms called *srstivada* is a fact of existence and is unchangeable. The root cause of worldly existence is the interaction of soul (*jiv*) and karmic matter (*ajiv*) within the naturally occurring *srstivada*. Soul and karma are eternal and both are susceptible to transformation: the soul influences and transforms karma and vice versa, a phenomenon called *Vyanjana Paryaya*. Their transformation is the very cause of all 'cre-ation.' Karma covers the soul's consciousness, and deludes and obstructs its innate power. *Mohaniya* (delusory) karma is the keystone of the whole structure in that it gives rise to emotions – and emotions are responsible for the endurance and tenacity of karma. In the absence of emotions, karma and soul would not 'stick' together. Thus the destruc-tion of *mohaniya* karma paves the way for the elimination of other variet-ies of karma (Dundas, 1992: 85). The soul is the progenitor of karmic bondage and also the enjoyer of its fruits. It is responsible for the attrac-tion of both good and bad karma, and karma is the root cause of the transmigration of the soul. Thus, if Jains claim passivity before an un-towardly expression of desire, it does not mean they were 'overcome' by their passionate 'animal nature'; instead, it signifies the agent is exter-nal (e.g., *bhuts*/possession). In the West, emotional outbursts are either outside of reason (e.g., 'wild') or 'eruptions within the physical self' (in which case responsibility is averted), or they are under the tutelage of 'reason' (in which case responsibility cannot be deflected). In Jainism, if passion originates in an external agent (e.g., a *bhut*), responsibility is averted. If its source is the self/soul, responsibility cannot be deflected. Samani Asha's unconventional behaviour is the result of demonic possession, and therefore she cannot be held responsible for it. But not all violations of protocol are as quietly tolerated, simply because not all violations can be absolved. The following is an example from my field notes:

> Tonight Muniji [Muni Dulharaji] and I were talking about disobedient ascetics, and he told me of a *sadhvi* who was expelled not long ago. She was in her mid-thirties and was known to have a short temper. She was often reprimanded by her superiors, and was warned that she needed to control herself or she would be expelled. Her anger would express itself in small ways – she would snap at fellow *sadhvis* or refuse to do her chores. One night, when her family was visiting the monastery, she became enraged and ripped off her sari and *muhpatti*. She put on 'householders' clothes and her family took her home. Some weeks later, she returned to the monastery and begged Guru Dev to allow her back into the order. She apologized and said that she had made a terrible error; she wanted to lead a spiritual life as a *sadhvi* again. Guru Dev said that he would allow her back in, but on one condition: if she returns, she must take *santara* (fasting unto death). She has not [yet] been able to accept this, evincing her weakness and nonpreparedness for spiritual life.

Responsibility for her unorthodox behaviour was all her own, and her disagreeable, passionate personality reflected a spiritually immature soul. *Santara* is the preeminent expression of ascetic strength, in that it is the supreme renunciation of worldly existence. Settar (1989) writes that Jains 'commend' death and advocate 'positive compulsions for ending life' (xxv). He writes, 'Those who invited death, without violating the code of conduct and without ever thinking of giving up the valiant fight in the middle, became models for the Sangha as well as the society' (xxvi). Because the troublesome *sadhvi* had demonstrated her unsuitability for ascetic life in such an aggressive manner, nothing less than *santara* could now vindicate her. Had her behaviour been the result of an external force (*bhut*), her spiritual purity would not have been in question.

Of course, the ascetics hope never to be in such an emotional quagmire to begin with, as it would reveal a lack of individual spiritual fortitude and undermine the general ascetic claim of purity and distinctiveness. Ascetics represent an elite, a tiny fraction of all the worldly souls from the heavens, hells, and middle world who are actually on the right path to emancipation. They are surrounded by souls more enmeshed in worldly existence than they – souls of the gods, infernal beings, other humans, animal, insects, and plants. The ascetic exceeds all of them. Some beings are aware but incapable of pursuing the spiritual life, whereas others are completely submerged in ignorance. Most lay Jains would fall into the former category – that is, cognizant of the right path, but not strong enough to pursue it themselves in this life. Most of the remainder of worldly existence would be lumped into the second category, viz. that of ignorance. In other words, to the Jain ascetic, the world around her is primarily filled with deluded souls – those with 'perverted beliefs' (*mithyadristi*) – and they are at the lowest level of spiritual advancement (the first *gunasthana*). The ascetic, by virtue of her initiation, is said to have reached the ninth *gunasthana* – 'self-restraint with remissness' (*pramatt samyat*) – or the seventh *gunasthana* – 'self-restraint without remissness' (*apramatt samyat*). The demons, as polar extremes, are among the most deluded of all beings: they are powerful as a result of austerities they performed in past lives, but they are misguided and relish tormenting others. Demons therefore do not represent an extraordinary state of being. They are the worldly counterparts to the spiritual ascetics, and in this sense they are very 'ordinary.' Their distinctiveness from humans is more quantitative than qualitative. They are severely burdened with worldly delusion and passion, whereas the rest of worldly beings are somewhat less so (e.g., most plants and animals are heavily burdened; most human beings are moderately so, and Jain ascetics are only minimally impeded) (see Babb, 1996).[11] But ascetics are not inherently pure; they can only establish their spiritual maturity through their ethical, ascetic behaviour. As argued in chapter 3, ascetics strive to be – and are seen as – creators of the distinction between the *laukik* (worldly) and the *lokottar* (transcendent), as embodiments of spirituality. Possession, therefore, is very distressing – not because it denotes the 'occupancy' of an individual by another spiritual being, which is accepted as possible, but, I suggest, because it threatens to blur the distinction between the spiritual and the worldly – to collapse the boundary between ascetics and *shravaks*. And this distinction is at the heart of Jain ontology.

During the period when Asha was 'indisposed,' the *samanis* were determined to convince me that possession was exceptional, that in fact celestial beings typically seek to honour, not harm, ascetics. And besides, they would claim, even in the case of the most dreadful of demonic attacks, the ascetics are almost always capable of withstanding them. The majority of the *samanis* had either heard the odious and terrifying sounds of *bhuts*, or seen their effects, but only a handful had had direct contact with the beings. But whatever form their encounters took, the *bhuts* were always subdued through the *samanis' tapas* (austerities).

The *samanis* took pleasure in enumerating the seemingly endless cases of ascetic victories. To my initial astonishment, in several of the cases, the ascetics' victories came at the price of their lives. It appeared that death was not particularly significant within the overall theme of mastery. Control and the conquering of passions resulted in triumph; it resulted in the clear demarcation between the *laukik* and the *lokottar*. Death was but the means to this glorious end.

Triumph through Death: The Case of Kirin

The demonic attack of *mumukshu* Kirin is probably the most celebrated case in the order's recent history. The events leading to her death occurred over a decade ago (1987), and have already become part of Terapanthi folklore, with at least two books in circulation documenting her trials and ultimate victory. Not long after she became a *mumukshu*, Kirin began to be tormented by a *bhut* who claimed to be her lover from a past life. The troubles were initially minor but increased in their occurrence and seriousness as time went on.

I had already known that Urmilla had become a close friend to Kirin during her troubles, supporting her throughout her ordeal with the *bhut*. Urmilla's fearlessness, though presented as a common ascetic trait, is in fact exceptional in the order. Most of the *mumukshus* and *samanis* were terrified to be near Kirin, as they were now with Asha, leaving Urmilla again to assume the burden of care. And because of her courage, she has had more indirect experience with *bhuts* than any other *samani* in the order. On the third evening of Asha's possession, I was able to meet with Urmilla after the *pratikraman* prayers for a couple of hours. While we talked, a householder kept watch over Asha. I wanted to know more about Kirin, and Urmilla was happy to tell of a tale more meritorious than the present one. She laughed at the thought of herself as a *bhut*-basher, though she was not surprised to find herself in this role. 'I have never been afraid,' she said, leaning against the back wall of her room exhausted, her eyes betraying a smile beneath her *muhpatti*.

'Like Lord Mahavir himself!?' I teased.

'No! Even when I was a householder, as a child, I was very bold. My mother always said I was a bad child,' she laughed. 'You would not believe it was me.' She described how she delighted in worldly things as a young girl, dressing up in fashionable clothes and wearing dark charcoal eyeliner. She sported both a nose ring and ear rings and didn't care what her mother and aunts thought. 'I was so bold,' she repeated. I found it interesting that she saw her courage in the face of demons not to be a product of the ascetic, detached worldview, but stemming from her 'boldness,' her confident, if not cocky, worldly personality. 'I have never been afraid of *bhuts* and so they don't trouble me. The *samanis* and *mumukshus* were so terrified of Kirin's *bhut*, but I was not.' She recalled some of the events leading up to Kirin's death:

> One night the *samanis* were in a room doing *pratikramin*, and Kirin was alone in *this* room [Urmilla indicated it was the room in which we were now sitting] doing *samayik* [a 48-minute period of absolute nonviolence]. Suddenly, just moments after we had finished our prayers, we heard a terrible scream coming from the room. We knew it was probably the *bhut*. The other *samanis* were too terrified to move so I went. When I opened the doors I could see there was a fire in the middle of the room. Kirin was screaming. Soon the fire went away. When I went over to Kirin she was trembling. She told me that her head hurt, and when I looked behind the hood of her sari, her *choti* (ponytail) had been torn out and there was much blood. Days later, when Kirin was chanting mantras, the hair fell from out of the air and onto her lap. The *bhut* claimed that in her past life she had (unintentionally) killed him when she threw a stone and hit him on the head. Though he still loved her, he also wanted revenge. He planned to kill her so that they would be together again.

Urmilla remained close to Kirin after that until the very end. Most of the other *mumukshus* and *samanis* were afraid to be alone with Kirin, or in the presence of her terrifying *bhut*, but Urmilla was not. She explained how she would accompany Kirin outside the residence at night so she could speak with the *bhut*:

> I could not see or hear the *bhut*, but I could understand what they were talking about by what Kirin was saying to him. He loved her and wanted to be with her, and so he wanted her to die – but not as a religious person because then they could not be together. If she had a good rebirth, they

would not be together. I held onto Kirin as she stared up at him. Sometimes she would pull her body closer to me, away from him, because he
wanted to touch her. He always wanted to touch her, but she never allowed
him.

Over the next couple of months Kirin suffered terribly at the hands of
the *bhut.* A number of other fires were started; objects were thrown at
her, blotches of blood appeared on her *mumukshu* saris, and sometimes
he would strangle her, leaving marks on her neck. Kirin found peace
only in her *sadhana* (spiritual practices). It was only through her ascetic
practices that she could disempower him. Urmilla explained:

> Early on, whenever she was in meditation, the *bhut* could not harm her.
> Her *sadhana* caused him pain. Her *tapas* [heat] caused him to feel as
> though he was being burnt alive. He would beg her to stop hurting him,
> reminding her how much she loved him in their past lives. But she knew
> that her ascetic life was the right one, and continued to do her *tapas.* But
> between *sadhanas* was dangerous for her – that was the time the *bhut*
> increased his attacks.

In the last year, Kirin became very anxious to be allowed to take *diksa*
(to become a *sadhvi*). She was afraid the *bhut* would soon kill her, and
that if she died a *mumukshu,* she might be forever entangled with him.
Becoming a *sadhvi* would sever connections to worldly existence and
would elevate her spiritually. By renouncing her 'householder' status,
she would be rejecting worldly existence forever, and would enter an
area of purity where the *bhut* would be unable to harm her. While she
believed that the *bhut* might still be capable of physically harming her as
a nun, he could not affect her next birth. But Guru Dev was not in Ladnun during this time, and she knew she would have to take her request
to him in Delhi. Most of the *mumukshus, samanis,* and *sadhvis,* including Sadhvi Kanak Prabha, cautiously supported her request, but they
did not share her sense of urgency. She should wait until the festival of
Maryada Mahotsva.[12]

A few years earlier, a similar request had been made by a *mumukshu*
who was caught up in a celestial battle between demonic gods who were
tormenting her and benevolent gods who were assisting her. Her dead
father communicated to her via a celestial being that she would soon
die, and that she should not die a 'householder,' but as a *sadhvi.* Guru
Dev did not believe that she would soon die because she was very young

and seemingly healthy. But sure enough, on the day and at the exact time she predicted, she died. The entire community was shocked and everyone deeply regretted neglecting her appeal. When Kirin made her request, it was not as readily dismissed. Weeks passed, and the attacks increased. One night after a bad episode in which rocks were hurled at her from nowhere, cutting her badly, Kirin decided that the only way she could defeat the *bhut* would be through *santara*. Urmilla explained:

> She could not wait to become a *sadhvi*, he was going to kill her. When she stopped *sadhana*, even to sleep, he would attack. She knew she must continue *sadhana* always, so she decided to fast. When she would fast, he could not hurt her. She started to fast for ten days and then to do *santara*.

Once she began her fast, the *bhut* was unable to torment her. She knew that if she were to stop the fast and resume her normal life, he would never leave her until he killed her. Since a *mumuhshu* cannot even wash her clothes without explicit approval from her superiors, let alone embark on *santara*, her superiors must have tacitly approved of her decision. After two weeks on her fast, she was taken to meet Guru Dev for his consent. The story goes that he was very severe with her at first, challenging her decision. But by the end of their meeting, he gave her his blessing and she returned to Ladnun knowing she would continue her fast until death.

Urmilla recalls that the weeks passed quietly and slowly. Kirin grew weak, and was unable to speak because her mouth became filled with sores. But the *bhut* was gone, and she was at peace. The Sadhvi Pramukha (head nun) made a request to Guru Dev to allow Kirin to take *diksa* in his absence, and he agreed. After forty-five days without food and only the smallest quantity of water, Kirin was initiated as a *sadhvi* in a ceremony from her bed, surrounded by monks and nuns. Four days later she died. The streets of Ladnun were filled with cheering crowds of householders as the procession carrying her body moved slowly towards the cremation grounds. The body sat in a open chariot, her *muhpatti* tied to the post behind her head to keep her upright. Her legs were folded, and she looked to be in meditation. Kirin's death represented the victory of asceticism over worldliness; of dispassion over passion; of good over evil. According to Kendall Folkert, *santara or sallekhana* is an 'ideally passionless death' which 'ensures that one will not void one's spiritual progress by clinging to material existence at the end of one's lifetime' (1987: 266). Through *santara*, Kirin died a dispassionate death, in total control of her emotions and thereby immune and impervious to demonic attack. Kirin and asceticism had won, and it was an occasion for celebration.

Samani Asha's possession continued. She remained secluded in the same room on the second floor of the Gautam Shalla. She ate infrequently and was unable to perform the *pratikraman* prayers, so Urmilla said them on her behalf. Most of the *samanis* were terrified and stayed away. Urmilla, together with a few courageous *sadhvis*, tried to rid Asha of the *bhut* on their own. They used the familiar methods of chanting special mantras,[13] sticking a leather shoe in her mouth, and of pinching the large toe of her left foot. That such methods and others like them are well known – and are even outlined in detail in the ascetic order's guidebook, the *Amrit Kalash*[14] – suggests the *non*-extraordinary nature of possession. But nothing worked. After a period of silence, Asha would still suddenly burst into a tremendous rage, and then a moment later sob uncontrollably. On the third night the *bhut* spoke. He told Urmilla and the two householders who were present that he was attracted to Asha because of her beauty. He said he was happy 'occupying' her and that he would never leave. At last the nuns admitted they were overpowered, and decided they would have to make arrangements to have a *sayana* (ghost doctor or exorcist) come to their assistance.

As with Kirin (among many others), the *bhut* desires Asha for her womanliness. He wants to possess her because he is physically attracted to her, not so much because her spiritual practice vexes him. Contrary to the official ascetic view on demons, it is not her asceticism but her worldliness (her sexuality) that prompted him to action. Within the walls of the desert monastery in Ladnun, the *bhuts* that tease and torment the ascetics are, I suggest, metaphors of desire.[15] They are undoubtedly other things to other peoples of different communities (see Kakar, 1996), but in the ascetic world, where desire is the main obstacle to liberation, *bhuts* are embodied desire – and flagrantly so. In the famous stories of the *Tirthankaras*, the *bhuts* represent anger, jealousy, and greed. But among the nuns of the Terapanthi, they often represent sexual desire. Indeed, a common theme running through most accounts of demonic attacks and possession of the nuns is desire. Unlike Lord Mahavir's demonic encounters, these *bhuts* often get personal with the nuns, hoping to establish intimacy.

The *mumukshus*, *samanis*, and *sadhvis* had no difficulty telling me about instances of demonic attack, whereas the monks were far more tight-lipped about admitting its occurrence within their male order. I could never get more than a foggy response from the nuns about whether or not they knew of any cases of possession among the monks. Only one nun told me she was certain a *muni* had once, years ago, been 'caught.' The monks themselves resolutely denied it. While the monks all firmly believe in the existence of the *bhuts*, and accept that braving a demonic attack reveals spiritual power (Lord Mahavir's afflictions are a well-known case in point), they claim that attacks and possession are more common among nuns. They put a decidedly gendered spin on the phenomenon of possession: possession symbolizes a loss of control, and women's emotional nature cause them to be more unstable. Demons, as beings of passion, prey on fear and desire. And because women are more emotional and more fearful than men, the monks assert, they are more vulnerable to demonic possession. Just as their emotional nature made them better devotees, it makes them easier to 'control.' Reynell's research on Jain female sexuality is pertinent here. She writes:

> The Jains regard this issue of [sexual] control as imperative, not only because of the feared repercussions if a woman follows the wrong course of action, but also because women are seen as emotionally vulnerable in the first place. It is believed that their greater depth of emotional feeling increases their liability of being led astray by male admirers declaring their 'love.' (1985: 180)

Women's perceived emotional nature is considered a source of danger to them (and society), whether in the household or ascetic life. The nuns do not dispute their natures as being more emotional than the monks, and they accept that they are more subject to demonic attack and possession.

At least as far as *bhuts* are expressions of sexual desire, their penchant for women may be understandable within the context of ascetic life.[16] Female desire is far more circumscribed than male sexual desire, and *bhuts* can and do openly express desire that nuns could not even admit to feeling. Conquering sexual desire is not considered an obstacle for *sadhvis*, as it is for *munis*, because female desire (among ascetics) is considered to be nonexistent (see pages 81–2). It is repudiated and disavowed. Monks openly talk about the difficulties of renouncing sexual desire, including even Guru Dev himself. If a monk's resolve is weakened, or he feels temptation, he can acknowledge it and perform austerities to weaken his desire. I suggest that a nun will have to channel such desires elsewhere, disguise them to make them acceptable. In a male-dominant ascetic culture, women are considered as objects, rather than as subjects, of desire. And ascetic women in these traditions may also come to regard themselves in this way. Routes that would normally be available to lay women to express desire (e.g., marriage) are not available to *sadhvis*. Demonic attack, therefore, in addition to allowing nuns a legitimate experience of being a 'subject' of desire, affirms them as traditional 'objects' of desire.

Desire is differently interpreted and experienced among nuns and monks. For monks, to experience desire (however unfortunate it may be to them) presents an opportunity to measure a spiritual advance; for nuns, it represents worldliness, attachment, and depravity. It is not just that nuns project their own desires onto the demonic realm; they may come to experience desire as inappropriate, frightening, and in this sense, 'other.' Catherine Lutz provides a basic anthropological insight:

> Culturally provided knowledge systems constitute the structures of exist-
> ence in a fundamental way; they determine how people experience them-
> selves and each other ... [C]ultural knowledge is not merely a tool used by
> the thinking person, it is rather both the form and substance of conscious-
> ness. This characteristic makes it invisible, in large part, to its bearer. (1985:
> 65)

Where monks might interpret/experience sexual desire as the self's arousal by a passive threat (e.g., another human being), nuns might interpret/experience it as an active, external one (i.e., *bhuts*). These experiences would be entirely fitting with cultural understandings of men's and women's 'natures.'

The local *sayana* finally arrived on the fourth night of Asha's posses-sion. He was said to be very powerful, and adept in *tantra*. Immediately he understood what type of demon he was dealing with, and knew exactly which mantras to use to exorcize the demon. The *sayana* spoke with the *bhut*, demanding him to leave Asha. The *bhut* answered that he found her so beautiful, he would never leave her. He also demanded all sorts of sweets, but no one brought him any.[17] But the *sayana* was stron-ger than the *bhut*, and within a few hours, he had driven him away and Asha was released. She was deeply distraught after learning what had happened to her, and did not participate in the usual ascetic practices for a number of days. But she was not punished. Her behaviour had been decidedly contrary to the ascetic ideal, and yet it was condoned because she could simply not be blamed. Accountability lay elsewhere.

In a world where emotions are banished, demons are familiar fellows.

I suggest that *bhuts* are metaphors of the 'worldly' in general, and of passions/desire in particular. They provide an example of the antithesis to the ascetic life, and embody worldliness in all its debauchery and immorality – and in an unambiguous manner.

Demons possess souls, as do all beings, and will endure innumerable incarnations until they one day achieve emancipation. We see that in Jainism, therefore, demons are considerably different from the embodiments of evil we in the West understand by that name. Our understanding of demons in far more essential and absolute, centring on a 'type' of 'nature,' whereas in Jainism it represents a degree. In Jainism, human beings and demons are functionally, but not essentially, opposed. They form part of the same continuum, albeit at polar extremes. Like animals and plants, demons and humans are all part of the same drama. And since Jain moral identity is defined negatively vis-à-vis external worldliness, *bhuts* – as worldly counterparts to the other-worldly ascetic – are central players in the demarcation between good and evil, between the *lokottar* and *laukik*. Indeed, if withstanding the passive worldly temptation of 'householders' is what constitutes an ascetic, enduring the extraordinary 'active' worldly threat of demons establishes greatness.

Bhuts are a micro-discourse on Jain ontology. The battle of the ascetic against the *bhut* is essentially the conflict between the worldly and the transcendent writ small. It is the cosmic battle fought on the individual battlefield between discipline and desire.

PART THREE
BEING OF THE WORLD

6

The Worldly Life of Renunciants[1]

From the guesthouse roof, I was in a privileged position to see the monastery turn from sober to near frenetic as everyone rushed for cover from the impending storm. A monk was in near-trot as he made his way past the guesthouse, balancing a stack of full *patras* in the swaying *jholi*. Two *samanis*, dressed in their *kavatchan*, strode vigorously, keeping their heads down to evade the whipping sand. The householders, less bound by protocol, were in full gait. The peacocks were already in the trees, looking rather precarious as they stood motionless on the branches, determined not to lose their balance. The camels feigned indifference. They were in no rush as their riders herded them under a large tree. The jaded creatures folded their legs and eased their immense bodies to the ground, allowing the harried riders, who were construction workers at a nearby site, to dismount and dash off.

The sky was so black it looked as if it were filled with soot, and the trees swayed violently as the winds picked up. I carried my clothes downstairs just in time. I joined others on the open veranda of the guesthouse and together we watched the gale raging just feet away. The storm instantly became a shared event and washed away reserve as easily as it did sand. Everyone spoke spontaneously and warmly, but soon we were engulfed in whorled hot sand and had to flee back to our rooms. I could see nothing in the pitch darkness of my room, but could hear sand thrashing into my small washroom through a chink in the wall. Within moments the sounds of the generator spurted and the lights and fan struggled to life. In the flickering light I could see a blanket of wet sand covering my floor!

From the very start, I had noticed small amounts of the desert sand, along with insects of every variety, freely entering my abode through a hole in the wall. The hole was no bigger than a shoebox – perhaps the first efforts to make a window. I had asked the superintendent, Mr Gupta, for help in blocking it, but nothing was done. In the winter months, I had used a piece of cardboard to block out the cool air, but now the strong gusts of hot sand were enough to collapse my makeshift barricade. After each incident, I would ask Mr Gupta for help.

'Oh, yes, yes. Dreadful. I will have Bapu fix it,' he would say so earnestly that, for the first two months, I believed him every time. But nothing ever happened. I taped newspaper sheets to the cement walls, but they were child's play before the mildest gusts. Again, this morning, I called Mr Gupta in to see the mess. 'Dreadful,' he said shaking his head. Then he bellowed for Bapu, who came shuffling, in the same way all the servants did – bent forward slightly, arms hanging limply by his side, and with a deliberately indifferent look on his face. Like every other time, Bapu was shown the problem, instructed, and sent off.

I was irritated as I headed over to Gautam Shalla. The *samanis* were already occupied with their regular chores and appeared to have weathered the storm effortlessly. A sweeper woman was busily whisking sand into tidy dunes in the open courtyard and another was swashing a wet mop over the marble terrace. The *samanis* never could wash the floors themselves, for it required raw ('live') water and a disinfectant, which would result in the death of innumerable beings. The sweeper women were from the Harijan village on the outskirts of Ladnun and, I was told, were not concerned with the rules of *ahimsa*. Appalled, the *samanis* would tell me that they even ate meat and drank alcohol.[2] When I entered Urmilla's room, she was not there. She and several others had been called to *Rishabdwar* for a meeting with Sadhvi Kanak Prabha. But Samani Shanta sat quietly near the window, reading. She looked up as I approached. 'You do not look well today,' she said flatly, interrupting my words of obeisance to her. I bowed and then sat crossed-legged on the floor in front of her. I knew I must have looked like a chimney sweep. My hair was filled with sand and, since I had been unable to bathe after the storm, my clothes were dingy and dirty brown. She, like all the ascetics, radiated cleanliness. It astonished me how they managed it. To 'bathe,' they were allowed only a damp cloth (with *ajiv* or 'dead' water), and many of them insisted on using only a dry cloth for their faces and arms.[3]

'I am fine,' I said, but almost immediately began to recount the story of my disagreeable room. At first I was hesitant with my words – trying to downplay my frustration somewhat. I feared she might resent being drawn into so trivial and worldly a problem. But she asked many questions and had stories of her own to tell. In the end she advised me, 'Tell Muniji tonight when you meet with him.'

'Muniji?!' I was surprised. 'He instructs me in *dharma*; why should he want to hear of my domestic problems?' She closed her eyes and shook her head – as if in annoyance with my naïvety. 'He will want to know' was all she said.

Muniji was sitting at his usual place on the open terrace of the monks' residence, leaning against one of the pillars with his eyes closed, a light bulb dangling from the wall above him. As I approached I resolved to tell him about my room immediately. It would be easier that way than trying to find a way to raise the mundane subject in the midst of a talk about karma or *ahimsa*. After paying him homage, he asked how I was keeping, providing me with my opportunity.

'I am fine,' I said, 'except for some problems with my room. I am not sure who to speak to about it.'

'What problems?' he asked seriously, as if such matters were entirely within his concern, and sounding like a school principal.

'Sand is coming into my room through a hole in the wall. There are several inches of sand and mud on the floor. And now the drain is completely blocked.'

'You have told Mr Gupta?' he asked. His knowledge of the superintendent's name surprised me, for it seemed to reflect a familiarity with the mundane and the worldly. I had expected him to say something about the evils of attachment to place or to body.

'Yes, many times. I suppose he is busy,' I said trying to be magnanimous before the holy man. But Muniji shook his head in irritation and said, 'I will speak with him.'

The remainder of our talk centred on the weather. He explained how terrible the sandstorms in Rajasthan can be – how no one dares venture outdoors during a bad one. He said that even from a chink in a wall, a room can be swamped with sand. But sand was more manageable than water; he recounted terrible tales of floods in the south. I told him about Canadian winters, which made him feel that sand was better than snow. Then the sounds of a young monk calling all to prayer broke into our discussion – forty minutes had passed and we hadn't got around to talking about *dharma*. There was a feeling of strain as I joined my hands to pay respect, and lowered my head. Then the young monk appeared. Muniji held onto the youth's arm as he struggled to his feet. Just before turning to walk away, he said curtly, 'Tomorrow, bring your questions.'

The next morning I returned from breakfast to find my room in perfect condition: the opening was boarded up with wood, the floor swept clean. I was flabbergasted. I turned on the faucet and watched the water flow freely down the wide drain. Divine intervention!

Later that day when I saw Shanta entering the library with another *samani*, I caught up with her to tell her the good news. After recounting the story, she said with a wan smile, 'Now you see how things work here.' I was taken aback by what appeared to be her cynicism. Raising my joined palms in thanks and in farewell, I watched her and the other *samani* disappear into the small, poorly lit building, and I wondered what she had meant, and whether or not I misunderstood her.

For six months I had tried in vain to resolve my mundane problem through the avenues and mechanisms of the *laukik* (social) realm. Yet it was only by tapping into the domain of *lokottar* (transcendent) that the problem was resolved. The social power of the religious elite and, concomitantly, the influence of lay elites in religious matters is as well established as it is inevitable (Babb, 1996: 52; Cort, 1991b; Flügel, 1995–6; Folkert, 1993c: 167–86). The interdependence of society and religion is a conspicuous feature of the Terapanthi community despite the order's uncompromising insistence on the doctrinal separation of the two realms (Flügel, 1995–6).[4] Indeed, the order's insistence on the rigid demarcation of religion and society may paradoxically exacerbate interdependence, as Flügel suggests:

> [T]he new doctrine of Bhiksu has effectively not been able to overcome the fundamental problem of routinization as described by Weber (1985: 142–8). It merely generated a new set of practical paradoxes. Generally, the increased degree of differentiation of religion and society produced both a greater immediacy and a greater indirectness of the links between the *dharmasangh* and the laity. (1995–6: 127)[5]

Muniji is a respected senior monk with the reputation of being a very learned scholar. His intellectual accomplishments and seniority have earned him considerable reverence from the more junior ascetics, and from the lay community generally. All are eager to receive his wisdom, and consequently he has to regulate his time assiduously. To have him intervene on my behalf meant instant success, and it also meant an elevation in my own status among the guesthouse workers.[6] It is a paradox of monastic life that the more successful one is as a renunciant, the more surely one is pulled into worldly concerns. The higher one's position in the ascetic organization, the more time one spends with *shravaks*. Guru Dev, Acharyasri, Yuvacharya, Sadhvi Pramukha, and all senior or charismatic ascetics have very little time for their own spiritual practices. Indeed, they must learn to practise their *sadhana* in public.[7]

Baldly stated, the ascetics *must* be concerned with the daily lives of the householders because they are the lifeblood of the order (Folkert, 1993b: 167–74). But social forces conspire to shift the focus of ascetic life away from detachment and aloneness towards public management. With each 'success' for the order – that is, with each new ascetic initiate – the order is brought a step closer to 'society,' from which it tries to stand opposed. The larger the order, the more dependent it is on the laity. Interaction with *shravaks* is neither random nor incidental, as it was with the great ascetic heroes, but rather it has become highly managed (see Reynell, 1985: 218). Only a few hours of each day remain 'off limits' to householders. At all other times, the ascetics find themselves surrounded by householders and drawn into their worldly problems – just as Muniji was to mine. Furthermore, the more charismatic an ascetic, the larger his following. And the more time he spends with *shravaks* means less time for his own *sadhana*.

Even though the socioeconomic foundation of ascetic organization rests in the socially circulated, validated, and accepted ethical formulation of reciprocity, the ideology of world renunciation remains legitimate only to the extent that outright reciprocity is denied (see chapter 3). There seems to be an unspoken agreement between householders and ascetics to valorize the ideological over the material, and to not examine the material basis of their shared existence. The reality of interdependence leads a shadowy, 'behind-the-scenes' existence, so that *moksa marg* (liberation path) and *laukik marg* (worldly path) remain fundamentally separate and distinct.

Kenneth Oldfield depicts ascetics and householders in this idealized manner – like billiard-balls that come together briefly, perhaps beneficially, only to return to their essentially separate existences. He writes:

> The lives of the laity caught up in business, journalism, medicine and education, all occupations which involve them deeply in the pragmatic decision-making which is part of living in the world, contrasts sharply with the lives of the monks and nuns who wholeheartedly pursue the path of purification that leads to *moksa* (release). This contrast represents a tension that lies at the very heart of the religion, a heart which ... is concerned with resolving the conflict between the path of *dharma* followed by the laity and

the path of *moksa* followed by the ascetics. The meeting place of the two paths is the *stanak* (building) or the temple where ascetics and laity encounter each other. The meeting is a *tirtha*, a crossing over point between the commercial world of the Jain businessman and the sacred world of the monks and nuns pursuing their path of purification ... Jains are preoccupied with the idea of achieving release from the evils of this world and the meetings with the ascetics for the laity appear symbolically to represent that quest, for in the meetings the boundaries and conflicts between the path of *dharma* and *moksa* are dissolved and the laity can glimpse into the world of purity and peace. (1982: 95–6)

The *shravak* and ascetic represent the opposed 'worldly orientation' (*laukik pravrtti*) and spiritual orientation (*lokottar pravrtti*) metaphorically. Nevertheless, no matter how stubbornly the *laukik–lokottar* polarity is affirmed, and no matter how significant the ideological realm in shaping interpretations and informing actions, day-to-day practices undermine it, exposing the intertwined nature of lay and ascetic life.

Power in the monastic order translates into power in lay society, and ascetics are 'utilized' for both spiritual and material gain. Charismatic ascetics may initially be in demand to give blessings or advice, but with time they are sought after because their popularity itself makes them important 'brokers' in the community. They become 'spiritual' conduits, legitimating individuals, families, and businesses (Flügel, 1995–6). Local political leaders, for example, have found it in their interest to publicly endorse Guru Dev's Anuvrat movement, for this in turn translates into popular support. Business leaders make enormous donations to the order – not only because of the good spiritual merit that will result from it, but from the very worldly benefits as well, in terms of reputation, alliances and so on. And conversely, the monastic order has extended itself deeply into lay life to make use of lay resources in order to secure support for its own religious projects. Flügel writes:

[T]ime enduring structures have emerged amongst Jains through the development of permanent links between ascetic groups and certain lay elites, who support religious networks and pilgrimages not only for religious purposes but also as means of both status acquisition and political and economic integration. (1995–6: 120)

Jains believe that the appearance of interdependence between the *laukik* and *lokottar* in day-to-day life is the outcome of *samsar*'s obfuscations. In reality, the two are distinct. The community's motivations to keep latent these mechanisms of reciprocity are rooted in an attempt to uphold their conceptions of reality.

When the 'infrastructure' of reciprocity is glimpsed (or perhaps, acknowledged), as it is on certain occasions, the fragile boundary between the *lokottar* and the *laukik* is threatened with dissolution. On several occasions, under Acharya Tulsi's (Guru Dev's) leadership, the Terapanthi order became entangled in a controversy over such 'boundary maintenance.' Acharya Tulsi embarked on a number of 'modernizations,' all of which were controversial precisely because they were perceived by some as blurring the distinctions between the *lokottar* and the *laukik*. On Tulsi's reforms, Flügel states:

> Compared to Bhiksu's vision of a purely ascetic Jainism, the Terapanth of today has considerably changed, particularly through a series of controversial innovations that were introduced by *acarya* Tulsi in the first decades after Indian Independence (1949–1981). In order to secure the growing influence of the Terapanth under the changed social conditions, Tulsi gradually reverted back to a traditional Jain system by forming closer bonds with the laity and promoting programs of religious and moral education for the society as a whole. He showed great ingenuity in the construction of an all-inclusive corporative sectarian organization by creating a new network of 'socio-religious' institutions for the laity, to carry the *Anuvrat* (small vow, 1949), *Preksa Dhyan* (insight meditation, 1975) and *Jivan Vijnan* (science of living, 1980) movements, without directly violating Bhiksu's principles. (1995–6: 127)

These changes were met by intense criticism on the part of many Terapanthi householders and some ascetics. Satish Kumar, for example, in an autobiographical account of his years as a Terapanthi monk, writes:

> During the eight years I had been a monk I was always with my guru (Tulasi). He treated me as his son and I treated him as my father. People thought that I was being groomed as his successor. But I was beginning to feel overpowered by him. His answers no longer satisfied me. *Ever since his decision to modernize the order, I felt he was travelling in two boats at the same time – denouncing the world and also seeking its recognition.* (cited in Oldfield, 1982: 88; italics added)

Dissent over Tulsi's modernizations culminated in the defection of a group of *sadhvis* and *munis* in 1981. The breakaway group became the most recent Jain ascetic order, calling themselves the 'New' or 'Naya'

Terapanthi. I quote at length from Oldfield, who was in Rajasthan in 1982 and followed the controversy:

> To develop the [*Anuvrat*] movement on a national scale, trust funds were established under Acharya Tulasi's control and Jain businessmen in particular contributed generously to them. It is Tulasi's use of these trusts and his involvement in the administration and finance of the movement, rather than in the rigours of the ascetic life, that much of the new schism has developed ...
>
> According to press reports, the schism had been simmering for about five years, but only became public knowledge in October 1981 when a number of monks and nuns submitted their 'muh-patras' (letters of resignation). Matters reached a head when Tulasi nominated his 'yubacharya' (his successor) at a public function in 1977. Apparently in 1972 Tulasi had agreed that he would nominate Muni Rupchand as his yubacharya but at a public function for the formal naming in 1977 Tulasi nominated Muni Nathmal, a monk closely involved with Anuvrata and a biographer of Acharya Bhiksu. Muni Rupchand and his supporters have complained of favouritism and claim that the reason for the sudden switch rests in Rupchand's refusal to pay court to a rich business friend of Tulasi in Calcutta. A supporter of the 'Nav' Terapanth (New Terapanth – the name given to the breakaway group) claims that 'The rich sravakas (laymen) have a stake in getting a pliable yubacharya because he can ensure influential contracts for them ...
>
> The main thrust of criticism against Acharya Tulasi is that he has brought the Terapanth sect into disrepute by making it a meeting ground for businessmen and politicians and has flouted the basic Terapanth principles by living a less than austere life, enjoying pomp and show. Tulasi himself refuses to enter into answering his critics with people outside the order but in a signed interview published in a Jaipur daily he claimed that all the funds he had collected had been for the benefit of humanity and he urged his detractors to 'move with the times' ...
>
> In his letter of resignation, Rupchand's co-leader in the breakaway group, Muni Chandmal, wrote, 'my soul does not any longer endorse the utterance of such benedictions to you every morning as "My Lord you are the essence of the organization. I have the highest respect for you." My heart trembles to utter such non-truths. (1982: 86–7)

Oldfield adds:

> During January of this year [1982] my informants were receiving letters from both sections of the schism explaining their position and seeking

their support. Most of my informants were impatient with the dispute, claiming that it represented a clash of personalities which reflected a decline in the quality of the ascetic order, who on entering the ranks renounce the world of ego. Muni Chandmal, speaking for the rebels, said in January: 'We have resolved not to let politics and business enter our precincts. We don't want a dictator around us so we have decided not to have an acharya-for-life.' (88)

Oldfield claims that much of the criticisms of the breakaway appear to have been substantiated by news reports, but he nevertheless sees the controversy within a wider historical context. He writes:

> The strength of Jainism that has already been noted, of a harshly ascetic monastic order being supported by and having its roots in a wealthy commercial-class laity, contains also the incipient danger of constant dissension and division, particularly when the ascetics attempt, as Tulasi has, to reinterpret the ancient rigid tradition in response to the needs of a new generation. In his attempt to present Jainism to a wider audience and make it more relevant to the needs of India today, as he sees it, Tulasi has found himself, inevitably, compromising with the world of big business and politics, a world which some of his laity and his mendicants consider he renounced when becoming a monk. Yet schisms of this nature can be interpreted as reflecting the liveliness and healthiness of the tradition and can be seen as pointing to the fact that the faith continues to be a vital force in Indian society today. (91)

Not surprisingly, according to the ascetics of the Terapanthi order, the schism did not stem from the order's involvement in worldly affairs, but from the *maan* (egoism) of a few disobedient members. Every time I raised the subject, I was told the same thing: Muni Rupchand was jealous of Acharyasri Mahaprajna's nomination for Yuvacharya, and he was very egotistical and felt he ought to be successor. Unable to bear the decision, he said all sorts of bad things about Guru Dev and turned others against the order. Eventually he and his followers left.

The Importance of Obedience

A couple of weeks after my room had been 'miraculously' repaired, Samanis Urmilla and Shanta and I sat talking outdoors in the sandy courtyard of the Gautam Shalla. It was an especially mild afternoon and they had just finished the weekly chore of washing their groups' saris.

They both sat crossed-legged on top of semi-dry saris, which, tightly folded and piled several high, looked like a square white cushion. With the weight of their own bodies, they 'ironed' the saris – and did a marvellous job of it too. I had just come back from a few days in Delhi, where I had visited the Naya Terapanthi order. I had met with the head nun and found her to be very open and friendly. She inquired about what was happening in Ladnun, and about my work. Urmilla and Shanta listened with interest, and then told me that that 'head nun' was Sadhvi Pramukha's sister. She had left with Munis Rupchand and Chandmal, and encouraged other *sadhvis* to leave with her.

'Guru Dev did not wish for them to go,' Urmilla said, 'but because of their *maan* (egoism), they were blinded.' Shanta sat quietly mending her *kavatchan*, saying very little.

'Without discipline,' Urmilla continued, 'we would be nothing. Who are we to challenge our leaders?' After a long pause, and some advice to Shanta on her patchwork, Urmilla soberly added, 'I have experienced Guru Dev's hard and soft eyes. We all have. He is strict with us because he cares about us. We must learn discipline, otherwise how can we succeed?'

I asked her why she had felt his 'hard eyes' and she explained that a few years back when Guru Dev was spending his *chaturmas* in Jaipur, she had disobeyed him. The congregation was gathered for the *pravachan* (sermon) but Guru Dev was sick with a sore throat and was having difficulty speaking. After just a few moments into his lecture, he called upon a *samani* to sing a song. Then, at its close, he called upon Urmilla to say something to the congregation. She recalls:

> He called me to stand up and speak before him, before the whole order and audience. I had nothing planned and I was startled. I could think of nothing, my mind was blank with fear ... So, I kept my eyes down and asked the *samani* beside me to stand. At first she said 'No! You must go' – but I could not. It happened quickly, but the time passed slowly. Everyone's eyes were on me. I could not move. I could not even look up at Guru Dev. Finally the *samani* beside me stood to speak. I have no memory of what she said. I felt so terrible. I could not lift my head.

She explained how after the sermon, all the *samanis* and *sadhvis* scolded her for her disobedience, which made her feel even more wretched. Later that same day, when she and the other *samanis* met with Sadhvi Pramukha, she was publicly reprimanded. The head nun used her error as an important lesson in obedience. She said that it was a matter of discipline and therefore very significant to both ascetics and householders. During that week and the one that followed, when she joined the *samanis* in doing *vandana* to Guru Dev, he ignored her. He gave all the others his blessing – by looking directly at them or raising his hand towards them in acknowledgment – but he entirely disregarded Urmilla. She said it was one of the most difficult periods in her life. Finally one day he called for her, and told her he had some important work for her to do. She was grateful that he had included her in his fold once again. She told him that she was sorry for her disobedience, and in the end, he gave her his blessing. She said:

> It would not have mattered what I would have said that day when he called me – even something very short. I should not have gone against Guru Dev. It is a matter of discipline. Guru Dev always says that if the bricks of a building are not strong it will disintegrate; we must not neglect the small things. It is never the great vows that are broken – only the small rules and regulations. So we must be alert!

Another *samani* came out of a room to collect the 'pressed' saris. Shanta and Urmilla rocked forward on their knees, and she pulled the saris from beneath their bottoms. When Urmilla left to fetch another bundle of saris for 'pressing,' I stayed back with Shanta for a few moments longer, watching her finish her mending job. Finally she too got up to leave, and as she did, she said in a very soft voice, 'Can you come and visit me tonight?'

'Of course,' I said, 'I will come after prayers.'

Shanta struck me as a deeply reserved person, someone who preferred to listen than to actively participate in conversations. Her smile was bashful, and – even when wearing the *muhpatti* – she would only laugh with her hand covering her mouth. That evening, I followed her into her room after the *Arhat Vandana* had been recited, a time when all the *samanis* return to their rooms for study or meditation. It was one of the few quiet times of the day, when they could catch up on their work or studies. And if there was no work to be done or no meetings being called, they could sit and talk with other *samanis*, meditate, or read. The *samanis* who shared Shanta's room were at a meeting with Niyojikaji, so we sat alone in her tiny, windowless chamber. Along the back wall were metal cabinets that resembled high-school lockers. But instead of posters of movie stars on the inside of the doors there were posters of

Acharya Bhikshu, Guru Dev, and the other Terapanthi leaders. She
pulled open one of the doors and took out a book from a large pile, and
handed it to me. It was an English-language textbook on contemporary
ethics. It had chapters on euthanasia, abortion, freedom of speech,
among others.

'Would you like to read it?' she asked.

'Sure,' I said. 'Have you read it?'

'No. I don't understand it. Do you have other books that might be
easier?'

'On this subject?'

'Yes,' she said equivocally.

'Not here in Ladnun. I could send you something from home.'

'I cannot answer you if you write to me,' she said quickly, and then
looked away from me.[8] Our conversation appeared artificial and she
seemed very nervous. After what felt like a long silence, she said, 'What
Urmilla explained to you today – about discipline – it is true. It is everything.'

I nodded, recalling Urmilla's words.

'It is not what I had thought,' she continued. 'Discipline *is* necessary
in an order, but here it is *mostly* about discipline and order.'

I still just kept looking at her, trying to make sense of what she was saying. Her critical words contrasted sharply with my image of her as a doc-
ile and devoted disciple. It took me some time before I abandoned my
framework. Our exchange two weeks earlier (after Muniji had my room
repaired) came back to my mind. Maybe her words, 'Now you see how
things work here,' were meant to be cynical after all, I thought.

She continued: 'Most of what we do has nothing to do with spirituality. It is about order, about living together.'

'Are you not happy in the order?' My artless question was too direct
and unambiguous, and she flinched.

'I do not know … I wish I could live as a *samnyasi* in the forest.' She
smiled timidly. Her words astonished me. I did not feel as though I knew
her well enough to hear them. I realized the enormity of what she was
saying. I also realized that, as an outsider, I was probably one of the very
few people to whom she could talk like this. Her body was trembling –
not from fear, I believe, but from the portentousness of what she was saying.

We sat staring: my eyes fixed on her, and her eyes glued to the book
she had taken out of the locker. Then – seemingly out of the night sky –
a family appeared at the open door. They were hunched forward in def-

erence waiting to be invited in. Their hands, in supplication, covered their mouths. The smallest among them, a boy of no more than three, stood by his mother with his hands joined and held high. On his mother's cue, he charged in and stood in front of Shanta. His palms together, he swirled his tiny arms in three circles, and then fell to his knees and ceremoniously lowered his head to the ground. He kept it there long after Shanta raised her hand in blessing and invited them in. The boy's father then scooped him up and praised his efforts. Delighted with himself, he began to perform the routine all over again. Hands held high ... three swirls ... but this time his mother sternly grabbed hold of his little hands and put a stop to it. Shanta handed me the book on ethics, and with a look of apology she said, 'Can you come tomorrow night?'

I nodded as I bowed to her before the householders, and then left. I returned to my room that night feeling especially anxious. I felt desperate for Shanta, but did not know how I could possibly help her.

Shanta was grappling with what is surely the single greatest paradox of monastic life – namely, the more one tries to step outside of society, the more one is in it. As G.S. Ghurye writes in the introduction of his book on Indian ascetics,

> Monastic life leads to the endeavour of creating social organization peculiarly fitted for the ascetic life. Thus asceticism leading in its growth to monastic life creates the paradoxical phenomenon of social organization for those who not only negatived but also renounced social connections and individual wants. ([1953]1995: 1)

The ascetic rhetoric of aloneness and detachment is a discourse, an ideal framework through which life's events are interpreted, and even to a large extent, experienced. But there is a huge distance between the ideal and the real. The ascetics' schedule allows for very little free time and – even within those rare unregulated moments – it is seldom spent alone. Their days are not spent isolated in meditation, study, and penance – as those of the ascetic heroes were – but, rather in group activities such as alms collecting, prayers, and chores. Their days are minutely regulated from sunrise to sunset, so that even 'free time' is supervised. After observing Terapanthi monastic life, Holmstrom stated:

> So much of the training for the *sadhvis* and many of the rules or conventions of their everyday life are concerned paradoxically with communal liv-

ing, with co-operation and sisterhood *between* sadhvis. It is then a society contained within, and delimited against, the 'social.' (1988: 36)

Communal living requires 'social' rules of cooperation, but it also breeds the 'social' vices of competition and ambition. Most ascetics are deeply immersed in these 'social' dimensions of monastic life – in the day-to-day rules and regulations for communal living *and* in ambitious efforts to stand out as individuals in a rigidly hierarchical order. These social factors dominate ascetic life every bit as much as they do lay life.

Although Shanta was surely not alone in her disillusionment with ascetic life, for many, it is the very social nature of the order that attracts them. In fact, there is little doubt that most would not have pursued asceticism if, in fact, it entailed a life of isolation. Paul Dundas writes:

One thing seems certain. Nobody today becomes a Jain ascetic to enter a state of contemplative solitude, for the lives of monks and nuns seldom offer an opportunity for sustained privacy. (1992: 132–3).

In the Terapanthi hierarchical structure, everyone's role is clearly delineated and upward mobility is encouraged. Discipline and obedience to one's superior are absolutely essential to the smooth functioning of the order, and yet, ironically, it reintroduces those rules and regulations for communal living that the renunciant is said to renounce. Dundas writes:

'Discipline is the root of religious practice' (DVS 9.2.2.). From a relatively ancient period, the Jains produced collections of rules which were designed not just to instruct the ascetic how to carry out the obligations entailed in his vows but also to regulate inter-monastic relationships, delineate acceptable forms of connection with lay supporters, and enable senior monks to impose penances for misdemeanours. (1992: 153)

Renunciation, therefore, involves the negation of society 'out there' and a concomitant recreation of society from 'A to Z' behind monastery walls.

The Terapanthi Hierarchy

All monastic life, based as it is on the *guru–shishya* (teacher–disciple) relationship, is inherently hierarchical. But the Terapanthi is unique among all Jain sects in its degree of centralization. Nalini Balbir describes the organization of the order:

Les Tp (Terapanthin) forment une organization 'de type à la fois central-isée et socialiste,' 'alliance de dictature et de socialisme démocratique' selon les propres termes des documents officiels. Un pontife se trouve à la tête de l'ensemble moines + nonnes, contrairement aux injonctions les plus répandues des textes canoniques où l'on ne voit pas qu'il soit question d'une direction centrale. Il préside aux actes religieux essentiels: lui seul a pouvoir d'ordonner des disciples, de les exclure, de désigner son success-eur, aujourd'hui un moine presque aussi ancien en religion que Tulsi lui-même – le Muni Nathmal, dont la personnalité semble bien plus effacée que la sienne. Une monial principale est à la tête des nonnes, aujourd'hui Kanakprabha sadhvi, mais elle-même est hiérarchiquement dépendante de lAcarya, et lui doit presque autant de déférence que n'importe laquelle de ses compagnes. (1983: 43)

The monastic order is organized hierarchically (see chart on page 158) under the absolute leadership of the *acharya*, who 'fulfils both spir-itual and administrative, legislative and judicative functions within the order' (Flügel, 1995–6: 130). The *yuvacharya* (successor) is next in the chain of command and serves as an important assistant in all religious and administrative matters. Beneath him is the *mahasraman* (leader of monks and generally assumed to be future *yuvacharya*). The leader of the nuns, the *mahasramani* (or Sadhvi Pramukha) is the formal equiv-alent of the *mahasraman*, but in practice her role is considerably differ-ent. She has greater autonomy than the *mahasraman* because her contact with the male hierarchy is limited. She presides over the *sadhvis* in an area separate from the *acharya* and *yuvacharya*, and so, among the *sadhvis*, her position is supreme and akin to that of the *acharya*. But within the Terapanthi *dharmasangh* in general, her role is considered to be subordinate even to that of the *mahasraman*. Whereas she has reached her pinnacle, he will likely assume the *acaryaship* in the future. Beneath the position of the *mahasraman* and *mahasramani* are the *sing-harpatis* (also called *agranis*), senior ascetics in charge of small groups of ascetics (*singhars*). Flügel writes: 'The *sadhus* and *sadhvis* are at the moment [1991] divided into 126 *singhars* (Skt.samghata – gathering), which are small itinerant groups of 3–5 ascetics, each led by a senior called a *singharpati* or *agrani* (chief)' (1995–6: 130–1).[9]

Beneath the *singharpatis* and their junior *sadhvis* and *sadhus* are the leaders of the *samanis* and *samans* called *Niyojika* and *Niyojak*, respec-tively. In 1996, there were eighty-one *samanis* and just four *samans* (most male aspirants become *sadhus* directly, without this intermediary stage).

Ācārya Śrī Pūjyajī Mahārāj

Yuvācārya

Mahāśramaṇ	Sādhvī Pramukhā
	(Mahāśramaṇī)
Agraṇī (Singhārpati)	Agraṇī (Singhārpati)
Sādhu	Sādhvī
Niyojak	Niyojikā
Samaṇ	Samaṇī
Sanyojak	Sanyojikā
Yojak	Yojikā
Mumukṣu Bhāī	Mumukṣu Bahan
Upāsak	Upāsikā

Source: Flügel (1995–6: 131)

Given the large number of *samanis,* leaders are assigned for each room when at the monastery in Ladnun and, when travelling, for each group. Beneath the *samanis* are the *mumukshus* and *upasikas,* who are formally outside the ascetic hierarchy because they have not yet taken *diksa.* In practice, however, they are treated as low-status novices in the hierarchy. The leader of the *mumukshu* sisters is called the *Nirdeshika* or *Sanyojika,* and in 1996 she was responsible for fifty-three sisters. The male equivalent is the *Nirdeshik* or *Sanyojik,* who in 1996 was responsible for just three *mumukshu* brothers. Beneath them are the *Yojikas,* who are essentially 'room leaders' responsible for three to five sisters (the *mumukshu* brothers were too few in number to require *Yojaks*).

Finally, there are the first-year female and male novices called *upasikas* and *upasiks,* respectively. Among the sixteen *upasikas* in 1996, one was designated leader (there were no *upasiks*). To be given a leadership position is an honour, but it is always temporary.[10] Each year at the *Maryada Mahotsav* (festival of restraint), new leaders are designated (the *mumukshu* and *upasika* leadership cycle is less structured, and can occur at any time). Flügel writes that one of 'the main organizational tasks of the MM [*maryada mahotsav*] [is] the rotating of the ascetics among the *singhars*' (1995–6: 134). A leadership role entails monitoring one's subordinates and reporting to one's superiors, as well as being responsible for the well-being of those in one's charge. During the eight months of their *vihar* (ritualized wandering), the *singharpatis* and *samani/saman* group leaders are required to keep diaries of their group's activities, which they then submit to the *acharya* at the *Maryada Mahotsav.* Flügel writes:

> The *agranis* keep diaries (*kul yatra vivaran*) in which they write the names of the villages they visited, how many days they stayed, how much cloth (*vastr*) and medicine (*ausadhi*) they received, and from whom, special achievements of each ascetic (*tapasya, svadhyaya*), religious programmes (*preksa dhyan*), pacifications of quarrels (vigrah saman), the number and type of vow administered, and the services given and received from other ascetic groups (*bhakti*).These diaries have to be scrutinized every year during MM by the *acarya*, who then evaluates the conduct of each ascetic (*sarana varana*), and distributes rewards (so called *kalyanak* points) and punishments (*prayascitt*) accordingly. (1995–6: 138)

One of the most important functions of the 'diaries' is to oversee the methods the ascetics are using to inspire the *shravaks*[11] and to keep track of potential *anuvratis* (those who have taken *anuvrat* vows) and renunciants. For example, when a *sadhvi* inspires a young person to consider joining the order, she records it. This information will be used to maintain contact between the ascetic aspirant and the order, and eventually to facilitate contact with the *acharya.* The *sadhvi*'s efforts will later be publicly acknowledged and honoured.

Group leaders are essential to the working of the Terapanthi order with its absolute centralization of power in the *acharya.* All groups – even if composed of just two – will have a leader, resulting in the establishment of a very intricate and hierarchical network of superiors and subordinates. Balbir describes this 'micro-structure':

> Le pontife règle également, en début d'année, la vie des religieux, en désignant l'*agrani,* 'le chef' chargé de diriger, pour les affaires courantes, les petites groupes plus ou moins autonomes de trois à cinq membre … C'est cette micro-structure qui forme la base de la vie quotidienne où les huit religieuses les plus agées sont prises en charge par un groupe de treize, nommé et renouvelé chaque année. (1983: 43)

The policy of consolidating all power in the hands of one Acharya makes the Terapanthi unique among Jain orders, and obtains legitimization through its 238-year-old constitution, the Maryada Patra. The Maryada Patra is a fixed code of ascetic practice, written by Acharya Bhikshu, to which all ascetics must pledge allegiance each morning through the recitation of the *lekh patr.*[12] Paul Dundas writes:

The Terapanth *maryada* [constitution] is to a large extent unsurprising in its strict delineation of regulations governing begging, dress, possessions, and the permitted relationships between monks and nuns and the laity ... What is distinctly new, however, is its insistence on the total centrality of the acarya, the assumption by him of all monastic offices and the total subordination of all Terapanth ascetics to him. It is the acarya alone who is responsible for the administration of discipline, for the appointment of his successor, for the giving of initiation ... and it is the same figure who every year instructs each ascetic about his mendicant itinerary and the location of his place of rain retreat. Through this total concentration of power in the hands of the acarya, Bhikshu hoped to prevent the tendencies towards fission and the emergence of rival ascetic lineages which he saw as leading to the corruption of the Jain community and the impeding of a correct understanding of Mahavira's teachings. (1992: 222)

Flügel explains how discipline is maintained in Terapanthi monastic life through a multi-faceted system of ritualized rules:

In order to guarantee the continuous implementation of these [Bhikshu's] rules, he [Jayacarya, 1804–1881] set up a system of three interconnected rituals: the *likhat*, the *hajari*, and the *maryada mahotsav*, each being based on the compulsory performance of an oath of acceptance of certain rules peculiar to the Terapanth monastic organization. The *lekh patr* or *likhat* (formular) contains the thirteen essential rules of the order and has to be individually recited and signed first thing every morning. The *hajari* (presence) is a ceremony of group purification cum teaching (*ganvisuddhikaran*). It was first organized by Jayacarya in 1853 as a fortnightly assembly of all the ascetics of the *raj* (and each *singhar*) for the recitation, explanation and acceptance of the *likhat* and other rules, as well as for public examinations of novices. Nowadays the *hajari* is only performed at special occasions, and the *maryada patr* – the new compilation of Bhiksu's and Jayacarya's rules made by Tulsi – is read out in the presence of a large audience. In this way the general public is made familiar with the *maryadas* and can monitor the conduct of the ascetics independently. Afterwards the sadhus and sadhvis, all standing in a row according to the seniority of initiation (*diksa paryaya*), recite the *lekh patr* and accept it one after the other ... However, the most important ceremony of the Terapanth is the annual *maryada mahotsav* (= MM) (festival of restraint). Like the *hajari*, it was originally (1864) a ritual for the ascetics only, but has developed into a meeting of the whole fourfold assembly, which takes place for three or more days in January/February, and often attracts up to 50,000 pilgrims. The festival celebrates the date of the recording of Bhiksu's last *likhat*, the constitution of the sect, through the recitation of the original text (*samuhik maryada*) and the performance of an oath of allegiance to the '*dharma, gan, acarya,* and the *maryada*' by the ascetics. (1995–6: 132–3)

Hajari, which translates as 'presence,' denotes the public, social nature of affirmation. When the ritual is performed, the Acharya (or *singharpati*) reads out a series of statements and questions (on the left in the list shown below), to which the ascetics respond in unison (on the right). There are slightly different versions and lengths of *hajaris*. The following is a condensed form:

1 Don't say a single bad word.	'*tyag hai*'[a]
2 Don't say words which create doubt about the order.	'*tyag hai*'
3 Don't do practices that counter those of the order.	'*tyag hai*'
4 Don't take any other ascetic with you if you leave the order.	'*tyag hai*'
5 Don't form factions or groups.	'*tyag hai*'
6 Don't break the order's regulations.	'*tyag hai*'
7 Don't break with the order of the *acharya*.	'*tyag hai*'
8 Do you do your *swadhi*[b] four times daily?	'*upiyog sahit kie*'[c]
9 Do you say '*avarshi nisihi*'[d] when travelling?	'*upiyog sahit kie*'
10 Are you giving respect to seniors at proper time daily?	'*upiyog sahit kie*'
11 Are you sleeping at proper time?	'*upiyog sahit kie*'
12 Do you speak with lay women or nuns [men/monks]?	'*upiyog sahit kie*'
13 Are you reciting the *likhat*[e] daily?	'*upiyog sahit kie*'
14 Have you taken *alochana*?[f]	'*upiyog sahit kie*'
15 Are you following the rules carefully?	'*upiyog sahit kie*'
16 Are you observing the *samitis* and *guptis*[g] carefully?	'*upiyog sahit kie*'
17 Have you observed the rules and regulations of the organization carefully?	'*upiyog sahit kie*'

[a] '*Tyag hai*' = 'it is renounced.'
[b] *Swadhi* = memorization of scriptures.
[c] '*Upiyog sahit kie*' = 'we do so carefully, though lapses may exist.'
[d] Ascetics must say '*avarshi avarshi*' when going outside, which means 'I am going with purpose.' When returning, they say '*nisihi nisihi*,' meaning ' I am returning with purpose.'
[e] *likhat* = *likh-patr* (*maryada patr*) = the letter of rules recited daily.
[f] *alochana* = critical self-examination, following the recitation of the *pratikramana* (confession).
[g] There are five *samitis*, or 'codes of conduct'– one must be careful when walking, speaking, taking alms, handing objects, and in excretory functions. There are three *guptis*, or 'restraints' – one must curb the activities of the mind, body, and speech.

The Terapanthi ascetics are immensely proud of the discipline that centralization brings, and commonly dismiss other orders thus: 'One acharya for every four monks.' A publication on the Terapanthi states,

> The Terapanth order is known as a well-knit and harmonious organization among the Jains. It owes its success to the code of conduct for the monks and nuns of this Dharm Sangh as enunciated in the Maryada Patra written by Acharya Bhkishu himself. The main features of this historical document are that Terapanth Dharm Sangh will have one Acharya and that all its monks and nuns will have invariably to submit to the discipline enjoined on them by him. They will move about under his authority and the place where they have chaturmas will be decided by him alone. The mandatory powers bestowed upon the Acharya by this document sound autocratic but they are not so, for these monks and nuns enjoy full freedom of discussion within the order. (Bhatnagar, 1985: Preface)

Although the ascetic ideal is one of the single 'I' located outside of 'society,' in day-to-day monastic life, the ascetic is defined through her position within the order, vis-à-vis other ascetics and by a myriad of roles and statuses. Her rank is determined by *when* she took initiation (*diksa paryaya*) and by *what* she has contributed to the order, as judged by the authority. Concerning the first and most basic form of rank, the most recent initiate is obliged to pay homage to all those her senior – in terms of years initiated. So, for instance, a mother is obliged to pay homage to her daughter if the latter initiated first. The daily ritual of *Guru Vandana* (homage to teachers/superiors), which occurs after the sunset *pratikraman* prayers, dramatizes this form of 'initiation hierarchy.' Goonasekera writes:

> In this ritual, monastic seniority is observed and emphasized. Every junior ascetic must worship every senior ascetic in the monastic dwelling. This is irrespective of an ascetic's chronological age. I have watched sixty year old juniors worshipping eighteen year old seniors. Here the gerontocratic authority of the lay society is negated and replaced by an alternative authority system based on seniority by initiation ... Guru Vandana re-establishes daily the authority of the monastic hierarchy and removes *maan* [egoism] from the minds of junior ascetics. (1986: 170)

Guru Vandana reminds each ascetic where she stands in the order of initiation, but I would argue that it does little to remove *maan*. The real authority of the monastic hierarchy is not based on *diksa paryaya*. Instead, as mentioned above, the prestigious, administrative, and leadership roles are assigned. One may be very senior in terms of initiation, but low in status, and vice versa. Guru Dev, for example, had to pay homage to monks 'senior' (in initiation) to him. The real power is in ascribed statuses, delegated by the more senior ascetics to those who have 'earned' them by contributing to the order in some way (through translation of important scriptures, writings on important ascetics, heroic fasts, selfless work for other ascetics, etc.). Honours and titles have nothing to do with *diksa paryaya* and, in fact, lead to competition and feelings of *maan* among the ascetics – feelings that the *Guru Vandana* ritual can do little to alter.

Maan and Monasticism

Most ascetics uphold the official view that the Terapanthi's hierarchical structure disciplines and helps to destroy egotistical tendencies. A Terapanthi textbook states, 'The spirit behind the *Maryada Patra* is to enable a *sadhak* to annihilate his or her ego that obstructs spiritual progress' (Bhatnagar, 1985: Preface). Even so, all ascetics whom I spoke with readily admitted that *maan* or ego remains a problem in monastic life. The behaviour is commonly explained away by saying that it is difficult to completely eradicate *maan*. Goonasekera concurs:

> Field investigations indicated that *Maan* (pride/egoism) is a constant problem in the lives of renouncers as well as in the functioning of the monastic system ... Senior and important ascetics who are close to the Acharya and who are involved with monastic administration stated that *Maan* caused much of the internal conflicts of the monastic system. Ascetics who fail to control their *Maan* often disobey the Acharya and contradict him. They forget why they renounced the world ... According to these administrative ascetics, such egoistic ascetics cause monastic schisms. Muni Mahendra Kumar, a senior, highly educated and erudite, intellectual monk, said 'Egoism, *Maan*, is the basic problem of these monks and nuns who break away from the group and form their own groups. Instead of disciplining themselves they want to discipline others, become heads of schools, Acharyas, and be important. What else is that except *Maan*?' (1986: 169)

It is not altogether surprising that the senior ascetics with leadership and administrative positions may interpret internal conflict as an expression of 'egoism.' Goonasekera adds:

Jaina monastic law, as stated in the Uttardhyayana Sutra, Dasavaikalika
Sutra, Brhath Kalpa Bhashya and Vyavahara Sutra, demands that the
renouncers get rid of their pride and egoism lest monasticism and its spiritual benefits become impossible. Every time an ascetic feels Maan he/she
is advised to confess to the appropriate senior ascetic and atone for his/her
emotional misconduct. (1986: 169)

But it may be the competitive, hierarchical order and the very existence of 'seniors' that gives rise to egotistical feelings in the first place.
The following is a description of how a rather inconsequential event
revealed to me the degree to which hierarchically structured monastic
life can foster competition, jealousy, and *maan* rather than negate it.

About halfway into my stay, I began to collect poetry written by the
nuns. I was particularly interested in its devotional content. I learned
from one of the *samanis* that a particular *sadhvi*, Sarala, wrote poetry in
English. I was interested in seeing it and asked another *sadhvi* – Dipika,
with whom I was quite friendly – to introduce me. When she inquired
why, I told her frankly that I was interested in reading Sadhvi Sarala's
English poetry. Immediately she dismissed the idea – stating that I was
wrong about the *sadhvi*, that in fact her English was terrible and her
poems, therefore, would be of no interest to me. I insisted that I would
still like to see them, but she said that I should forget it or take the matter up with Sadhvi Promukha.

That same afternoon Sadhvi Promukha happened by, and I
approached her with my request. At first she just seemed to be smiling at
my awkward Hindi, but then Sadhvi Dipika joined me and began to
argue against my request. There was an active exchange, and many *sadhvis* looked on. I could not make most of it out. All I understood was that
Dipika was concerned with me reading such poor-quality work. Sadhviji
Promukha then raised her hand to us in a blessing and moved on – without saying another word. I looked to Dipika, but she too said nothing. It
wasn't until a few moments later when we were sitting at her mini-desk
again, that I asked,

'Did she say it would be alright?'

'No. Don't bother with this matter any more' was what she answered
without explaining. But another plumpish and elderly *sadhvi* who had
entered the room after Sadhvi Promukha left started talking to Dipika.
She appeared upset, her face becoming increasingly flushed. The two
spoke in their native Marwari and appeared to be in a tense exchange,
and then the elderly nun abruptly left the room. Immediately, Dipika

turned to what we had been working on, and said no more. I left the nun's residence that afternoon feeling agitated. When I met up with Urmilla shortly after, she told me that the plump elderly nun must have been Sadhvi Sarala herself. They told me my mistake was to have asked Dipika for an introduction because she is extremely jealous of others who can speak English.

'She likes to think that she alone can speak English,' Urmilla said. 'She just wants to impress Achayrasri.' Their faces revealed scorn for her. Several weeks later, Urmillla did something that surprised me. She had arranged with Sarala to copy the poems for me (see Appendix 3 for some examples.). During *pravachan*, sitting in a large group, Urmilla hastily transcribed. Dipika was present but, of course, unaware.

Ego, discord, and pride are considered among the greatest threats to spiritual advancement, and yet, ironically, monastic life is a fertile ground for their development. *Maan* is not simply a stubborn 'worldly' weakness to be tamed and disciplined through ascetic discipline; monastic life itself nurtures it.

The order has a variety of ways to separate out the extraordinary from the ordinary: it rewards them with titles, administrative positions, leadership roles, and so on. As a consequence, monastic life is highly competitive. The ascetics compete among each other in a variety of ways: in fasting, knowledge of scriptures, austerities, distances travelled during *vihar* ('*padyatra* miles'), the number of conversions they inspired to take the ascetic path, and so on (Flügel, 1995–6: 138). The Terapanthi also makes use of a 'currency' or merit/debit (*kalyanak/gatha*) point system which operates on a 'reward and punishment' basis and which is competitive in nature. Each year, the *sadhvis* and *munis* are required to contribute something of practical benefit to the order. These are gender- based tasks: the *sadhvis* are responsible for making all the *patras, rajoharan,* and *muhpattis* for the order.[13] A fixed number of new bowls, brooms, and mouth-shields are set every year – depending on the state of the current year's stock. Monks are required to transcribe a fixed set of scriptures. Each of these chores is 'worth' something in the point or '*gatha*'system; so, for instance, if a particular nun must make twenty *rajoharan*, this may represent 100 points or *gatha* 'owed' to her guru. If she does something considered exceptional or meritorious by the leaders, Guru Dev may give her *kalyanak* (say, twenty points) with which she can use against her task burden, if she so wishes. She then would only have eighty points worth of *rajoharan* to make, or sixteen brooms. Or she may use her 'credited' points in any way she wishes. Muniji gave me an example: if the disposal of the chamber pot at sunrise is an unpleasant chore, an ascetic can trade in points to be exempt from it. She may 'pay' another *sadhvi* five points to do the job. Even if she never makes use of the points she has earned, she is honoured publicly by gaining them. On special occasions, Guru Dev was known to give all the ascetics additional *kalyanak* when he was generally pleased with them. Of course, the system works the other way too – an ascetic can be punished by receiving 'debit points.'

Whatever the function, the point system is inherently social, hierarchical, and competitive. The *kalyanak/gatha* system is but one of a myriad number of mechanisms through which the ascetics try to distinguish themselves as special, as individuals. Whether in captivating lectures, scholarly works, or artistic endeavours, each ascetic strives to earn the affection of the guru – and with it the respect of the order and veneration of the householders. Others turn their own bodies into projects and through penance demonstrate their worth. Fasting, in particular, is the 'easiest,' or at least the most popular, method to demonstrate commitment and fidelity – especially among the *sadhvis*, who for so long were all but excluded from scholarly and administrative pursuits.

Dr A.N. Pandeya is a Hindu pundit and lay adviser to the ascetic leaders of the Terapanthi. He lives in Delhi, but is often called to Ladnun for special meetings and has had the ear of Guru Dev and Acharyasri for decades. Because of this, many of the monks and nuns believe he has been privy to information about them. They try to meet with him to find out where they 'stand' in the hierarchy. He told me that most of the ascetics are obsessed with trying to know their position within the order and with what the elite really thinks of them. If ascetic equanimity is damaged by the existence of *maan*, the fault lies not in the 'vestiges of worldly' pride, but rather, in the very nature of monastic life itself (see Cort, 1991b: 665, for a discussion of the ascetic hierarchy).

When I met with Shanta the following evening, two other *samanis* were in the room. They appeared to be busy memorizing something, and paid no attention to us.

'Did you read the book?' she asked.

'I haven't even looked at it yet. Do you want to know what it is about?'

'No. I just want to read something English. Maybe you can read it to me. My pronunciation is very bad.'

'We can read it together, starting tomorrow.'

'Actually I have no interest in English. But Guru Dev wants us to learn it,' she said. I recalled that early on in my stay, Guru Dev announced to his congregation that he was assigning me the 'job' of English teacher to the nuns. I remembered feeling troubled with that task, since I was eager to minimize my use of English and learn Hindi.

'English is the most important language today to change the world,' Shanta continued. 'Everywhere people speak English. To spread the Anuvrat movement, even in south India, we need English.'

'Doesn't this interest you?' I asked.

'No. I am only interested in Jain scriptures – in Sanskrit and Prakrit. First I must do my own *sadhana.* And learn about myself before I can change other people. All knowledge and all power is within me; within all of us. Books and such things are just information, not real knowledge – they don't make us happy.'

Soon the two *samanis* went to their meeting with Niyojikaji and we were left alone. Shanta stood up and looked out into the dark courtyard before closing the door. 'Tonight I hope no people will come,' she said and then paused before adding, 'We must welcome householders, they do so much for us. But it is difficult, we have so little time for our own *sadhana.* This is why I cannot become a *sadhvi.*'

'Why can't you?' I asked, misunderstanding her to mean she was for some reason barred from moving up.

'I don't want to. It is difficult,' she said. 'So much time is spent on small things – *panchami, gochari, yatra** ...'

'But what is so different from your life?' I asked.

'Oh, it is very different! *Sadhvis* spend so much time with householders, they are almost in the world!' she said with a touch of disdain. 'Householders come to them with their problems – sometimes very terrible problems, and the *sadhvis* become involved. They are never alone.' (See Appendix 6 for a description of the *sadhvis'* daily routine.)

For *samanis,* interaction with householders is certainly less intense. Because they are only partial renunciants, they have less prestige and (it is assumed) less power than those in the *sadhvi* and *muni* orders. As a result, their time is less in demand.

'Don't most *samanis* want to become *sadhvis?*' I asked, echoing the official view on the ascetic hierarchy (namely, that since ascetics yearn only for *moksa,* they strive to lead a life of total and absolute renuncia-

---

*Panchami = the term used by the ascetics for their excretory functions, which, like all other things, are rule-bound. For *samanis* it is called *kayiki; yatra or vihar* = pilgrimage/travelling; *gochari* = alms collecting.

tion of all things worldly). She hesitated before answering, as if considering the matter herself.

'It depends what they want. To get closer to Guru Dev and Acharyasri, yes. For their *sadhana*, it is better here. You see,' she said looking around her room, 'I have time to study and practise my *sadhana*. Our *gochari* rounds do not take so long – we can collect all our foods from one home if we need. They spend so much time collecting. They travel all year, except *chaturmas*, and have only a few scriptures to read. It is very difficult. When they stay in one place, they are with householders all the time. Even *panchami* takes them a long time!'

Full ascetics – *sadhvis* and *munis* – must perform their *panchami* in places completely devoid of water, grass, or insects. They must first sweep the ground to make sure nothing alive is present, and when they are finished, they must cover their excreta with sand. And a *sadhvi* must always have another *sadhvi* accompany her, wherever she goes. Thus, it can be a time-consuming procedure several times a day.[14] As 'semi'-ascetics, the *samanis* are allowed to use flush toilets, even though the use of water entails violence. For Shanta, *panchami* represented just one of the many drudgeries of *sadhvi* life.

'If you don't want to be a *sadhvi*, what will you do?' I asked Shanta.

'Sometimes I think of leaving here. It would be very difficult. I don't know.'

'Are there people to help you if you want to leave?'

'Help me? How?'

'I don't know. What do you want to do? Work? Marry?'

'No. I cannot work. I don't want to marry – it would be impossible. I don't want to be in *worldly* life. I want to devote myself to my *sadhana*.'

'Do you want to stay a nun?'

'I want to study and practise *sadhana*. I don't want to be in the world at all. If I can stay a *samani*, it will be OK. Our life has many restraints.* Maybe I cannot find a better one.'

'Can you request to remain as a *samani*?' I asked. The expression on her face was doubtful.

'I don't know ...' she began. The door swung open.

'Come now. Niyojikaji is calling you,' a *samani* said to me.

I looked over at Shanta. She had lowered her head and was studying the palms of her hands. It felt terrible to walk away from her at this moment. To have trusted me enough to reveal her troubles took confi-

---

*See Appendix 2 for examples of some of these 'restraints.'

dence. I felt the least I owed her in return was to be a good listener. I wanted to ask the *samani* to tell Niyojikaji that I'd be there shortly – that I was having an important discussion with Shanta, but clearly that would have been outrageous, and would not have been appreciated by anyone. To understand and respect the Terapanthi Jains was to honour their structure of authority. I bowed to Shanta and closed the door behind me.[15]

In the Jain ascetic tradition, the highest ideal is the singular 'I' – one who doesn't engage in any 'culture' (agriculture or other) to survive. In the search for the authentic 'I,' the ascetic acts as a reproach to all social classification and ordering; only the self is truth (A.N. Pandeya, pers. comm., 1996). Others are eliminated in the ascetic epistemology because all things worth knowing are derived through introspection. The ascetic search, therefore, is a romantic pursuit (see Kakar, 1981) for the authentic self; it asserts that truth can only be found if one goes deep inside the self and withdraws from others. A more common way of realizing the self, in most cultures, is through active social involvement, because integration and interacting are the most fundamental resources of the human self. The ascetic way is the total rejection of this path. But, I argue, in its actual structure, it parallels and duplicates the process on a highly controlled and focused pattern (see Cort, 1991b: 664). Indeed, much of ascetic life centres on classification and ordering within its own boundaries, as well as a preoccupation with defining and maintaining boundaries. Mary Douglas suggests why the singular 'I' is a precarious position to maintain:

> Timid or gregarious, we accept more [social] pressure than we exert ... Somewhere mid-way between strong bond and no classification provided by society, the individual is free to make up his own rules and to classify the universe as he pleases. The only requirement is to accept the personal pressures of his fellows. In this range the religious sects are founded whose only rule is 'love ye one another,' but ... this [position] is inherently unstable. Sooner or later some hard lines and boundaries are drawn, starting with the line between saints and sinners ... The thought of zero point, of perfect freedom in love, exerts an extraordinary seductive power. Caught by the dilemma of how to exist in community without rules, people resort to the paradox of legislating for rulelessness. (1975: 219–21)

Rules, regulations, discipline, and obedience form an integral part of Terapanthi spirituality, and, for the majority of the ascetics, they represent the foundation of the *moksa marg*. In order to discipline the self and subdue *maan*, the ascetics argue, group living is necessary. 'It is easy for a forest dweller to think he has subdued his *maan*,' a *samani* once explained, 'but how does he know for sure he has succeeded unless it is tested? *Maan* is only tested in a group.'

My fieldwork would suggest that the workings of day-to-day monastic life are testimony to the fact that the rejection of society is not totally possible or desirable; one cannot simply drop out of orbit. The Terapanthi ascetics are fond of quoting Acharya Bhikshu's motto: *Grnam mem rahui, akela nirdavo* – 'Living in a group, I feel my aloneness.' Through it, what once appeared paradoxical, becomes reasonable.

In monastic life, the goal of detachment becomes secondary to the efforts to keep the *laukik* at bay. The constructed 'untouchability' of worldly life requires vigilance, administration, and rigour. And, with time, it grows increasingly complex to ensure that no gaps remain. The ontological isolation of the soul does not find expression in the social isolation of the individual as it once did (Dundas, 1992: 131), but in an environment closer to totalitarianism than to solitude. And the search for the authentic 'I' occurs within a rule-bound, hierarchically structured 'society.' The separation of the *laukik/ lokottar*, however, continues to dominate ascetic discourse no matter how inseparable the two are.

7
Devotion and Divinity

'You draw, I'll colour,' Samani Mallipregya* commanded, lowering her handkerchief to reveal a big smile. Though she had been jovial over the past couple of weeks, I still found her smile and mood unexpected. Ordinarily, she appeared so dour and distracted that I didn't quite know what to make of her transformation. I wondered if her recent and more frequent use of a handkerchief, in place of the *muhpatti*, was a deliberate effort to reveal her good humour to everyone. Unlike the *sadhvis* and *munis*, the *samanis* and *samans* do not have to wear the *muhpatti* at all times. They alternate between it and a handheld handkerchief to cover their mouths – such as the householders do when speaking with the ascetics. Indeed, one of the big observable differences between *samanis* and householders is in the former's deftness with the handkerchief. For them, the practice of covering their mouths when speaking appears as natural as breathing itself – a small skill they master over the years at the PSS.[1] The householders, in contrast, often forget themselves when their speech becomes animated and do away with the handkerchief altogether – waving it about until they realize with embarrassment and cover up again.

Mallipregya and I were making colourful posters for Guru Dev's birthday celebration, which was less than two weeks away. Everyone was in high gear for the occasion, but lots remained to be done. Posters had to be drawn, poems and devotional songs had to be composed. Mallipregya and I had several more drawings and cutouts to make – mostly variations of Guru Dev nestled among colourfully drawn flowers. The task

*I write *'pregya'* instead of *'prajna'* to follow Samani Mallipregya's own usage. See below.

was simple enough as we had dozens of colour photos of Guru Dev to chose from – from poster to wallet size.

We sat close together, our folded legs slightly overlapping, and got to work on our collages. A few *samanis* were stretched out for a nap – covered from head to toe in old saris that substituted for sheets. We, like most of the *samanis*, were taking advantage of the afternoon lull in activities and were busy preparing for the celebrations. The cold marble floor upon which we sat was strewn with the art materials – coloured pencils, markers, cardboard sheets, a bottle of glue, and, of course, posters of Guru Dev. I was 'commissioned' to do a drawing of Guru Dev surrounded by adoring devotees – a group that included gods, humans, and animals of every sort. Mallipregya was cutting out a beautiful latticed paper design that we would use to decorate the sides of the drawing. She sang softly as she created, and then laid down the scissors to show me her design. It was lovely. I continued to draw when she said, 'You are *also* very fortunate.' She then took hold of my left hand, looking intently at my palm.

'Why do you think so?' I asked.

'Because Guru Dev and Acharyasri are pleased with you,' she said, inspecting my hand. Then, looking up at me, she declared, 'You have so many lines!'

I said nothing and continued to draw. It was not the first time Mallipregya had tried to decode my hand lines for a hidden truth, but as a novice she was as yet unable. The supernatural and the mystical interested her immensely. Indeed, earlier that morning we spent so much time talking about numerology that it got too late for our meditation lesson.

Several months earlier Mallipregya had volunteered to teach me *Preksha Dhyan* (Jain meditation). She would talk me through a meditation, forcing me to concentrate on her words as a way to reign in my straying, undisciplined thoughts. Then we would sit motionless, focused on our breathing until the sun rose to warm our bodies. Together we would end by repeating *'Om shanti'* ('peace') several times. It was a perfect time: the day was just beginning and the air was still fresh; we were in our meditative cocoon overlooking the monastery. And very often in this sheltered state, Mallipregya would talk about her tireless quest for *shakti* (spiritual power). She interpreted her life as a narrative of ever-increasing strength, emphasizing the augmentation of power rather than the reduction of karma – the standard Jain ascetic idiom. She would often say, 'Each of us is a god. We must realize this.' She was engaged in meditation, devotion, austerities (*tapas*), astrology, palmistry, and, most recently, numerology, all to harness *shakti*.

We would meet each morning before sunrise and sit on the roof of *Gautam Shalla,* in the cool, pre-dawn desert air. On this particular morning, when we met on the roof for our meditation lesson, she appeared so full of cheer that I asked her, 'Malli, what is making you so happy these days?' Though it was not yet light, I saw a smile come across her face; then with quiet confidence she lowered herself onto her meditation mat. She sat in a lotus position, and pulled her feet up so they touched her belly, making her legs look like a pretzel. She began to breathe deeply and slowly, inhaling, exhaling, inhaling, until, looking absolutely calm, she slipped her *muhpatti* over her mouth and said:

'Yes. Things are better for me now.' I waited, and soon she added, 'Things were not easy for me. Physically I am not strong.' She took my hand to touch the thinness of her calves, 'Often I get sick. Once I nearly died.'

My face must have shown surprise, for she continued, 'Yes, my family was called and everyone thought that I was going to die. I couldn't eat. I only slept ... and besides that – with other *samanis*, it was not easy for me.'

I strained to see her face clearly but it was still quite dark. 'My numbers were not good,' she said, beginning her tale of numerology. 'Like all the *samanis*, I spelled my name 'p-r-a-j-n-a.'* I did not know it gave me a very *ashubh* (inauspicious) number. If I spell it 'p-r-e-g-y-a' it gives me a number one – a very *shubh* (auspicious) number.'[2]

'And? What difference does it make?' I asked.

'This number has *shakti.* Everything is better now. Before I was living under an inauspicious number – and things were very difficult. Big things like when I became sick, but also many little things were hard for me. [pause] The other *samanis* would accuse me of writing in their notepads, and ripping pages out of their books. It was difficult. Now this does not happen. Now everything is good. I am very lucky, and Acharyasri encourages me in my work.'

'When did you change your name?' I asked.

'September 10th, my birthday. Everything has been easy since.'

I wondered if she wasn't being rather hasty in her celebrations, as this was only a little over a month ago. But the period did coincide with what I thought was her transformation. 'Does Guru Dev know?' I asked.

'Yes, and Acharyasri. They allowed me to change it,' she said, her eyes

---

*All *samanis* end their names with the suffix '*prajna*,' meaning 'wisdom' – e.g., Samani Shardaprajna.

showing delight. She went on to illustrate how much her life had changed for the better: Guru Dev and Acharyashri had since praised her work and had allowed her to pursue intensive studies of *Preksha Dhyan*, for example. And her relationship with the *samanis* improved.

Mallipregya's interest in connecting with an 'external' power, though far removed from ascetic discourse, is a common one within the order. All ascetics, like householders, acknowledge the existence of supernatural powers. The world is filled with *devas* and *bhuts* – mystical powers, the auspicious and inauspicious – and *shakti* to be harnessed by those with 'know-how.' Like householders, who depend on the 'magico-cosmic' to arrange their practical affairs such as marriage, education, health, and so forth, the ascetics rely on it for their own purposes. Some examples of this are that no *sadhvi* or *muni* is without a special calendar that indicates auspicious and inauspicious days of the year. And after *chaturmas*, they consult it very earnestly to decide which day to set out on their travels. Also, daily, the *sadhvis* pay homage to a 'Muslim *deva*' that they believe inhabits their dwelling with them. A small shrine on the first floor of their residence (Rishabdwar) is dedicated to him, and although they insist that the ascetic path is one of 'aloneness,' they acknowledge the *deva*'s power and mollify his temper by showing respect. (For example, when leaving and returning to the building, they acknowledge him with a blessing. There are many stories of the *deva* becoming agitated if he is not properly propitiated.) And in private, many ascetics recite special *mantras* and make clandestine *yantras* to harness the powers around them. But Jainism teaches that one's destiny is determined by one's moral actions alone – not celestial bodies or mystical powers. Therefore, the conventional representation of Jainism does not include these 'magico-cosmic' dimensions because they appear to conflict with its public ideology of 'aloneness' and 'detachment.' This is an area where Jain and non-Jain representations have colluded with the tradition's hegemonic discourse to exclude *phenomenological* Jainism – the realm of subjectivity and experience. Efforts are made by both Jains themselves and Jain observers to reign in and mould the mystical, devotional, and divine (what I call the 'magico-devotional') according to the dictates of the ascetic ideal. However, for most Jains – lay and ascetic – public ideology and private belief are not in conflict; both are 'correct' in some manner. And, as we shall see below, the two are rarely juxtaposed.

By the time Mallipregya and I were finished talking, the sun was already high in the sky, too late for meditation, and time to be going on. Our conversation would have to wait till the afternoon ...

We were working on posters for Guru Dev's birthday. Mallipregya took hold of my left hand and said with authority, 'You have a very auspicious guru line.'

Turning from my drawing, I asked, 'What is a "guru line"?'

'You have good fortune in finding a guru. It is true. You have come all the way here because of Guru Dev!'

Maybe it was true, I thought. I smiled at her. 'Let's get this finished,' I said, turning back to the drawing.

She picked up the pair of scissors and began to sing softly again until she had cut out another delicate design. '*Is* he your guru?'

I hesitated before answering, 'Yes, I suppose he is. All of Jainism is my guru.'

'When you return home, you can keep his photo in your house,' she said. 'You will not feel so far away.'

I looked at my carry-bag in which that morning I had put a few of my own treasured photos. I had taken family photos from my room to show Mrs Gupta, my wonderful Hindi teacher with whom I met every afternoon. She was an elderly Hindu woman who lived in Ladnun only with the greatest reluctance. She and her husband, a retired librarian, came here in 1995 because he was invited to run the small library at the monastery. She had no interest in Jainism, considering it to be a minor offshoot of Hinduism. But she believed that Guru Dev and a few of the senior ascetics were spiritually very powerful, so occasionally she would go to see them to receive their *darshan*. Meeting with her for a couple of hours each day was like entering another culture where an entirely different dialect predominated; we would talk about family life, romance, marriage, children, and delicious foods – all the things formally tabooed for the ascetics. Most days my Hindi lesson would be combined with a cooking lesson: we would cut the 'live' vegetables and wash them with 'live' water before cooking and eating them together. It was all very *himsa* and very worldly. Many times she asked questions about my family, and today I remembered to bring some snaps. I hadn't any intention of showing them to the nuns, but at this moment with Mallipregya, something made me think it would be a good idea.

'Would you like to see the family photos I keep with me in India?' I asked.

Although she didn't say a word, her eyes appeared to follow my hand with interest. I passed her the few snaps. 'Ohhhh,' she sang as she flicked through them. Then quickly she jumped to her feet. 'I will show Niyojikaji.'

'Must you?' I said with some exasperation, knowing that they would then likely circulate the order.

'Yes' was all she said and turned to leave the room. Her steps were small but fast, and I could hear the sound of her tightly wrapped cotton sari swishing all the way to Niyojikaji's room next door. I continued my drawing, but it didn't take long before I was summoned into Niyojikaji's room.

'Mitri,* why do you keep these photos with you?'

'So that I feel they are not very far away' I answered, still standing, carrying my drawing.

'*Purisa! Tummev tumam mittam, kim bahiya mittam icchasi?*' (Man! You are your own friend, why search for one without?) She spoke the words slowly, in rhythmic Prakrit. This is so common a verse it almost qualifies as being a Jain manifesto. It is part of the *Arhat Vandana* mantra the ascetics say twice daily, and it had been recited to me many, many times before.

I lay my drawing on the ground before me, knelt down, and whispered '*Vandami namung samani*' to pay homage as was expected.

Niyojikaji continued, 'You know that we renounce our families when we take *diksa*. In Jainism, we teach that we are born alone and die alone. You only take your karmic bondage with you.'

Samani Chaitanya, who was sitting with Niyojikaji, was surprised that I should want family photos with me at all. 'I thought that Westerners are not close with their families!' she said. Westerners' perceived lack of attachment to family is considered to be of an entirely different matter to that of ascetic detachment. Western 'detachment,' I was told, stems from selfishness and disrespect of family values and is ego-oriented. For an ascetic, detachment comes from self-sacrifice and from a desire to emancipate the soul.

'The greatest of all threats is attachment,' Niyojikaji continued. 'It binds you to this world. Without attachment, there would be no violence. It is the root of all problems, the source of our *samsara*.'

Niyojikaji sat with her back against the wall of the room, her mini wooden desk in front of her crossed legs. Posters of Guru Dev and

*Mitri, meaning 'friendship,' was the Hindi name that Mahasramani, or the 'head nun,' Sadhvi KanakPrabha, had given me. The nuns used it interchangeably with my English name, which they pronounced 'Annee.'

Acharyashri, of all sizes, lined the walls and decorated the covers of the books on her desk. The walls of my own small room at the guest house were similarly inundated with posters and photos of Guru Dev, Acharayshri, Mahasaman, and Mahashramani, and the few family photos that I had brought with me from home were engulfed by them. They even looked odd sitting on the shelf next to the saintly ascetics: the unabashed and generous smiles on their faces appeared incongruous and maybe even a little indecorous next to the *muhpattied* gurus. I was always being given some sort of devotional icon from the ascetics,[3] who, in turn, had received them from householders – a calendar, a note pad, wallet-sized snaps, cassettes of mantras, stickers, and even pens – all bearing images of the gurus. Most were of the gentle face of Guru Dev, often with his right hand raised as in a benediction. As I sat and listened to Niyojikaji, her talk of the 'sins of attachment' and 'aloneness' seemed to clash with the avalanche of devotional materials on display.

Looking up at the images surrounding us and then at the one I was drawing, I asked, 'What about these?' Niyojikaji followed my eyes up to the images of Guru Dev and then returned to look at me without saying a word. I continued, 'You have photos of Guru Dev close to you, and I keep photos of those I love close to me.'

She appeared stunned by the comparison. She lay my photos down on her desk and shook her head. She had been using a cotton handkerchief as a *muhpatti*, but now put on the proper one. She secured the elastic bands behind her ears. With assurance she said, 'They are not the same thing. You *depend* on these people. You need them, you are very *attached*, but we are not. We are devoted to our *guru* because he shows us how to lead a spiritual life. He is our teacher, and that is why we are devoted to him. We learn from him. But we are independent and not attached, as you are.'

The Terapanthi Jains do not practise idol worship.[4] In addition to the violence inherent in their construction, they argue that since the great emancipated heroes, the *Jinas*, do not interfere in worldly existence, there is no point in worshipping statues of them. But photos of the living gurus abound (see Babb, 1996). Samani Chaitanyaprajna added, 'He is our god, and we are his devotees. He is everything to us. He knows everything about us, and cares about us more than our own parents! Whatever he says, we do. We have no worries. He always knows what is best. So of course we feel very happy to have his picture near us.'

Mallipregya, forever focused on spiritual power, said, 'You are attached to your photos. As a *shravak*, this is normal. But the photos are nothing. These photos (she pointed to those of Guru Dev on the walls) have so much *shakti*. You can feel his *shakti* from the photos. Many times …'

Niyojikaji interrupted forcefully, 'He is our *inspiration*. He makes us exert ourselves. By having him there, he is always in our mind. We are always alert, and never forget why we have chosen this path.

I nodded in acquiescence; clearly my few photos were no match for those of Guru Dev. But it was obvious that the *samanis*' positions on devotional images were not identical – and, in fact, could be seen as competing interpretations. Niyojikaji's statement tried to contain the other *samanis*' interpretations, just as the public ideology of ascetic life quells or reigns in beliefs and practices about gods, devotion, and the supernatural. By emphasizing the guru's 'inspirational' role, she interpreted devotion – which might otherwise be seen as an effort to connect with someone/something *outside* oneself – in terms of ascetic self-help. By contrast, Chaitanya spoke of Guru Dev's protective, even divine, role and the devotee's passiveness before him, whereas Mallipregya's interpretation was furthest from the official ascetic narrative in its acceptance of the propitiation of miracles as an important part of ascetic life. Chaitanya's and Mallipregya's understandings spoke of the experiential level, and provided insight into what constitutes a meaningful life for the majority of ascetics. Despite the rhetoric of the hegemonic discourse, most ascetics do not feel as though they are treading a lonely path in isolation but, instead, one filled with potential friends and foes.

The ways in which the 'magico-devotional' is 'reigned in' is interesting and reveals the coexistence of competing ideologies within monastic life. First, the 'magico-devotional' is conspicuous by its absence in the Jain ascetic literature, which stresses the aloneness of the ascetic path, mirroring the ontological aloneness of the soul. But within monastic life, efforts to connect with someone/something greater that the self are commonplace. According to the 'public ideology' of asceticism, the 'magico-devotional' – a profoundly other-oriented set of discourses – is translated into a discourse of *self*-realization. This is the view espoused by the most learned ascetics of the order (e.g., Niyojikaji), who recognize a contradiction in proclamations of independence *and* dependence; detachment *and* attachment; the *lokottar* (transcendent) and the *laukik* (worldly). But for the majority of nuns and monks, *nivrtti-marg* (the ascetic path) and the 'magico-devotional' do not need reconciling or translating; they are already compatible. Indeed, the two are inseparable.

Discussion of devotion and divinity in the context of Jain asceticism is rare (see Babb, 1993; 1996 for a notable exception). Little in the ascetic literature suggests its relevance, and Jains themselves when presenting their tradition in ideal terms, downplay its significance or omit it altogether. Muniji provided me with the standard position when he explained, 'If one wants to attain *moksa*, then he must exert himself. He receives no help from anyone. Neither society nor god can help. Only individual effort alone, not divine efforts, can lead to liberation.'

The image of a lone mendicant wandering through the Indian forest looms large in the ascetic imagination, leaving little room for divine intervention or anything resembling outside assistance. Jain asceticism is characterized by its own brand of rugged individualism. Its dominant metaphors are those of separation, detachment, and disconnection; of isolation, aloneness, and independence. (See, for example, the poem 'The Utopia' in Appendix 4, which catalogues the characteristics of the 'ideal monk' and, in so doing, provides a good illustration of the conventional representation of Jain asceticism.) The discourse of Jain asceticism is of *self*-realization and total aloneness, relegating all other dimensions to the periphery. The ascetic rhetoric exhorts, 'Ponder thus: I am alone. Nobody was mine in the past, nor will ever be in the future. It is because of my karmas that I delude myself and consider others as mine. The truth is that I was alone in the past and will ever be all alone' [annotation to 4.3.32, Acaranga Sutra] (Holmstrom, 1988: 36).

But this is the realm of the ideal. The public ideology of asceticism is a fixed, logical, ahistorical, and archetypal portrait. It delineates the 'formal grammar' of ascetic life and is distinct from the dynamic, 'discursive' fabric of monastic life, where divinity, devotion, and – in general – efforts to 'connect' rather than 'disconnect' govern day-to-day life. The daily lives of the ascetics are consumed by efforts to *connect* with something greater than themselves, to *not* be alone – neither in the order nor in the universe. It is a mistake to assume that because Jains have no conception of a creator god they have no belief in divinity or a divine power. As Paul Dundas writes,

> While Jainism is, as we have seen, atheist in the limited sense of rejection of both the existence of a creator god and the possibility of the intervention of such a being in human affairs, it nonetheless must be regarded as a theist religion in the more profound sense that it accepts the existence of a divine principle, the *paramatman*, often in fact referred to as 'god' (e.g. ParPr 114–16), existing in potential state within all beings. (1992: 94)

Similarly, Kendall Folkert writes that in Jainism, 'There is no deity; Jains do, however, venerate the Tirthankaras and some saints, and a temple cultus exists around these figures, who are not seen as intervening in any way in the lives of the devotee' (1993a: 24).

I suggest that the effort to extend *beyond* the immediate self and connect with divinity and the 'magico-devotional' is a central part of Jain ascetic life, though it is sometimes masqueraded as something else, more along the lines of self-realization. The actual practice of daily life is made to fit the ideal of asceticism so that all experiences become subsumed within its grasp, even discordant and competing ones. Practices of devotion and the mystical are not treated (in the public ideology) as efforts to connect with something greater than the self, but rather as utilitarian tools of spiritual self-help.

In studies of Hindu renunciation, by way of contrast, the role of divinity is considered as central. Divine power *must* be tapped into in order for asceticism to be complete. In her study on Karnataka Hindu asceticism, Lise Vail claims that renunciation is

> not or is hardly possible *without* the assistance of that greater power. The reason why renunciation as a whole is so important in defining the Karnataka swami is precisely to create conditions which allow for the influx and nourishing of a divine presence. (1987: 396)

Connecting with divine power is fundamental because it

> offers a powerful buffer and protection against slipping back into an old lifestyle and samsaric ways of thinking. For this reason, a renouncer is generally not supposed to become a guru until that power or presence has been revealed within him. (395)

For the Jain ascetic, connecting with divine power is merely more circuitous: miracles and boons are supposed to be *by-products* of a religious path, not its aim, and the experience of divinity is sought from *within* the self, not from without.

The ascetics who are most revered, idolized by all, and sought after for blessings are those believed to possess *shakti* (Babb, 1996; Flügel, 1995–6). Other than Guru Dev and Acharyasri, a number of senior ascetics have gained prominence in the order and attract a large lay following. When I would ask lay devotees why they followed one particular ascetic rather than another, they would invariably cite 'their maharaja's' *shakti.* It may be that the ascetic is believed to intuitively understand the problems the devotee is suffering, or possesses clairvoyance, or is able to bestow boons on the followers.[5] However, these more mystical elements have been eclipsed due to the tendency of both Jains and Jain observers to focus singularly on the *fact* of renunciation – the necessity of renunciation and the austerities – over the mysterious and devotional elements of religious practice and experience. Indeed, the efforts of Jains to present their religion as a battle with *oneself* (i.e., one's karma) and a path of total *self-reliance* is one of the factors that distinguishes them as Jains. In describing and delineating what constitutes Jain asceticism, the ascetics, laity, and scholars conspire to focus on this aspect alone, that of *nivrtti-marg*, the path of 'turning-away-from-the-world.' But efforts to connect with and experience divinity form as much a part of ascetic life as do the relentless efforts to burn away karma through *tapas* (austerities). Help is solicited, and the mysteries of the *atman* are sought in myriad ways. This is the realm of *bhakti* of attachment, devotion, divinity, *shakti*, and emotion. And through it we learn that the ascetic path is much more wondrous, and quite often less austere, than is normally perceived.

Nivrtti-marg is the cultivated and conventional representation of Jainism and has more to do with ideals striven for than the reality of everyday life. It represents the 'formal grammar' and is an ideal – the structure and the most public and visible aspect of ascetic life. But it is *bhakti* and the other means of *connecting* with other individuals, the guru, deities, supernatural power (as opposed to the rhetoric of disconnecting) that make up the practice of daily life and constitute the strength and spirit of the order.

Nivrtti-Marg: The Public Face of Jainism[6]

It is by its austere ascetic path that Jainism has been defined by both Jain and non-Jain observers – albeit for different reasons. Other dimensions of its religious life have appeared trivial in comparison to its ethic of renunciation, resulting in a distorted view of a tradition in which ascetics represent less than ten thousand individuals out of a population of approximately three million (Folkert, 1987: 256). The reasons for this are varied. First, Jains themselves overwhelmingly valorize the *nivrtti-marg*. Laidlaw writes: 'The defining figures in Jainism are ... not those hedonistic deities, but the ascetic renouncers. It is renouncers, both living and dead, who are the central objects of religious veneration' (1995:

3). Similarly, Babb states, 'This is the fundamental matter: Jains worship ascetics and this is the most important single fact about Jain ritual culture' (1996: 23).

Jains frequently assert that they are 'alone in this world,' by which they mean that they can rely on nothing but their own self-discipline to guide them along their spiritual path. Laidlaw cites lay Jains (from Jaipur) as saying, 'As Jains we know we are alone in this world. Only by our own actions can we gain help. Only by cleansing our own souls' (1995: 26). And:

> Jainism is the most difficult religion. In fact it is impossible. We get no help from any gods, or from anyone. We just have to cleanse our souls. Other religions are easy, but they are not very ambitious. In all other religions when you are in difficulty you can pray to God for help, and maybe God comes down to help. But Jainism is not a religion of coming down. In Jainism it is we who must go up. We have only to help ourselves. In Jainism we are supposed to become God. That is the only thing. (27)

The Jain individualistic attitude stems from an ontology preoccupied with the state of the soul's bondage. For example, a primer for children asks the question 'Who are you?' and then answers, 'I am a pure soul presently in the form of a human body,' followed by the question, 'Where did you come from and where shall you go?' and the answer, 'I have come from one of the four *gatis* (destinies)[7] and will go in one of them until *moksa*' (Jineshkumar 1990: 17). Laidlaw writes that the Jain conception of the human predicament

> calls forth the image of each soul locked into its own unique fate, which is fixed by its previous actions, labouring for release through ascetic practice. Asserting or accepting that everything depends upon *karma* is to take a particular stance with respect to oneself, with respect also to exemplars such as the Jinas: the stance of the individual striver (*shramana/shraman*) and ascetic (*tapasi/tapasvi*). (1995: 30)

The community's 'public face' hinges on its asceticism. Its uncompromising insistence on the ascetic path as the *only* truly religious one sets it apart from the larger Hindu community with its acceptance of more varied avenues. Jain self-identity, and the sense of their uniqueness within the larger Hindu world, is rooted in the centrality of this ascetic ideal.

Non-Jains have also been quick to stress Jainism's ascetic orientation.

Dundas writes that Hindu commentators have often emphasized the austere path in order to ridicule it (1992: 1). The classical Hindu stereotype of Jainism is as 'a religion practised by filthy and naked ascetics requiring pointless torture of the body, such as regular pulling out of the hair, and involving as part of its doctrine the subversion of basic Hindu values' (1). Dundas continues:

> As represented in many recent accounts, this view would see Jainism as unified in nearly all respects, essentially both ahistorical and eccentric, with its belief and practice revolving around extreme forms of ascetic behaviour, dietary restrictions and a near-pathological preoccupation with the minutiae of a doctrine of non-violence. This misconceived approach has been compounded by many contemporary Jain writers who, in an attempt to boost their religion's intellectual credibility, have often seemed principally concerned with presenting Jainism in purely metaphysical terms as little more than a gradualistic spiritual path. (2)

Early Western writers were also singularly interested in Jainism's asceticism and presented a rather negative view of the tradition, emphasizing its external practices and its 'morbid' philosophy (Dundas, 1992: 6). Dundas writes that the tendency to stereotype the Jain tradition has persisted into modern times:

> I do not refer to western jibes and misunderstandings for their own sake but wish rather to suggest that their legacy is still very much in place today, with Jainism as a rule being interpreted as either colourless and austere or with reference to a few 'exotic' customs such as the wearing of the mouth shield (*muhpatti*) to avoid violence to minute organisms living in the air. (8)

According to contemporary scholars, the problem lies in the absence of studies on the lay Jain community. For example, Dundas writes,

> The largely textual orientation of nineteenth century and subsequent western scholarship has also been responsible for the creation of a distorted perspective on Jain society and history ... Unfortunately, the Jain lay community has never been adequately studied and the history of Jainism, inevitably based on literature emanating almost exclusively from the ascetic environment, has been presented solely in terms of the preoccupations of the ascetic community, with the laity emerging only intermittently and in largely idealized fashion. (1992: 8–9)

And:

> [T]here can be no doubt that lay people have throughout Jain history always constituted by far the more substantial proportion of the community, and the ascetic vocation, whatever its prestige and vital role in the construction and promulgation of Jain culture, has been adopted by only a few. (1992: 9)

Although greater attention to lay Jains would undoubtedly help counter the ascetic bias prevalent in the presentation of the tradition, I believe that attention to the ascetic *community* – as opposed to simply the ascetic *literature* – would have a similar effect. The ascetic literature details the 'grammar' of ascetic life – the rules, regulations, taboos, and violations. It tells us nothing about motivation or the actual experience of asceticism. Indeed, attention to the lay community would uncover the same ascetic bias. The tendency to valorize and even publicize the 'ascetic-ness' of their lives is as commonplace among the laity as it is with the ascetics (Babb, 1996: 22–63). The discourse of *nivrtti-marg*, the 'thorny path of asceticism,' is emphasized because it is so central to Jain identity. It distinguishes Jains from non-Jains and the *laukik* from the *lokottar*. Laidlaw provides an example of a householder's dilemma of wanting to reveal some of the tradition's 'magico-devotional' dimensions but needing to uphold its public 'ascetic' face. He writes:

> Torn between wanting to impress me with the Guru Dev's power to grant favours, and the injunction to pursue *karmik* self-help through ascetic practice, she does not look for a causal explanation of miracles that will reconcile them logically with *karma*, but cites instead her own ethical imperfection and attachment as the reason she should want supernatural help. (1995: 75)

Our understanding of asceticism is largely derived from the rules and regulations that make up monastic discipline, and less on asceticism as lived practice. As such, the picture that we have of ascetic life is that of a pristine, even theoretical, ideal. The archetypal ascetic life is presented as one of solitary pilgrimage, withdrawal, renunciation, detachment, and penance. Each of these is a dimension of the *nivrtti-marg*, and it is through such a framework that Jain asceticism is most typically interpreted. Because Jainism envisions liberation as a revelatory process – a peeling away of karmic layers until the perfect soul is unveiled – the path to liberation is depicted as a process of undoing and negation, not creation. Patrick Olivelle explains:

> Renunciation is a negative state, consisting of the abandonment of what characterizes life-in-society. Therefore one is a renouncer not because one performs certain distinctive actions or conforms to certain characteristic habits and customs, but because one does not perform actions and does not conform to customs that characterize life-in-society. (1975: 35)

The *nivrtti-marg* presupposes a complete break with lay existence. Dundas claims that the choice to enter ascetic life is a 'radical reorientation of behaviour' (1992: 132) and,

> It is the adoption of the five *mahavratas*, the 'Great Vows,' and their integration into what must after ascetic initiation become a totally realigned way of life which is the central defining characteristic of the monk and the nun, governing their external, observable behaviour and providing a system of internal, spiritual control. (1992: 135)

The radically oriented new life of the ascetics is structured in order to observe *ahimsa* in all aspects of daily practice (see Jaini, 1990: 242). But beneath the rules, restraints, and penances, and beyond the public ideology and conventional representation of asceticism, exists the *bhakti* spirit of the order – the underbelly that animates and maintains the *nivrtti marg* of ascetic life and enables it to exist. *Bhakti* typically refers to the path of devotion, attachment, and divinity and, although generally not associated with Jain asceticism, forms an integral part of it. This is the world of devotion, of gods and demons, miracles, and the supernatural, and it is the lifeblood of the ascetic order as much as it is of householders' lives. Here, those distinctions which the official discourse seeks to maintain as separate – between ascetics and householders, between 'the transcendent' and 'the worldly,' even between Jains and Hindus – tend to blur. This is not clandestine, 'underground' Jainism – it is *phenomenological* Jainism instead of *discursive* Jainism. And though at times difficult to reconcile philosophically, the two coexist effortlessly and, in fact, are inseparable in practice. This is the murky dimension of Jainism, but also one of the most compelling and beautiful dimensions of monastic life. And just as the imposition of a codified grammar tidies up the spoken tongue, so too does an official framework become a grid through which monastic life is filtered. As Holmstrom notes,

> The Great Vows on monasticism order conduct and are invoked through
> conduct ... [they] are invoked, conscious, scriptural, literally formulated
> rules which are referred to *as such* in action, and which action is in part
> consciously trying to map onto. (Holmstrom, 1988: 31)

Efforts are made to 'map' the mystical and the devotional onto ascetic
values; a *nivrtti-marg* interpretation is imposed on them. But for the
majority of the ascetics, the different discourses do not conflict. Detachment is achieved *through* attachment to guru; independence and aloneness of the self are achieved through total dependence on guru. The
way of turning-away-from-the-world (*nivrtti-marg*) is achieved through
immersion in *bhakti.*

Nivrtti-Marg through Bhakti Marg

Days passed and now the countdown was on; just one week remained
before Guru Dev's birthday and there was still much to do. I arrived at
the Gautam Shalla early to visit Urmilla prior to settling down to work,
for I hadn't seen her in days. She was on our 'art team' – put together
to make posters for the birthday celebrations – but had been ill again
and was unable to participate. She had been recovering from another
bout of malaria when she came down with a bad head cold, and was
still not well enough to return to her own room. I had brought with
me a cold remedy from Canada that I wanted her to try. When I
entered the room, she was laying on her side, covered by a white sheet.
At first I thought she was asleep, because she didn't move when I
approached, but I could see that her eyes were open, listlessly staring
ahead.

'*Vandami namung samani,*' I said quietly as I knelt before her and
asked, 'How are you feeling?' She looked up and gestured for me to sit
in front of her. Another *samani* in the room came over to offer her
water, but she gestured her away. I presented the cold remedy and told
her I thought she should try it. It needed to be mixed with boiling water,
so the other *samani* left with a *patra* (alms bowl) to 'beg' a small quantity
from a nearby house. Urmilla was apathetic and I wasn't sure she would
take the remedy, but when the *samani* returned with the water, and I
mixed the powder into it, she obliged me by sipping slowly. Her throat
was sore and it hurt to swallow. She appeared lost in thought as I
watched her sip the remedy. Suddenly four *samanis* rushed in, creating a
stir. They knelt before Urmilla, quickly bowed and then told her the
good news: Guru Dev had asked about her! She pulled herself up until

she sat cross-legged and stared at them, wanting to hear more. But there was no more to tell, only to repeat: at the end of the morning *provochan* (sermon), Guru Dev asked the *samanis* how she was. When told she was feeling better, he appeared pleased. Energized by the news, Urmilla sat beaming on her cardboard mattress, her hands flustering about trying to find her *muhpatti.*

Looking at her, I recalled a conversation I had with Sadhvi Visrut Vipaji ('Sadhviji') earlier in the week. I was at Rishabdwar in the middle of a hot afternoon when the town had quietened down. I sat with Sadhviji and spoke quietly so as not to wake Sadhvi Vandana – the most recent and youngest *sadhvi* at just fourteen years old – who slept beside us. Vandana had gone from being an *upasika* directly to being a *sadhvi*, skipping all the intermediary stages and years. Beads of sweat covered her forehead as she slept. She looked suffocatingly hot with the top of her *sari* pulled over her head and the *muhpatti* snug around her small face. Sadhviji began to shake her gently to wake her. Still asleep, Vandana moved away until Sadhviji took hold of both her shoulders and shook her until she opened her eyes. Sadhviji began to tease her about being lazy, but she seemed in no mood to joke. Her body was swaying slightly, struggling to collect itself, but her eyelids kept on closing. Intuitively knowing how to snap her out of her slumber, Sadhviji said, 'Tell Mitri what happened this morning.' A tiny smile appeared on Vandana's face, and she shook her head bashfully. Sadhviji continued to tease her, nudging her gently. Vandana covered her face with her hands in embarrassment and rested her elbows on her miniature wooden desk. Clearly she was not going to talk. Sadhviji, her eyes scrunched up from smiling, extended her arm around Vandana's shoulder and said, 'She is our youngest. She is very special to all of us.' Vandana looked away. 'Today Guru Dev spoke to her directly. Didn't he Vandana?' She began to smile again. 'Today Guru Dev asked her to tell him how she is liking her new life. And he told all of us to take very good care of her.'

Now fully awake, Vandana sprang to her feet, shy but clearly enjoying Sadhviji's retelling, and walked over to the *mutki** outside the room. I watched as she took the small brass cup from top of the *mutki*, removed the stone lid, and scooped up some cool water. With her left hand she lowered her *muhpatti* and let the water pour effortlessly into her mouth. Sadhviji, also watching the new waif-like *sadhvi*, said smiling, 'If Guru Dev says something special to us, individually, we are *so* happy. Even if he

---

*A round earthenware container for water, slightly tapered at the top. The clay cools the water, making it refreshing, even in the scorching heat.

just asks how we are, we tell everyone. Everyone is anxious to get the grace of the guru.'

'And how does one do that?' I asked.

Still smiling, she turned her face towards me, 'Through *bhakti.* We surrender to our guru, and he takes care of us.'

Bhakti marg is the 'way of attachment.' It is characterized by dependence, surrender, and emotional catharsis, and therefore is often seen as the antithesis of the ascetic path of detachment, independence, and restraint. Chronologically, the path of 'turning away from the world' preceded that of *bhakti marg*, as a socially legitimate and established spiritual path, by several centuries. Jhingran contends that *bhakti* developed as a movement in contradistinction to Vedic religio-culture among the *sants*[8] of Karnataka, in the last two centuries before the common era, before spreading to Maharashtra and then north, where it dominated Hindu religious life and thought until the sixteenth century (1989: 147). Throughout, it flourished alongside the two other main traditions in the Indian religio-culture: the ritualistic, polytheistic, and world- and life-affirming tradition of the Vedas and Dharmasastras, and the soul-centric and world- and life-negating tradition of the philosophies of spiritual liberation (147).

Bhakti marg is typically regarded as a parallel but *distinct* path from that of asceticism, for a variety of reasons. Sudhir Kakar emphasizes the uniqueness of the ascetic path: '[T]he yogic vision offers a romantic quest. The new journey is a search and the seeker, if he withstands the perils of the road, will be rewarded by an exaltation beyond normal human experience' (1981: 29). But he adds that these practices are 'the province of a small religious élite, the 'talented' few who devote their entire lives to the realization of moksa through systematic unswerving introspection' (29).

Kakar goes on to delineate other, more traditionally sanctioned, 'paths' which the majority of Indians have followed to lead them toward the ideal state of liberation, namely, the way of *bhakti* (intense devotion) and the way of *karmayoga* or selfless work. We find the ascetic and devotional path treated as distinct, and even conflicting. Schomer and McLeod, in their book on devotional traditions in India, distinguish them by their methods of attaining *moksa.* They write:

> From ritual observance and the performance of prescribed duties, or alternately, ascetic withdrawal in search of speculative knowledge of the divine, the heart of religion became the cultivation of a loving relationship between the individual and a personally conceived supreme god. (1987: 2)

Others note that the paths present different conceptions of the ultimate state of liberation. The *bhakti* concept of *moksa* stems from its unique perception of the relation between the individual soul and the 'Ultimate Self.' It can even be seen as an opposite interpretation from that of the *nivrtti marg.* Jhingran writes that in *bhakti marg,*

> *Moksa* is neither the realization by the soul of its total aloofness and transcendence (*kaivalya*), nor its complete merger into Brahman; rather, it is the realization by the soul of its essential 'creatureliness' or dependence on the Lord. This concept of absolute dependence in 'creatureliness' of the soul (*karpanya*) emphasizes the volitional nature of the soul. Liberation is therefore conceived not as a mere cognitive experience (*jnana*), as in the philosophies of liberation, but as freedom from all passions and sin, as also knowing, loving and serving (or attaining) God. (1989: 151)

Contrast this with the *nivrtti-marg* conception of *moksa:*

> [Its] concept of liberation is derived from their concept of the self which is an ultimate, transcendent reality and which, like the monads of Leibniz, is self-sufficient and alone or unrelated to the world and other selves. The self's involvement in the transmigratory existence is considered its bondage, and its liberation consists in getting rid of this false involvement and realizing its original and pure nature or aloneness. (118)

Perhaps the most significant difference lies in the way the ascetic and devotional paths envision the role that human effort should play in spiritual life. Jhingran writes:

> As against the self-reliance in the way of knowledge, the theistic tradition insists on man's incapacity to emancipate himself on his own and the need of God's grace. To quote Narada, 'And also because God dislikes the reliance on one's own unaided effort and likes the complete feeling of misery due to the consciousness of one's helplessness in independently working out one's salvation, *bhakti* is greater.' (152)

Contrast this with the archetypal image of the Jain ascetic:

> The Jain monk is portrayed in the earliest texts as being fully responsible for his destiny and in control of his life, and his isolation and independence, which mirror the state of the soul as conceived by Jainism, are conveyed in stark terms. (Dundas, 1992: 37)

These distinct convictions give rise to rather different religious dispositions. The *bhakti marg* asserts that

> the ideal religious attitude is conceived as that of total surrender (*prapatti*) which is understood as a profound religious feeling of one's helplessness and total dependence (*karpanya*) on the Lord. (Jhingran, 1987: 152)

Whereas *nivrtti marg* maintains

> When the monk realizes that he is alone, that he has no connection with anyone and that no one has any connection with him, in the same way he should realize that his self is also alone. (*Acarangasutra*, cited in Dundas, 1992: 37)

It is easy to see why *bhakti marg* and *nivrtti marg* have been depicted as contrary. On the face of it, they do appear to be distinct and even opposing paths. But at their most basic levels, both are about connecting with a divine power – tapping into it, experiencing it, and benefiting from it.[9] In Hindu *bhakti*, dissolution in an external god leads to self-realization. In Terapanthi monastic life, intermediaries are sought to help and guide, and the guru plays a nearly equivalent role to that of a god. Devotion and surrender to the guru is the first step to self-realization.

Despite the protests from the *samanis* in the room, Urmilla now insisted that she felt well enough to do some work for Guru Dev's birthday. Just as with Vandana, I could now witness the effect of Guru Dev's special attention on her. Moments before, she was languishing from the heat and her illness, but now was instantly rejuvenated by words of kindness from her guru.

'You're feeling better already? Was it Guru Dev's words?' I asked.

'He cares about us. More than our family! He inspires us to work hard,' she replied.

Mallipregya and the other *samanis* who had delivered the good news went to fetch the art supplies and drawings. Soon Urmilla was busy cutting, pasting, and colouring posters.

'What did you feel the first time you met Guru Dev?' one of the newly initiated *samanis* asked me. This was a question I had grown very accustomed to answering, so without hesitation I said, 'He has such kind eyes. He spoke such kind words to me that I felt calm.'

'You must tell him so,' she said.

'No. I'm sure he knows how I feel,' I answered.

'It is true. He knows everything about us,' Mallipregya responded.

'Yes! His eyes. Everyone says his eyes. They are very powerful,' said another, who then began to recount a recent incident: 'There is a very good family in Jaipur who are devotees of Guru Dev. They have a big house , and burglars entered it to rob it. When they got in, they gathered up lots of expensive jewellery, but one of them saw a picture of Guru Dev hanging on the wall and it disturbed him. He tried to ignore it and continue to take the jewellery from the drawers, but he felt Guru Dev's eyes on him and was unable. He got angry with the family and wanted to know who the picture was. He couldn't steal a thing!'

'It was the picture that had the power?' I asked.

'Yes surely!' Urmilla added matter-of-factly, 'Many times such things happened. Not just his photos, also his name. When the *sadhvis* were in Haridwar they were staying in a small room. There were holes in the wooden door ... a very thin door. Late at night while they were meditating, a group of drunken men came banging on the door. They yelled for the *sadhvis* to let them in. They could do terrible things. The *sadhvis* were terrified. They began to tremble. Then Sadhvi Venita said they must chant Guru Dev's name. So they began chanting his name over and over together. The men were bashing the door with their bodies, but they could not break it open!'

Soon the circle of *samanis* were each recounting their own miracles associated with Guru Dev as well as with Acharya Bhikshu. It became a chorus of wondrous testimonials. But miracles (*camatkar*), like devotion, are on shaky ground within the ascetic discourse. For example, in a discussion of the supernatural, Laidlaw quotes a nun who, after explaining the powers of *yantras*, insists that ascetics 'don't believe in miracles (*camatkar*), only karma.' He then goes on to write:

> The problems Jains have with miracles is not whether or not they are possible in causal and mechanical terms ... The problem is that they are not allowed. They are, in Moore's terms 'real really: the way that common knowledge, common sense, and common experience all suggest that things must be. But they are not 'really real,' they do not figure in the understanding of the way things are which informs ascetic renunciation. From the latter point of view they should be renounced, along with other worldly things, even if all one does is acknowledge and assert this, without necessarily giving them up in practice. The interdiction does the necessary work, even if you don't always follow it. (1995: 79)

According to the authoritative *Tattvartha Sutra*, methods to inhibit or 'burn away' karma

> have been specified in order to *exclude* practices and rituals such as religious pilgrimage, sacred ablution, deluded ordination, offering one's head to the deity as a gift, worship of gods and demi-gods and so on. Such practices and rituals are inspired by attachment, hatred and delusion which attract rather than inhibit karma. (*TS*, 1994: 219; italics added)

All forms of 'extending oneself' or 'connecting' are either denied by the official ascetic discourse or transformed according to its ideal. For example, the learned Muni Mahendra explains miracles according to a combination of individual efforts and modern psychology. He said:

> Someone who has a strong faith in some ideal, or in some divinity, then, by praying to this person, the power is actually his own soul developing. Nothing else. He develops extra-sensory power. Scientifically, our deep concentration will increase our own vital energy, which is otherwise dormant. For example, the recitation of mantras – the repetition increases our mental power.

But, as we saw in the case of devotion, monastic life is not a coherent monolithic system, but is a site for competing discourses (see Holmstrom, 1988: 4). One day, for instance, Mahasraman heard a group of *samanis* reciting a simple prayer common to both Hindus and Jains: 'I pray to God for the pureness of the moon, the brightness of the sun, the sincerity of the ocean.' Mahasraman told the *samanis* that it was wrong for a Jain ascetic to say a prayer entreating of a god. Jains, he reminded them, do not believe in miracles, only in karma and self-exertion. But when one of the *samanis* asked Acharyasri Mahaprajna his opinion, he told them that they could continue to recite it. He said it was fine as a technique to 'subdue the ego.' We see that even among the most senior ascetics of the order, consensus is not present. For Acharyasri, the prayer's acceptability depended on the motive underlying it. By interpreting efforts to 'connect' with something greater than the self in terms of tools of self-realization, the magico-devotional can be rationalized and contained. Therefore, even though deities 'continue to play a very prominent part in religious life,' as Laidlaw writes, 'they occupy a rather hazy domain in Jain culture' (1995: 72).

We must bear in mind, however, that these rationalizations are occurring only on the discursive level – that is, in the public ideology of Jain asceticism, and among its literati. Miracles and efforts to connect with divinity, like devotional practices, are seen to conflict with the ascetic rhetoric of aloneness and detachment on the *discursive* level only. Within the monastery, 'competing' ideologies coexist and even thrive, as the following talk of the *samanis* makes clear. Samani Chaitanya said: 'Four of us [*samanis*] were in a car going to a camp to give a talk. The road was so narrow and we were going so fast when a big truck appeared. There was no room for both. And the truck was coming so fast. We thought we would surely die, so we started chanting "Om Bhikshu, om Bhikshu, om Bhikshu" ... over and over, with our eyes closed ... "om Bhikshu, om Bhikshu" ... and when we opened our eyes we were on the other side. The truck was gone.'

'What had happened?' I asked. 'What did the driver say happened?'

Her eyes were wide in the retelling, 'The driver said he thought we would all die. He heard us saying "Om Bhikshu" and then the car was lifted over the truck and put down safely.'

'Acharya Bhikshu caused this to happen?' I asked.

'Yes,' she answered, but then quickly qualified by saying, 'Not Acharya Bhikshu, but the *devas* who honour him. Bhikanji is in the fifth heaven; he does not interfere with us; he is not concerned at all with worldly matters. But the *devas* who want to honour him, they help.'

'Such things happen all the time. Ask anyone, they will tell you,' Urmilla said. 'We pray to Lord Mahavira, or Acharya Bhikshu because it purifies us to do so; and if we die chanting their names, we will have a good rebirth. Our minds will be focused on spirituality at the moment of death – this is very important. We do not ask for help, but the *devas* help us because we are Bhikshu's devotees and they also honour him; they bow down to him.'

The newly initiated *samani* added, 'The *devas* honour Guru Dev by moving the clouds to shield him from the hot sun. When he walks – even in the bright day light – he is always in shade.'

'Was it the *devas* who helped the family in Jaipur from the robbers?' I asked.

'We do not know,' she answered. 'It may be. Or maybe it is Guru Dev's aura. Mahasaman says Guru Dev's aura is very powerful.'

Samani Savita said that Guru Dev's 'aura' helps them in all sorts of ways. She said that once when she was in Bombay she had to give a talk and felt very nervous and didn't know what she would say to the huge audience. As she sat on the stage before being called to speak, she chanted Guru Dev's name and then felt calm. When she was called to speak, she spoke without fear.

'Yes, it is not always the *devas*,' Urmilla added. 'Sometimes Bhikshu can appear – it is according to him. He appeared before Muni Mahendra's father and told him to take *santara*.* When *Muniji's* father asked him how can he be sure what he sees is real, Bhikshu said, "Only do as I say if two *sadhvis* come to your home for alms tomorrow." The *sadhvis* were not supposed to be in the town; they made a special trip because they knew he was sick. So they went to his house. And he then took *santara*.'

Mallipregya leafed through the posters on the floor and said, 'Everything about Guru Dev is auspicious. His words, his image, his name. Householders even collect the sand from where his feet have been – and there are many miracles from it.'

Looking at the photos, trying to decide how best to make a collage, the *samanis* began to comment on Guru Dev's features – his large ears, his sloped shoulders, his head shape. 'You can know by these things that he is very special person,' one said.

'Guru Dev has certain marks on his body that very few people have. And his ears are long like the Tirthtankaras. Everything about him is special,' Mallipregya confirmed.

'Yes,' added another, 'the way his shoulders go down, his arms, the shape of his forehead are different … and show his greatness.'

Soon the talk quieted down. Mallipregya began to sing softly and we spent the rest of the morning drawing, cutting, and pasting. In the end we had completely finished two posters, and had only one more to make before Guru Dev's birthday.

Asceticism *as* Devotion

Devotion permeates ascetic life. It motivates Jains of all ages to 'renounce the world' and join monastic life; it motivates parents to 'give their children away';[10] it motivates *tapas* and even *santara*. The discourse of devotion that underpins ascetic practices suggests that a desire to belong to or connect with someone or something greater than the self is central to the monastic life. Devotion makes the more austere aspects of ascetic life comprehensible and desirable by making them immediate and personal. Although the ultimate purpose of the ascetic life is to

---

*Santara or *sallekhana* refers to the Jain ritual fast until death.

wear away karma and prepare the soul for emancipation, devotion makes these transcendental and abstruse goals concrete, coherent, and even joyous.

Bhakti structures the lives of the devotees. They learn to see their spiritual progress as a result of their guru's grace and benevolence as much as, if not more than, their own efforts. And perhaps even more important, the ascetics embark on ascetic practices *as devotional practices.* For example, when I asked a group of *mumukshu* sisters how they were capable of regular eight-day fasts, one said, 'If I feel hunger, I think about Guru Dev and it becomes so easy for me. I know that he is happy when we make spiritual progress.' And from one who had extended her fast to fifteen days, 'He inspires me when I feel weak. When he told everyone how strong I am, I felt I could continue for one year!'

The elderly Sadhvi Pannaji – the most celebrated 'faster' in the order – openly describes her life as a dedication to her guru. In a book written about her, entitled *Tapasvini*, she is reported as attributing all her strength and courage to Guru Dev. The book was written and published by a local layperson; it details her heroic austerities and the supernatural powers she gained as a result of them. It demonstrates that the narrative of her life has been informed as much by the discourse of *prapatti* (surrender) as that of *nivrtti* (detachment). To separate the motivations underlying her fasting would be meaningless. Clearly she did not distinguish between devotion and the wearing away of karma – the two were inseparable to her.

In the day-to-day life at the monastery, devotion underpins, inspires, and invigorates ascetic practices. In the nuns' more private moments, when they are not giving lectures on Jain *dharma* to the householders or counselling them on their worldly troubles, *nivrtti* recedes into the background of their talk, and *bhakti* – the basis of their asceticism – emerges forcefully. Their talk becomes peppered with devotional idioms:

- 'We do everything for him, and he knows what is best for us.'
- 'As a *samani* I may only have five minutes' notice to get prepared to go to south India for a lecture. If Guru Dev decides it, we know it is for our best interest.'
- 'Whenever one of us is away from our gurus, we find it very difficult. Here we have peace. We always want to be near him,' a *samani* said, looking in the direction of Guru Dev's residence.
- 'We have no existence without our guru.'

- 'When he looks our way, or says something directly to us, we feel ...' She shuts her eyes and smiles, and doesn't finish her sentence. 'We feel inspired,' another finishes her sentence. 'We feel we can do anything.'

Just as Urmilla was motivated to continue working despite a serious illness, ascetics typically embark on *tapas* (most quintessentially, fasting) for the approval they will receive *and* for the karma it will burn. Because nothing occurs in monastic life without prior consent, private austerities are always public performances. This makes the distinction between a desire for spiritual advancement and a desire for public approval difficult to tease apart. For example, when a *mumukshu* decides to embark on a fast, she must first get approval from her superior. All will know about it, encourage her, praise her to others and fuss over her at its termination. Her individual austerities gain group approval. And exceptional individual efforts are rewarded in a public ceremony, often with the designation of a special title – reflecting the importance of group acknowledgment. For example, Guru Dev gave Acharyasri (formerly Muni Nathmal) the title 'Mahaprajna' meaning 'great knowledge' for his extraordinary literary works on Terapanthi Jainism. And Sadhvi Pannaji was given the title 'Tapasvini' in recognition of her heroic austerities (i.e., fasts).

Dundas cites a survey conducted on the motivations for renunciation among Svetambar nuns. He writes:

[The study] produced an interesting mixture of spiritual and social reasons for rejection of the world and subsequent initiation. Out of answers garnered from one hundred nuns interviewed about why they had chosen to reject the world, twenty-one expressed themselves as having been attracted to this attitude for personal reasons, fourteen were impressed by the general ambiance of the ascetic community, nineteen were spiritually drawn to a prominent female teacher, nineteen were spiritually drawn to a particular nun, seventeen were orphans who regarded ascetic life as preferable to that with relatives, and five were attracted by the outward appearance of ascetic life, such as the initiation ceremony itself. With regard to reasons for initiation, fifty-nine nuns stated themselves to have been spiritually motivated, eleven sought increase of knowledge to gain a specifically religious end, ten wanted to be of service to the community, three to escape from marriage and seventeen to find some sort of refuge, presumably because they were widows. (1992: 132)

The survey, however, bifurcates motivation in a way the average ascetic does not. Within the order, desire to belong to the group, or attraction to a charismatic leader, is not treated as 'social' motivation, stemming from worldliness. Instead, it too is seen as evidence of a spiritual purity. Indeed, any expression of interest in monastic life – however worldly the motivation – is seen as inchoate, burgeoning spirituality in need of direction and nurture. *Attraction* to any aspect of the order is interpreted as embryonic *devotion* to the ascetic ideal, which in turn is seen to represent worldly detachment. And *disdain* for any aspect of worldly life is seen as outright evidence of worldly *detachment* – even if the disdain was very narrowly focused. The PSS is a school through which the young women's motivations all come to be interpreted via a discourse of *nivrtti marg*. As we saw in chapter 4, Mumukshu Promika's motivation to join the order was her attraction to the uniform – a white-hooded tunic or *kavatchan*. But this was treated as a sign, an expression of vestigial spirituality, and her subsequent happiness at the PSS confirmed it. Another example of motivation, this time stemming from disdain, is that of Mumukshu Kamala. When we first talked about her motivation for joining the PSS, she was still an *upasika*, and had been at the order only several months. She said:

I saw my aunt have a baby. I was too young to see this, and there was so much blood, and she was in so much pain. Then she died. I was terrified, but the baby was fine and very lovely. But I knew that I never wanted to have a baby, so I would never get married. I told my mother this. And then one day when my mother went to the nuns, I went with her. The *mumukshu* sisters were also there – and they looked so proper and lovely together. I knew I wanted to be part of that.

By the end of my stay in Ladnun, Kamala had progressed to the stage of *mumukshu*. When we talked again about her motivations, they had already become more 'other-worldly' sophisticated:

Seeing my aunt give birth, I was struck by the uselessness of worldly life. It is just birth, death, rebirth. Everyone does this, over and over again. There is nothing special in this. It is a terrible cycle that never ends and causes so much pain. I wanted to end this cycle. I wanted to end the cycle of *samsara* and do something special with my life. When I saw Guru Dev and all the *sadhvis* and *mumukshus*, I knew immediately that I wanted to be part of the order.

For most of the young women entering the PSS, it is difficult to discern the difference between being *attracted* to the charismatic order and wanting to *renounce* worldly life (see Goonasekere, 1986). To many, their attraction to the guru, a particular nun, the clothes, the order, the discipline, and so forth signifies a 'this-worldly' disdain. Devotion and asceticism form two sides of the same coin.

Goonasekera's dissertation explored the psychological motivations for renunciation among Terapanthi Jains. He writes:

> Many young renouncers declared that they became motivated to join ascetic orders because they were inspired by '*Gurus and Guruvanis.*' Some ascetics of both sexes have a strong appeal to young people. Whenever these ascetics visited their home towns these young women had gone to pay them respect and to listen to their sermons. They had discovered a certain magic in the presence of these ascetics and became enchanted by it. As one nun said: 'When the Acharya visited our town I went to see him with my parents. When I saw the Acharya something happened to me. It was if I got an electric shock. There was a light radiating from his face. We listened to his Pravachan. Everything he said made sense to me. I realized that the Acharya knew everything about the world, about the truths, about me. He was talking to *me*. I immediately decided to follow him.' (1986: 96–7)

We will recall that Muni Dulaharaji tells a similar story. He explained that he was once a 'worldly man' and enjoyed all sorts of worldly pleasures. He never thought about renouncing – the idea was ludicrous to him. When he was a young man he married. Several months after, as is common among Jain newlyweds, he and his wife made the trip from Maharashtra to Rajasthan to receive the Acharya's blessing. He said that something very strange happened to him that evening, while he sat and listened to the guru's speech. Out of the blue, he was struck by the righteousness of the ascetic path. He wanted to renounce the world at that moment. He felt torn. He was now a husband and soon to be a father. So how could be renounce? He decided he must honour his obligations, but he explained to his wife his desire to renounce, and they both decided to lead religious, celibate lives from that day on. A year later, he and his wife returned to see their guru again with their child. On that occasion, his wife became suddenly ill and died while on their visit. He then decided to become a monk.[11]

Many ascetics, like Muniji, emphasized their *mystical* transformation in the presence of Guru Dev. Confronted by his spiritual might, they experienced the power of asceticism firsthand and were deeply attracted by it. Many hope that they too can develop *shakti* through *tapas*. Goonasekera describes a young *mumukshu* sister who decided to join the PSS because 'she thought she would be able to better her next birth while achieving various supernatural powers such as clairvoyance if she practised asceticism and purified her soul' (1986: 99). When she and her family visited the Acharya to inform him of her intentions,

> She felt that there was *Shanthi* (peace) near him. She was convinced that he had *Karuna* (compassion) for her. There was something about the Acharya which filled her heart with religious devotion. Something radiated from his face. Something emanated from him and entered her intensifying her piety and devotion to him. Her conviction became stronger. (99)

The ascetics inspire devotion not simply because they represent an ideal, but because of the power they possess (Babb, 1996). Devotion benefits the devotee by providing her with knowledge, peace, and, importantly, *shakti*. Whereas the householder hopes to receive some of the guru's power through his blessings, the ascetic in addition hopes to generate her own power through *tapas*. Austerities, most quintessentially fasting, are a source of creativity and of unassailable power. Through the 'heat' that they generate, they not only burn away karma but also produce tremendous power and creativity (Holmstrom, 1988; Reynell, 1985). Householders and ascetics are equally interested in both. Sadhvi 'Tapasvini' Pannaji derives her title from her heroic and famous fasts, but what fascinates householders most about her are the powers of clairvoyance and healing that she has acquired as a result of her fasting. Wherever she travels, individuals flock to her to receive her blessing. They come because they are sick, or are troubled by *bhuts* (demons), or simply want a blessing of good fortune.

Goonasekera's dissertation includes an autobiographical story written in the 1930s by a young Terapanthi monk Bhairavdan (Bhairun to his family). He includes it as part of a discussion on the role of charismatic ascetics in inspiring others to renounce the world. Even though it is quite long, I include it here, omitting only small sections, because it demonstrates rather excellently how the devotional, mystical, and the transcendent are interwoven in monastic life – how the *laukik* and *lokottar* are, in many ways, inseparable. In addition, it provides us with a sense of the fabric of lay Terapanthi life and the context in which the decision to renounce takes place. Goonasekera begins by writing that

Bhairavdan was a child-renouncer who joined the order because he was attracted to charismatic ascetics.

I followed my mother like her own shadow. I went wherever she went. I was part of her body. She breast fed me until I was two years old. She massaged my body daily with sesame oil. I slept in the same bed as my mother and always ate off her plate. Mother rose at four in the morning and meditated for 48 minutes, the prescribed period in the Jaina religion, the religion of our family. She sat alone on the veranda with the glass timer, and meditated partly in silence and partly chanting the Mantra of Surrender:

I surrender to the One who is enlightened and therefore has no enemy
I surrender to the Released Spirit
I surrender to the Wise Guru
I surrender to the Spiritual Teacher
I surrender to the Seekers of Enlightenment

During her meditation she took a daily vow of limitation, such as today I will eat rice, lentils, wheat, mango, melon, cucumber, cumin, chilli, salt, water, milk, butter and nothing else. Today I will not travel more than ten miles, and only towards the east ...

When I was seven a group of monks came to spend the 'chathurmas' (the four monsoon months) in our town. The news of the monks' arrival travelled by word of mouth and a group of people, including my mother and myself, went along the desert path to greet them, singing songs of welcome –

Today the sun is golden
because our gurus are coming
with a message of peace ...

Suddenly out of the sand and bushes, I saw three monks in their white robes walking barefoot and carrying a few belongings on their backs. They were walking fast, their faces impassive to the crowds around them. I had to run to keep up. People had gathered in the courtyard of the house where the monks were staying to hear their first sermon. One of the monks, monk Kundan, who was sitting on a table, started speaking:

'Seekers, we have come to show you the path to liberate your souls. The soul is wrapped up in good and bad karma which imprison it. We have to break away from these illusions. Sometimes we have to leave everything we know and love – mother, father, wife, children. These relationships are the expression of possessive love that destroys, maims and kills, rather than the expression of divine love that sustains the universe and has life in all of us' ...

At the end, men of the town went up to the monks, put their heads on their feet and asked for blessings. I went up to monk Kundan. He looked deep into my eyes and talked with me. I asked him if he would come to my home to receive food. He enquired the way. When I got home mother said that he wouldn't come because it was the first day and he would have been invited to many homes. I insisted we wait to eat and to keep the doors open since monks can only come into a house with an open door. I kept running out into the street to look for him. Nobody else thought he would come. After some time I saw him coming. He said to me, 'We're going to spend four months here. Will you come everyday to receive knowledge from us?'

... So I went to the monks in the morning and in the evening ... One evening, cool after the monsoon rain, before the story-telling began, the senior monk, Kundan, talked to my mother and me. He said that there was a line on my foot, the lotus line.

'We think he is the incarnation of a spiritual soul. He looks and behaves like a spiritual person. For many generations, no-one from your family has offered himself as a monk. Out of eight children surely you could contribute one?'

It was dark. I couldn't see mother's face.

Next day monk Kundan said to me, 'If you become a monk, the people will come to listen to your preaching, they will bow their heads at your feet. You will go to heaven and after heaven to nirvana.'

'What is nirvana?' I asked.

He said, 'No death.'

That impressed me – no death. Father's death had created a deep question in my mind. I couldn't understand where he had gone. Whenever I asked mother about him, she said I asked too many questions and didn't answer.

So I used to ask the monks about what happens after death. Monk Kundan described human life in '*samsara*' (the everlasting round of birth and death) and the souls of the monks who alone can free the individual from it.

It was October – cool and dry – the monsoon was over. The night before the monks left I couldn't sleep. After the sunrise mother was busy looking after the animals, but I went to see the monks. A crowd had gathered to see them off. Some people walked with them and I also followed. At the next village they stopped. Monks went to beg food for themselves. It was considered wrong to give it to a non-monk and the other followers didn't know I had come alone. So nobody worried about me. I was very hungry. It was the first time I had been out of town without mother. At home mother was worried. She searched everywhere. Eventually someone told her that they had seen me following the monks. She walked the ten miles to the village in the evening and found me.

'Did you eat?' she asked.

I said, 'I haven't eaten. I am hungry. Give me some food.'

She said 'You're stupid. Why didn't you ask someone to give you some food?'

I didn't tell mother that I wanted to be like the monks ...

One morning mother and I rode out on our camel to the land. The maize crop was ripe. We built a small hut with wood and rushes. There we could sleep and protect the crop while we were harvesting. Mother asked me why I looked so sad. I could not answer. She said: 'You don't listen properly. You're not interested in playing anymore. Look at other children. See how gay and cheerful they are while you mope around, you miserable little soul.'

When I was eight the head of our sect of the Jaina order, the guru Acharya Tulsi, spent the monsoon months in our town. Two rich families gave their homes to the guru for this period. Canvas tents were put up in the courtyard where the people could come to hear the guru preach and receive his blessings. Mother took me to welcome the guru. I saw Tulsi walking towards us across the desert. He was plump and short but his eyes were shining like big lights. His face was fair, calm and peaceful. Three deep lines cut across his forehead. His brows were bushy and black. His ears were long as I had seen on the statues of gods and hair grew on the outer edge denoting wisdom. His arms were too long; which meant a man of many resources. His step was firm. He alone among the monks wore snow white clothes. All other monks carried bags on their backs. He alone was free. He walked like a lion. He raised his hand to bless us.

After the guru walked forty monks, then sixty nuns, then the male disciples, then the women. Men and women sang welcome songs:

The sun is golden today
The guru comes to our town
O men and women gather together
And sing the songs of happiness
Now we can swim across
The Ocean of *Samsara*

The monks and nuns walked with their eyes on the ground and remained silent. They looked like glorious angels in their robes. Through the clouds of dust I looked for any monks I might know. I saw monk Kundan. He smiled and raised his hand. I felt as if the guru had come to rescue me from death.

A few weeks later monk Kundan took me to the guru. Normally the guru remained aloof, beyond reach, and talked only at sermon times but this day he looked at me with his kind and gentle eyes.

I said, 'The monks have told me that they feel something spiritual in me, a link with my previous life and that I should become a monk.'

The guru replied, 'A monk's life is very hard. You may have spiritual links from a previous life, but in order to continue these links you have to gather strength and dedication.'

His words reverberated in my mind. I felt I belonged to the guru. He would take me to nirvana. He would give me light. I longed to put myself in his hands.

I stopped going to school and sometimes I didn't even go home to eat. I no longer saw my friends and playmates. At night I walked in the desert thinking of Tulsi. In moonlight the sand shone like silver and sometimes I slept on the sand. During the day I wandered around. The town was quiet. Near the well under a Peepal tree sat a rich man smoking his hookah. Shepherd children rested under the trees with their goats and sheep. In the market women were buying monsoon fruits and vegetables and chatting. But all this did not attract me.

As every morning mother was making butter ... The beautiful sound of butter churning woke me up. I went to mother and sat by her. I wanted to tell her of my meeting with the guru but I just sat looking at the butter-making, waiting for the butter to come with a *chappati* in my hand.

Impatient, I interrupted her.

'The butter is ready. It's coming. Give it to me.'

She said, 'It isn't ready. Wait.'

I looked into the pot and pointed to some bubbles, 'See, it has come.'

Feeling my anxiety, she gave me some butter which was still not ready. After a while she said, 'What's the matter with you, little one?'

I said, 'I want to become a monk.'

Mother was shocked. There was silence. Then she said,

'I was dreading the day you would say this. But my son you are too young. You can become a monk later on.'

She burst into tears. We didn't speak any more about it.

The Brahmin came home to ask why I wasn't going to school. Mother told him that I wanted to become a monk and she could not prevent it. She told him of a vow she made when I had smallpox at the age of five (Small-pox is a deity called 'Mata' [mother]. So as not to offend her, and if some-one has smallpox we say 'Mother can come into the body.' Every year a special day is dedicated to her when the family doesn't cook but eats the previous day's food. If 'Mata' is offended she is supposed to come into the body in the form of smallpox.) When I had smallpox mother said she thought she had done something wrong and everyday prayed to 'Mata,' 'Please leave my beloved son.' In spite of herbal medicines I became so ill that mother feared I would die. She promised 'Mata,' 'If you leave my son I will never stand in the way of him leading a religious life.' From the day she made this vow I started getting better.

The Brahmin was angry with mother saying, 'Your son is not an animal to be sacrificed. You'll regret it later on.'

Although the Brahmin was very close to our family he was a Hindu, not a Jain, and therefore mother couldn't trust him on religious matters. I lis-tened to mother and the Brahmin arguing. She said that if she broke her vow, 'Mata' might come again and this time kill me. One day she said to me:

'Bhairun, the thought of your becoming a monk grieves me but I have given my word to "Mata." I will not interfere. You must decide for yourself.' And then she burst into tears again. My decision was already made.

Together with my mother and some prominent people of the town, I went to guru to make a formal request to become a monk. The guru said,

'You should wait. Think more. You are going to be a monk for your whole life and there will be no turning back.'

After a week I went to ask him again. Again he said, 'Wait more.' After many more pleas he said, 'I accept to consider your request and I will ask monk Kundan to teach you and examine your intention properly.'

A month later Kundan reported to the guru that I would make a good monk. I went to the guru with my final request. He pronounced,

'On the last day of the monsoon I will make you a monk.' (Goonasekera, 1986: 108–13)

Bhairavdan's story demonstrates how the goal of *self-realization* is often sought through *surrender* to the guru. As Richard Lannoy observed,

The active ideal of the spiritual 'teacher' is associated with the Indian con-cept of compassion, or *karuna*. He helps others attain liberation. He is a competent therapist and capable of supplying correct answers to the rid-dles of life. (1974: 349)

Attachment to the guru through devotion allows for *detachment* from worldly existence. In her discussion of Hindu renunciation, Vail makes a similar argument when she claims that dependence on, and dissolution in, God can lead to a sense of autonomy. She writes: 'the spiritual one-ness with God ... allows for an extreme amount of independence from ordinary social convention, fears or impurity, and so forth (1987: 297).

Bhairavdan's story also reveals that the desire to 'extend oneself' by connecting with something or someone greater than the empirical self is a powerful motivation to join monastic life, and a driving force within it – notwithstanding the rhetoric of asceticism's 'public ideology.'

Detached Devotion and the Attachment of Asceticism

Jainism's 'public ideology' interprets devotion in a utilitarian way, as functional within the *nivrtti marg*. It is about admiration, emulation, and inspiration, not attachment. Like Niyojikaji's view, which we saw at the start of this chapter, this is a rationalized interpretation that maps devotion according to the ascetic values of detachment and aloneness. For example, the learned Muni Mahendra Kumar explained devotion this way:

> When we accept someone as an ideal, as a role-model, *arihant, siddha, muni, acharya* ... we want to imitate that person. For imitation we must be humble, appreciate their achievements, and eulogize them.

Paul Dundas states that devotional activity was nonexistent in the old-est texts, but acknowledges that the eulogizing of the great ascetics came to play an important role early on in the tradition (1992: 147). However, he restricts his discussion to the worship of the Jinas, and there-fore claims that the motives underlying devotion are solely that of 'self-realization':

> Jain devotional worship of fordmakers,* who are frequently also referred to by the designation 'god,' should be interpreted as being directed towards this [i.e., the *paramatman* or 'supreme soul'] and as an acknowl-edgement of the spiritual principle within every individual. (1992: 94)

---

*A 'fordmaker' is used synonomously with *'Tirthankara,'* denoting one who creates a ford or passage across the ocean of *samsar.*

Dundas adds that the ancient tradition

> is emphatic that worship of fordmakers does not actually elicit a response
> from them but rather brings about an internal, spiritual purification in the
> worshipper ... So, while it may be the case that worship destroys karma,
> such an effect is regarded as having been brought about by the inner trans-
> formation which worship effects. (1992: 180)

On *bhakti*, Nalini Shântâ similarly confines her discussion to this narrow interpretation:

> Le *bhakti* jaina a son aspect propre, c'est-à-dire la louange, la dévotion,
> l'admiration – quelles que soient leurs expressions extérieures – s'adr-
> essent à la réalisation spirituelle d'êtres éminemment dignes de vénéra-
> tion, des vaillants, des victorieux, les *tîrthankara* et autres *paramesthin, dans
> le but ultime de les imiter, de les suivre, et par là, de se purifier, de se libérer.* (1985:
> 72; italics added)

A Jain textbook likewise emphasizes a functional motive behind devotion. It states:

> When a person worships the Lord he forgets his worries, his problems,
> even his whole existence. He starts praising and singing. He admires and
> does all sorts of adorations. Sometimes a layman gets more peace and joy
> by some sort of ritual worship than by reading scriptures which he may not
> even understand. (Kapashi, Shah, and Desai, 1994: 59)

In the public ideology, therefore, as these examples demonstrate,
devotion is seen to exist only as a tool in the ascetic's arsenal of self-puri-
fication.[12] In this view, devotion has nothing to do with emotion or with
attachment – the 'seed' of all worldly problems[13] – instead, it is focused
on the self. This, however, is not the dominant way it is experienced or
understood within the order. For most, their devotion is more conven-
tionally 'other-oriented' *bhakti* – involving love and surrender (*prapatti*)
to their gurus.

Devotion is an unquestioned and integral part of their lives *as* ascetics. When asked how their devotion is reconciled with the dominant
ascetic discourse of *nivrtti-marg*, most do not invoke the sophisticated
rationale of self-realization above. Many try to put into words something
that has always been apparent to them, but which they never thought to

define. When pressed to do so, many interpret it as *samyag darsana* or 'enlightened worldview,' one of the three pillars of the ascetic path – evincing its centrality in their minds. However Dundas writes that devotion, in any form, was not part of the early ascetic path (1992: 147), and the literature does not support the translation of *samyag darsana* as 'devotion.' Rather, according to the *Tattvartha Sutra*, *samyag darsana* means '[T]rue understanding, informing an individual's thoughts and actions in solving the ethical and spiritual problems of worldly bondage and of release from that bondage' (*TS*, 1994: 5).

But interestingly, the ascetics' interpretation is based less on the *definition* of *samyag darsana* than on its foundational role, its function as the bedrock for the creation of an ascetic life. The *Tattvartha Sutra* continues:

> Enlightened worldview (*samyag darsana*) begets enlightened knowledge, which in turn begets enlightened conduct. So enlightened worldview is the cause, enlightened knowledge and conduct the effect. The spiritual path is determined by this integrated trinity. (5)

The ascetics' interpretation is, in this sense, accurate: it mirrors their experience of ascetic life where devotion serves as the foundation upon which ascetic practices are carried out. For the majority of ascetics, reconciling *nivrtti* and *bhakti* is unproblematic. Most do not make a connection between emotional attachment and devotion. They profess their devotion as earnestly and vigorously as they denounce attachment and emotion. Clearly, they believe that their 'attachment' to the guru is fundamentally different from the evil of 'worldly attachment.' Since attachment is the chief villain of the ascetic discourse, something so obviously 'spiritual' to them as devotion could clearly never have anything to do with it. And the years the ascetics spend in the order do not teach them to tame their devotion, but, on the contrary, to extend, develop, and amplify it. Whatever contradiction this poses on the discursive, philosophical level for Jains and Jain observers, it is not experienced as such. Even in the story of Lord Mahavira's devoted disciple Gautama, where the connection between devotion and attachment is made explicit, the lessons are not.

Lord Mahavira, being omniscient, knew exactly when his own *moksa* would occur, and as the time approached, he sent his disciple Gautama away on the pretence of needing him elsewhere. Mahavira knew his disciple was deeply attached to him, and did not want him there when he left this world. Later, when Gautama learned of his guru's death, he went into a state of shock.

> He had immense devotion for Bhagavan Mahavira. In the presence of Bhagavan Mahavira, Gautam's consciousness experienced perfect protection; Bhagavan Mahavira found a dependable devotee in the latter. Gautama had much attachment to the mortal frame of Bhagavan Mahavira and was not prepared to bear separation from him. *His attachment to Bhagavan Mahavira never waned, even in his physical presence with the result that he could not attain the state of kaivalya.** His attachment knew no bounds on hearing the news of the nirvana of the master. Being overwhelmed, he grieved like an ordinary man. But this state lasted for a few moments only. Gautama was a great sage and was conversant in the *sutras* and was possessed of an insight into the Truth ... Such a wise man could not be lost in sorrow. He regained himself. The image of Bhagavan Mahavira symbolizing non-attachment flashed before his eyes. His attachment melted away. He became free from all attachments and attained the state of *kaivalya.*
> (Tulsi, 1995: 85; italics added)

Though Gautama was prevented from attaining liberation until he abandoned his attachment to his guru, without loyalty and devotion he would never have reached such spiritual heights. It is as though the ascetics accept that total detachment is for a future time, a time that their devotional practices will – ironically – prepare them for. This is how the two ideologies – one of aloneness, the other of dependence – come to coexist. Sadhviji once offered me an 'official' explanation of devotion. She said, 'Jain *bhakti* is different from Hindu *bhakti.* Jain *bhakti* is mental.[14] *Bhakti marg* is about pleasing the Lord with music, singing and it involves attachment. Jain devotion is not like this, it is not done to please.'

When I asked what the purpose was of Jain devotional songs, she replied, 'They lead to *samyag darsana* and encourage creative power; they are not to praise or to form attachments.' A discourse that demonizes attachment and emotion, yet embraces them in the expression of devotion, may appear contradictory and even disingenuous, but what we are observing are efforts to reconcile two discourses that exist on complementary levels of reality. The public ideology of Jainism, which

---

*kaivalya = state of omniscience. *Kevalin* or *Arhat* refers to one who has attained infinite knowledge.

emphasizes aloneness and detachment, naturally problematizes attachment, but within monastic life the discourse of *bhakti* prevails – the discourse of love, surrender, and attachment. 'Official' efforts at reconciliation attempt to reinterpret *bhakti* along the lines of ascetic detachment, and define it as a tool of self-realization. The more candid interpretations of the majority of ascetics see the two as inseparable: *bhakti* is the progenitor of asceticism, making it desirable and possible in the first place.

It would appear that for the majority of the ascetics – and despite the exhortations of the public ideology to the contrary – it is not so much that attachment and emotions are problematic, it is how they are directed. The critical factor, in effect, becomes the objects of these attachments – be they spiritual and acceptable, or worldly and not. Muniji's interpretation probably most accurately captured this when he said: 'Emotions which attach us to worldly pursuits, or sensual concerns are bad, but those that sweep us away in spiritual pursuits are good.'

Recognition of the coexistence and even complementarity of asceticism and devotion in monastic life challenges the more commonly espoused view which considers them as antithetical. Richard Lannoy, for example, in analysing the phenomenon of 'discipleship' in India from a psychological approach, treats the devotee and the ascetic as opposites. He writes: 'In acute cases of insecurity, there exist only two alternatives: the utter detachment of *kaivalya*, isolation, or utter attachment of guru-*shishya* relationship' (1974: 366). But in Terapanthi monastic life, the 'utter attachment' of the guru–disciple relationship is regarded as the best path to attain a state of utter detachment.

Guru Dev's Birthday

> You are the knower of superior conduct and you are perfect in conduct.
> You are the preceptor of religion, you are preeminent in religion.
> You have knowledge about everything, you are able to understand everything.
> You believe in truth, you are in right faith and with the controlling power of the mind and with peace.
> You are with eight types of good attributes and the knower of matter, of space, time and emotions.
> You are the disciplinarian-administrator of the four orders of this Religion.
> You are the representative of the Tirthankara.
> You have thirty-six virtues, Gannadapati Guru Dev Sri Tulsi and *vartaman* [contemporary] Acharya Sri Mahaprajna, I pay my respects humbly.

On the morning of Guru Dev's birthday, the *samanis* recited the *Guru Vandana* prayer (above) as they did every morning, but with greater enthusiasm. Then they added original poems written specially for the exceptional day:

> An earthen lamp in the night, an island in the sea
> A tree in the desert, fire in the snow
> Like these things you are to me,
> Your feet are lotus flowers, as is the sand which touches them.

> Moksa is not possible in this age. But if
> I live in your heart, I find it possible;
> But if You live in my heart,
> I want nothing else.

> A guru who awakens my intuition power
> Makes my heart pure and is identical with my
> Soul, I bow my head to him.

Many stayed kneeling for a few extra moments, softly speaking their own private words of devotion to their guru. Then we were off to Rishabdwar to meet up with (and pay respects to) the *sadhvis*. We didn't dawdle there, as the nuns too were moving in high gear. Everyone wanted to get to the assembly hall as quickly as possible. The sun was breaking through the splendid sky, providing us with the necessary light to begin our trek.[15] As our large group walked briskly in the cool morning air along the narrow Ladnun roads towards the monastery, sounds of excitement and cheer could already be heard. A car honked continuously in the distance, its volume increasing with our every step. Soon we saw a small jeep weaving its way down the main road, avoiding the *tongas* and sleepy dogs. A group of at least six young men sat in the open-top jeep, holding a life-size cardboard cutout of Guru Dev, and chanting slogans, '*Anuvrat Anushasana Yug Pradhan Ganadipatti Shri Guru Dev Ki*' and then responding '*Jay Ho!*'* The nuns paid no attention to the cheers, and kept up their fast pace right into the monastery grounds. As we entered, the buzz of the crowd around the main gates recalled a *diksa* ceremony. But nothing so momentous was going to occur today. It was simply a commemorative occasion, an opportunity to venerate the com-

---

* = 'Anuvrat Disciplinarian World Leader Religious Patriarch Guru Dev!' ... 'Victory!'

munity's aged and revered guru.* I was surprised to see how many had come for the morning prayers since the ceremony proper wouldn't begin until ten o'clock, after the *bhiksha* rounds. Perhaps receiving Guru Dev's morning blessing on this day was particularly auspicious. We entered the assembly hall from behind the monks' residence. I walked behind the nuns as they strode swiftly but silently in unison, their white gowns flapping in the gusts created by their own speed. Each approached Guru Dev and Acharyasri and paid homage on their knees:

Tikkhutto Ayahinman Payahinam Karemi
Vandami Namansami Sakkaremi Sammanemi
Kallanam Mangalam Devayam Cheiyam Pajjuvasami
Matthayena Vandami[16]

The day had finally arrived. It was 20 October and Guru Dev was now 82 years old. Some said that he was so uncomfortable with these annual birthday celebrations, that he decided to designate 20 October as 'Anuvrat Day,' and claimed that the celebrations were really about the peace movement, not him. For the occasion, many people active in the Anuvrat movement from all over India had arrived in Ladnun over the past few days. Later in the day, they would make speeches on the successes of the movement. Although all Terapanthis (lay and ascetic) are justly and immensely proud of the achievements of the movement, and are usually very eager to talk about them, for them this day was the birthday of their guru. In the weeks leading up to 20 October, they scarcely spoke of 'Anuvrat Day.' Nothing could detract from the significance of this special day, which would end up being Guru Dev's last birthday. The assembly hall was packed as Acharyasri and Guru Dev led the morning prayers.

To end the prayers, Guru Dev recited the *mangal path* (auspicious blessing). The monks disappeared behind the stage wall into their quarters, and a few *sadhvis* left to collect *bhiksha,* but most of the crowd were slow to move. The *samanis* were uncharacteristically slow in their steps as they headed to the rear of the monks' residence. There, they met with a group of *sadhvis, mumukshu* sisters, and a growing number of *shravaks.* Each morning, after the *mangal path* blessing, lay and ascetic devotees wait for Guru Dev and Acharyasri to emerge from their residence then

*The Terapanthi worship of the *acharya* has no real parallel in other Jain traditions, and would appear to bear more resemblance to the 'god-man' traditions in Hinduism. See Babb (1987, 1991) and Fuller (1992).

follow them through the western gate and out of the monastery grounds. The procession moves slowly and then comes to an abrupt halt, when the gurus turn into an open field, behind a large grey stone wall, to defecate. Nearly a year ago when I first found myself amidst that chanting morning crowd, I was sure we were all headed to some special event. I tagged along with the *samanis*, talking with Urmilla along the way, until I nearly walked into the back of a woman devotee who had abruptly come to a stop. I looked around and wondered what was going on. I couldn't see Guru Dev and Acharyasri, but the crowd was fairly large, and I assumed they were simply hidden from my view. But within a moment the crowd began to disperse – heading home into the village or returning to the monastery to meet with other ascetics. I was left standing with Urmilla and a few other *samanis*. I was aghast when they told me what was going on. My astonishment at what I considered to be an extreme invasion of privacy was met by laughter from the *samanis*, who simply saw the procession as an expression of *bhakti*. Devotees follow the ascetics at every opportunity. Clearly, the public display of devotion is part and parcel of the renunciant's life.

Today the crowd awaiting the gurus after the *mangal path* was as large as I had ever seen it, and there was definitely a degree of excitement in the air. The crowd lined up facing each other, forming an impromptu path – an alley of about four feet wide – providing just enough space for the gurus to walk side by side. Guru Dev had been frail for some time, and needed the support of another monk's arm to walk even short distances. For somewhat longer distances, householders had built a three-wheeled wagon in which he could sit and have two other monks push. I once saw him use it when he was visiting the PSS and Rishabdwar – but everyone said he was deeply embarrassed to have to do so. According to the rules of *ahimsa*, ascetics are forbidden to travel by any means other than by foot. The gurus finally appeared, and immediately the householders gathered tightly around them, chanting slogans of reverence, with many prostrating themselves at the gurus' feet. Acharyasri held onto Guru Dev, while a younger monk walked a few steps ahead of them and another walked immediately behind. When they are indoors, the monks and nuns always throw down their shawls for the leaders to walk on. For practical reasons this is not often done outdoors. Standing back with the *samanis*, I had difficulty seeing much of anything, but the crowd moved forward fairly quickly, the pace being dictated by the resolute monks. I stopped at the monastery gates, watched for a few moments as the especially large crowd shuffled its way towards the opening in the wall, and then I was off to join the *sadh-vis* for alms collections.

This morning on their *bhiksha* rounds, the ascetics would receive a variety of delectable delights – unquestionably prepared for the occasion – and they would not be so fast to pull their *patras* away from the householders' generous offerings. They would accept all with pleasure because they could then, in turn, offer what they collected to Guru Dev as an expression of their love. And at the end of the day, the sweets would be exchanged once again: Guru Dev would pass them out to each and every ascetic in his order. It was a wonderful time; it was a joyous day for all.

By ten o'clock the crowd was gathering in the assembly hall again. The sun was only a few hours in the sky and yet it was already warm, and the intensity of the crowd made it feel even warmer. The ceremony began with a group of neatly dressed schoolchildren belting out the *Anuvrat-Gita*, a lovely tune about Anuvrat that Guru Dev himself had composed. Then two little girls, dressed in fancy frocks, stood in front of a microphone and 'performed' a humorous song about the life of a pious Jain. When they sang about things Jains should not do, such as drink 'raw' water, they wagged their index fingers, as in censure, like matronly schoolmasters before a class. The audience of householders was delighted, and Guru Dev also appeared amused. Following them, a monk stood before the microphone to introduce a number of prominent lay speakers who wished to say something about their devotion to Guru Dev and the Terapanthi order. Time passed slowly until finally it was the ascetics' turn to speak. Monks and nuns made heartfelt devotional speeches of varying lengths, punctuated by an occasional song by the *mumukshus*.

When Sadhvi Kanak Prabha was called, she spoke of her devotion to her guru and of the importance of his Anuvrat movement. Acharyasri Mahaprajna's speech, which followed, lasted for half an hour until, at last, it was Guru Dev's turn. Unlike the others, his talk was brief. He spoke on the importance of the Anuvrat movement and of his pride in his monks and nuns. On cue, a small group of *samanis* with truly beautiful voices stood again to sing.

Women and Devotion

On this occasion of Guru Dev's birthday, the nuns played a much more prominent role than did the monks; they were 'centre stage' throughout. They prepared and presented artwork, performed their own songs, and recited poetry to mark the event. The monks were, by and large, spectators. The nuns' visibility on this day was customary, and reflected the monopoly they have on the expression of devotion in the order.

My research suggests that not only do monks display their devotion to a lesser degree, they *narrate* their lives less in terms of *bhakti* than do the nuns.[17] Their language is not saturated with idioms of surrender and devotion to the same degree. I use the word 'narrate' because I am referring specifically to the self-conscious presentation of their lives – accounts derived from looking at their own pasts. These narrative accounts structure past and present events in order to provide a coherent self-image and interpretation of renunciation. Although all ascetics are encouraged to interpret their lives through a framework of *nivrtti-marg* – as I have argued throughout this chapter – the nuns juxtapose the framework of *bhakti* alongside that of *nivrtti* to a much greater degree than do the monks.

One reason for the *sadhvis'* predominance in matters of devotion may be that there is a cultural assumption that women innately possess the virtues of the ideal devotee. And, because girls are socialized to see their self-worth as stemming from other-oriented actions, most of them 'naturally' accept this role. The 'archetypal' Indian woman is the loyal and virtuous wife (*pativrata*) and devoted mother. The value in her life is derived from her 'other-oriented' devotion and self-sacrifice. In *Women Images*, Pratibha Jain writes:

> Since marriage is regarded as the noblest avocation and the true destiny of Indian women, there is an enormous emphasis on the cultural ideal of faithful and uncomplaining wifehood ... The *pativrata* regards it as her *saubhagya* (good fortune) to willingly suffer all kinds of adversities and privations for the sake of her husband and accepts service (*sewa*) to her husband, in-laws and members of conjugal family as her basic gender duty (*stridharma*). (1996: 15)

Cross-cultural studies demonstrate that women's position in religion is very often a reflection of their status in society, that religious systems typically reinforce cultural values and patterns of social organization (Sinclair, 1986). However, given the fundamentally egalitarian religious doctrine of Jainism, and given that the status of female ascetics among the Svetambar Jains is highly atypical of other religious traditions in the Indian subcontinent – with nuns outnumbering monks three to one

(Balbir, 1994) – the life of a Jain *sadhvi* could appear as an alternative to the Indian woman's traditional roles as daughter, wife, and mother. Holmstrom suggests this very point when she writes:

> The same religious tenets of renunciation, self-discipline and *sakti*, which partly define the constraint of women can also, in posing renunciation as central to the whole cosmology of Jainism, offer women a means of escape – in some measure – from that constraint, by adopting renunciatory action *completely*, as ascetics. In a religion where enlightenment is attained by control over the self, and by not just controlling but increasing one's *sakti* through *tap*, it is women who overwhelmingly make up most of the community of Jain ascetics. Women as powerful [individuals] are not just controlled; they control too, but the nature of these relations involving many-meaninged powers, land[s] us in a whole complex of ambiguities and contradictions. (1988: 7)

I would agree with Holmstrom in maintaining that renunciation offers women an alternative – 'in some measure' from the dominant feminine norm. But I would add that in the Terapanthi monastic environment, renunciation is both a creative and a conservative institution. It is conservative in its alignment of women with *bhakti* – the vibrant but *subordinate* discourse of monastic life. As Jhingran writes,

> From the moral point of view, the most important aspect of the tradition of devotion (*bhakti*) is its universality ... It is repeatedly asserted that all, irrespective of their caste or sex, are freed from mundane existence by hearing and reciting God's names and qualities. No external qualification is required for practising devotion to God which is essentially *a matter of inner feelings or attitude*. (1989: 153; italics added)

It is precisely because devotion is 'essentially a matter of inner feelings' that it is considered to be quintessentially the domain of women, and why it is ultimately subordinate to *nivrtti marg* and its values of detachment and aloneness.

Sadhvis are regarded first and foremost as 'devotees.' Their role as 'ascetic' and 'guru' is rare and a relatively recent phenomenon. The nuns would often tell me that their lives are completely different from the previous generations of *sadhvis*. As recently as thirty years ago, nuns never learned Sanskrit or Prakrit, so they were unable to read the scriptures, and they were never taught to speak in public. Today's generation

of nuns attributes all the changes to Guru Dev, who was determined to
see the women of his order receive an education. Today Guru Dev mar-
vels at 'his' confident *sadhvis*. He tells them that in the early years of his
Acharyaship, if he would call upon a nun to answer a question, she
would be too bashful to even look at him, let alone speak. This change
in the nuns' behaviour, however, must be understood within a wider
context than that of Guru Dev's motivation alone. It is important to
note that asceticism as a freely chosen *vocation* by young unmarried
women is a relatively new phenomenon among Jain women, and parallels their new-found self-assurance. In P.S. Jaini's study of just twenty
years ago, he states that most Jain nuns are widows ([1979]1990: 247).
This is not the case today among the Terapanthi order. None of the current *samanis* or *mumukshu/upasika* sisters have ever been married. Reynell claims that Jaini's statement reflects a condition prevalent in the
past (1985a: 268). She writes:

> In general it is the older nuns who are widows. This suggests that widow-
> hood as a cause for taking *diks* was related in the past to the institution of
> child marriage whereby if a husband died still in his teens, before he had
> begun to work or accumulate wealth, then his widow would be left totally
> dependent of his affines. In addition to this many such widows would be
> childless which would increase their lowly status within their affinal family
> … In fact, in those days (fifty years ago) it was rare for a woman to take *diks*
> who had not previously been married. (1985a: 269)

Today, for most, nunhood is a highly esteemed vocational choice
within the Terapanthi community. And within the monastic organization, women are given opportunities that would not be available to them
in household life. Because of their long training at the PSS, for example, the nuns receive much more formal education than do their lay sisters. In addition, they tend to be much more 'book' educated than the
monks. But the nuns were quick to remind me that the knowledge the
monks learn at Guru Dev's feet is far more valuable. Although there
have been many important changes for Terapanthi nuns, the lay community still tends to regard them as devoted followers, more than powerful teachers.

Nuns are aligned with the devotional element of monastic life, and
dominate in its practices. This provides them with a visible and important function in monastic life, but it is in the realm of *bhakti* that the

position of nuns is most clearly seen as an extension of the house-holder's life. Devotion is the domain of the nuns because they are con-sidered to be 'natural' devotees. Surrender, sacrifice, and nurture are natural attributes of the ideal woman (Jain, 1996). Thus, it is in their sta-tus as devotees that they are *both* elevated and devalued; praised and per-manently subordinated. Devotion is expected of them; it is considered a normal rather than extraordinary attribute as it is with monks. Being a *bhakta* (devotee) is like being a *pativrata* (devoted wife) in that the vir-tues associated with both (devotion, self-surrender, self-sacrifice) are assumed to be natural to women. The monks, reflecting dominant patri-archal notions, generally consider nuns to be better devotees because of their 'emotional natures.' For example, the following are some observa-tions made by the monks:

- 'Monks are more rational.'
- 'Nuns make better devotees because they are not so argumentative as monks.'
- 'Women are more emotional than men, they cry more, for instance. This can be very bad for they can be dominated by their emotions. But for spiritual women, this means that they make excellent devotees.'
- 'They don't ask as many questions, they accept what the guru says.'
- 'Women make better devotees because they are more accepting and are fol-lowers.'

Nuns do not typically explain their superior 'devoteeship' in terms of being more 'emotional' – though when asked, most did accept this to be true. Instead they tend to emphasize positive values. The following are some observations made by the nuns:

- 'Women are more compassionate than men.'
- 'Women are more caring.'
- 'Nuns do not challenge as much because we accept what our guru says is right.'
- 'Women can endure more than men.'
- 'Women are kinder.'
- 'Nuns care more about others. Men can be selfish.'

Reflecting pan-Indian ideas of womanhood, nuns are considered bet-ter devotees because they are more emotional, less stubborn, and more nurturing. This idea is also advanced (by both *sadhvis* and *munis*) to explain their greater numbers in the order. Therefore, the fact that they outnumber the monks by over three to one is not generally perceived as a source of potential power, as Holmstrom suggested. Instead, it is simply seen as reflecting women's devotional/emotional natures. Rather than interpreting renunciation as a challenge to the orthodox feminine norm of marriage and childbearing, it is in many ways seen as an extension of it – even by nuns themselves.

Even in monastic life, though she has renounced family, marriage, and childbirth, the *sadhvi* is still evaluated according to the *pativrata* virtues of devotion, surrender, and self-sacrifice. These traditional virtues prescribed for women are not substituted for but rather supplemented with values more accordant with those of the ascetic ideal (i.e., detachment, independence). Asceticism therefore is not a negation of traditional feminine values, it is an extension of them. Although devotion is expected of all in the order, its alignment with emotions is ever-present. Male devotion, because it is not believed to come easily or naturally, is seen to represent extraordinary humility. For the nuns, it is commonplace and 'natural.' As a result, devotion serves as both a creative and conservative force in the nuns' lives; it allows them to play an active and pivotal role in monastic life, but it aligns them permanently with their bodies, emotions, and attachment.

Guru Dev's Divinity

At the morning birthday celebrations, the *samanis* sang proudly. The enthusiasm in their voices revealed their zeal and several among them were truly gifted singers. When they finished and returned to where they had been sitting, Guru Dev took the microphone again. He waved his long arms first in the direction of the *sadhvis* and *samanis,* and then towards the *munis* and *samans.* He spoke of pride in his disciples, whose path is the most difficult of all, but who tread it admirably. His speech was animated and full of good humour. Laughter came easily to the enthusiastic and adoring crowd. Today, he had 'gifts' for his ascetics. Before him, in a large pot, were great quantities of delicious sweets of all varieties. He beckoned his disciples to come. Laughter and smiles abounded; the serious ascetics were exuberant as they each went up to receive a sweet. The *mumukshus,* since they are still householders and not part of the receiving group, could only watch. But they appeared to share in the joy anyhow.

The ceremony had already gone on for several hours and would continue again in the afternoon with talks more specifically to do with the Anuvrat movement. But many had other plans: namely to visit Guru Dev's birthplace. I decided to follow a group of *mumukshu* sisters as they headed towards his home in the centre of Ladnun.

The house in which Guru Dev was born and grew up (until he took initiation on 5 December 1925 at the age of eleven) has now become a Terapanthi pilgrimage site. No one lives there anymore, but the building is maintained by the community. Most days it remains quiet, frequented only by a few devotees, but on this day it was crowded. Although I knew the story of Guru Dev's birth very well, and the *mumukshus* knew that I knew it well, I listened earnestly as they told it again with ebullience upon entering the old building. Mumukshu Promika gestured as she spoke, 'When Guru Dev's mother became pregnant – oooof!!' She flung both hands forward, fingers outstretched, as if describing an explosion, 'She knew he was different.'

We walked through the heavy iron gates of the house and entered a small, unlit landing. At one time, this area would have led to the courtyard, but now it was closed off. Only one room remained accessible; the room in which on 20 October 1914 Guru Dev Tulsi was born.

We stepped from the dark, grey stone landing into a bright, colourful room, crowded with photos and mural paintings of Guru Dev. There were photos of him as a young adult. In one photo he was without the *muhpatti*, and I couldn't stop staring at the large, white teeth and perfect smile of a man in his twenties. Another showed Guru Dev and a group of monks in a boat on a river! I looked to the *mumukshus* to explain such un-ascetic behaviour. It was an exceptional time, they told me, when the monks were being physically threatened by a hostile community, and their lives were in danger. Only by taking a boat could they be assured safety. I found it odd that the photo should have ended up in this pilgrimage site. Objects belonging to Guru Dev when he was a child were, like the photos, encased behind glass – the crib in which he lay, clothing that he had worn. Over the spot where he was born was a larger-than-life mural of a reclining woman with her eyes shut, dressed in a red sari. It took up the whole back wall. It was of Guru Dev's mother. Promika continued,

When his mother became pregnant she had many auspicious dreams. One night she dreamt of a god's beautiful golden chariot flying over her home. And then she dreamt of *kum kum* footprints [footprints made out of red powder] on the roof of her house, as if the god had stepped out of his chariot there. When she woke, she was startled by her dream. Immediately she climbed to the roof and there she found the *kum kum* marks!

The archetypal, auspicious 'dreams of the mother' are treated with respect and awe in Jainism, as they are indicative of future greatness. They are a regular part of all the Tirthankaras' and Kevalins' lives. The dreams of Bhagavan Mahavira's mother (Queen Trishala) are best known. She 'felt an unprecedented joy on the night of her conceiving the child. She saw a series of significant dreams in a half-waking state' (Tulsi, 1995: 12). She woke her husband and said, 'I saw an elephant and a bull and several other things in my dream. I feel a very pleasant sensation. The whole atmosphere seems to be throbbing with light and joy' (12). A soothsayer was called to decipher the Queen's dreams. He then presented himself to the king and said:

> The queen has seen very significant dreams. She will give birth to a son who will be a ... *dharma-cakravarti*, the Emperor of the Kingdom of religion, and will develop the ideals of *ahimsa*, freedom, relativism, co-existence and non-possessiveness. He will be a great exponent of these. (13)

Clearly, the birth of Guru Dev was not like that of an ordinary person; it, like the birth of Lord Mahavira, had a divine mark on it. He was destined for greatness.

I should like to have stayed longer in the room where Guru Dev was born and hear more about his life, but today there were many devotees waiting to come in for a visit. We headed back towards the monastery. Pictures of Guru Dev were in full force, lining the walls of the street and dangling from homes and shop windows.

Bhakti is treated as an alternate answer to the *sannyasi's* quest for the authentic self. The latter is the way of cognitive reason; the former is based on the human psychic resource: feeling emotions to judge the spurious from the authentic. According to Professor A.N. Pandeya, *bhakti marg* and *moksa marg* have been the two dominant paths in Indian culture (Pandeya, 1996, pers. comm.). *Bhakti* is rooted in the human experience of authentic belief and emotion which takes one away from the individual ego, enlarging one's range of concern to empathize with, and to merge in, the other – like falling in love. The model is from everyday experience, and uses the human emotion of love as the vehicle to realize the authentic self. To plumb the depths of human emotion is liberating because it allows total self-forgetfulness; it enables one to be totally free from ego. As such, the goal is the same as that of the ascetic path. *Moksa marg* and *bhakti marg* are treated as two parallel ways of authentication and discrimination, with *bhakti* the easier and more democratic path in that it does not require a special skill, only love. Ascetics are considered to be an elite, the 'talented few' to use Kakar's words. But, as I have argued throughout this chapter, within the Terapanthi ascetic order, an individual becomes an ascetic via both paths concomitantly: ascetics are made through a process in which they are progressively detached from 'worldly life' (or where worldliness is objectified, reified, and then exiled) and simultaneously attached, via devotion, to the order, guru, rules, hierarchy, and the like. Sadhvi Visrut Vipaji describes the ascetic path this way:

> We are so lucky to be his devotees. Otherwise why not stay in society? [Monastic] vows are adopted by people who are keen to uplift their souls and sacrifice all worldly pleasures for its sake. For this purpose they have to renounce the life of a layperson, give up all possessions and all ties of worldly attachment. It is a thorny path and an ordinary person would not dare to undertake these rules and regulations. But those who follow this path lead a happy life. They always live free from any kind of tension. They are not worried about their future because they have dedicated their lives to their guru. Their guru takes care of them. It is the guru who thinks to develop the internal power of his disciples.

Devotion, divinity, and asceticism are not separate religious paths to achieve *moksa*, they represent intimate dimensions of the one path.

8

Conclusion: Ascetic Women –
The Link in the *Laukik* and *Lokottar*

Austerity and Purity

A group of householders entered the room in which Samani Urmilla and I sat talking. At first they stood back, perhaps not wanting to intrude, but Urmilla gestured to them to come closer. Among the group was a woman in her thirties dressed in an ornate red sari. Her face was tranquil, unlike those of the accompanying group who beamed with pride. They were a local family from Ladnun, and Urmilla appeared very familiar with them. The men in the group stood a few feet back as the women took turns touching Urmilla's feet, paying her homage. The woman in the fancy sari was at the end of a sixteen-day fast, during which she had consumed only boiled water. She was being honoured by her family (natal and affinal), who today would escort her as she visited the ascetics for their blessings. Tomorrow her husband would have a feast in her honour and many relatives and friends would attend.[1] The woman, adorned with splendid jewellery, was silent and kept her eyes lowered as her family spoke of her virtues. Among the group were two of her sisters-in-law, a brother and mother-in-law as well as her natal sister and mother. Urmilla said a few words directly to the honoured woman, but most of what she said was for our ears. She explained that the woman was very pious and a real *tapasvini* (heroic faster). Last year she had completed the very arduous *maskaman* fast of thirty-one days. It is considered to be one of the most difficult of the many genres of Jain fasts, and, as Reynell points out, most women do it only once in their lifetime, if at all (1985a: 191).

The mother of the celebrated woman was carrying a photo album cataloguing her daughter's fasts. She passed it to me for a quick look while

Urmilla spoke to the family. I had been shown many such albums before by women proud of their achievements. Reynell writes, 'The photos of the fast symbolize the woman's continued purity of conduct after marriage, showing that she has proved worthy of wifehood within her affinal family and has brought them only honour and prestige' (1985a: 194). It was a particularly thick photo album, documenting several different fasts over a period of ten years. In one photo, the daughter was among a large group of women, all equally adorned with beautiful jewellery and ornate saris. Surrounded by a large audience of householders, they stood before Guru Dev with their heads lowered to receive his blessing.

Glancing at the photo I was looking at, Urmilla said, 'I have a niece who completed the same fast. She is just eleven years old and a real *tapasvini*! She wants to take *diksa*. Everyone can see she is very pure.'

Turning back to the family, Urmilla raised her hand as she gave them a blessing. The woman at the centre of the attention bowed deeply at her feet, prostrating herself so as to press her eyes against Urmilla's large toe – an auspicious and respectful act. She then left with her family to receive blessings from other *samanis* at the residence.

When we were alone again, Urmilla confided, 'I cannot fast so long. I become sick,' she said holding onto her head. 'Some *shravaks* are very pure; even more spiritual than us.'

Continuity vs. Rupture

Remarks like those that Urmilla made to me are not rare. Parallels are commonly drawn between the religiosity of lay and ascetic women. Both can be compared and even equated because their religious practices are analogous. Whether demonstrating suitability for the ascetic life or establishing female honour, the methods are the same: withdrawal from worldly activities, restrained bodily demeanour, and the performance of austerities. Practices of bodily renunciation demonstrate proper gender socialization as well as ascetic suitability; the behavioural expectations of lay women and *sadhvis* remain constant. For both lay and ascetic women, social legitimacy is sought through their *behavioural purity*. Balbir likewise grants that the preoccupation with female physical chastity 'to some extent removes the boundary between a woman in the world and a woman outside the world' (1994: 126). It is radically different for men, in that male gender socialization does not prepare them for a life in which controlled bodily comportment is of paramount importance. Indeed, male lay and ascetic lives call for competing and even contrary demands. I suggest that the gendered universes from which women and men 'opt out' are centrally implicated in the type of stance they take vis-à-vis the ascetic ideal.

Denial, difference, rejection, transformation, change – these are some of the idioms of renunciation used to define a process of un-doing which makes *diksa* so spectacular and makes the ascetic a symbol of otherness. For women, their denial of the world is more circumscribed than it is for men, and the fabric of their ascetic lives is less a renunciation than an extension of what came before. The religious lives of lay women is essentially ascetic in its ethos but – significantly – its renunciatory practices are expressed in terms of requirements in the management of female nature, reflecting a woman's need to restrain her body, not a will to renounce the world.

Women, because of their association with sexuality, corporeality, emotional bonds, and family ties, have always represented an obstacle to India's ascetic traditions (Goldman, 1991). Both the veneration and the vilification of women are centred on their physicality. As a symbol of attachment, she is condemned and portrayed as the greatest threat to ascetic discipline; as a symbol of fidelity, she is extolled for her celibacy and devotion. Jain stories involving women centre on these dualistic themes: women play the roles of the seductive temptress or the faithful *pativrati* (see Granoff, 1993). Devout queens, nurturing mothers, prostitutes, and temptresses – women serve as foils against which ascetic values can be demonstrated.

In the public ideology and religious imagination of Jainism, women are more closely associated with 'the worldly,' making their acts of renunciation less absolute and more ambiguous. Ascetic women are perceived as mediating between the worldly and the transcendent, as 'liminal' beings within the Jain moral universe. As symbols of renunciation *and* attachment, ascetic women represent the link in the *laukik* and the *lokottar.*

Sectarian Differences and Female Nature

The question of female religiosity represents one of the central differences between the Digambar and Svetambar Jain traditions and reveals ancient and deeply entrenched cultural beliefs about female nature. According to Digambar tenets, a woman is of inferior religious status to a man due to her anatomy – in particular, her reproductive system –

which is considered to be inherently violent (Jaini, 1991), and due to her mind which is considered to be of a fickle and deceitful nature (Reynell, 1984). Because of these 'innate flaws,' the Digambar argue that liberation can never be achieved from a female body – that a woman would have to be reborn as a man before liberation could occur (Jaini, 1991). The Svetambar tradition likewise holds that the female body is flawed and that to be born female is evidence of the sin of deceitfulness (Reynell, 1984: 21; Banks, 1997: 225–6). However, it does not deny women the possibility of liberation. Renunciation via a female body may be an encumbered process, it claims, but not an impossible one. The Svetambar's version of the story of the nineteenth Tirthankara 'Malli' (or, alternatively, Mallinath) reveals its ambivalence about female spirituality. It claims that, unique among the twenty-four Tirthankaras, Malli was female. The Digambar deny this possibility, and argue that all souls that have attained *moksa* were liberated from male bodies. The Svetambar belief, in spite of its position of ostensible gender equality, does not refute negative claims about women. Instead, in a circuitous way, it supports them. Reynell writes:

> The story goes that Mallinath, the female Tirthankara, was, in a previous birth, a Prince called Mahabal. He renounced the world together with six friends. His strict religious practices incorporated the twenty deeds necessary for accumulating Tirthankara Karma. However, he commits one small sin. He and his friend had vowed that they would all perform exactly the same penances. However, to accumulate more merit, Mahabal prolongs his fast by making excuses as to why he cannot break the fasts, when the allotted time to do so arrives. Through this deceitful action he does longer penances than his friends, but in the process he accumulates Striveda, namely that karma which leads to rebirth as a woman. His prior accumulation of Tirthankara karma destines him for birth as a Tirthankara. The fact that he is born also as a woman is almost accidental – a punishment for a sin committed at the last moment. In this way the existence of Mallinath serves rather to detract from female religious status rather than to support it by reaffirming the insidious association between women and sin. (1984: 24–5)

This debate over female religiosity, which is over two thousand years old, forms part of a more general dispute over ascetic practice. The Svetambar (white-clad) tradition claims that nudity is not essential for mendicancy and that the white garment worn by ascetics is not an obstacle to liberation. The Digambar (sky-clad) tradition, by contrast, asserts that the practice of nudity is essential for a Jain ascetic in order to fulfil the vows of nonattachment and nonpossession. Moreover, since nudity is 'unacceptable' for women, the Digambar concludes that women cannot attain salvation. Dundas writes that

> By establishing a direct connection between the fact that a woman cannot go naked and the affirmation of nudity as sine qua non condition for the attainment of emancipation, Kundakunda put forward the central argument of a debate that subsequently became a locus communis of the Digambar/Svetambar doctrinal rivalry, which has continued to the present day. (1992: 131)

The practical outcome of these theoretical debates is that among the Digambar, as with most ascetic traditions in India, women are denied full monastic vows and thereby are incapable of representing the tradition's highest cultural ideal.[2] In the Svetambar Jain tradition, by contrast, female asceticism has a long, stable, and even illustrious history. According to the scriptures, since the time of Rsabh (Jainism's first Tirthankara of mythic times), nuns have always outnumbered monks by more than two to one. Lord Mahavir, the last Tirthankara of our era, and a historical figure (599–527 BCE), is said to have had 36,000 nuns and 14,000 monks as disciples (Dundas, 1992: 49). Reynell writes:

> In view of the prevailing Hindu attitudes to women during the period in which the Svetambar sect arose, and in view of the influence of these ideas of new non Hindu religious groups, the Svetambar attitude is quite exceptional in that it went against the grain of contemporary thought. The Svetambars state that women are the religious equals to men and can attain enlightenment in their own right through religious action. As a result they recognize an order of female ascetics who are considered on a par with the monks. (1984: 7)

Theoretically, nuns are 'on a par with the monks,' as Reynell writes, but empirically, as well as on the level of symbolism, they are subordinate. Although the Svetambar and Digambar are often depicted as opposites with respect to their views on female religiosity, the ideas they share in common are as important as those on which they differ. Both hold the same negative understanding of a female nature as flawed, associated with sexuality and sin. The vigour and persistence of these ideas inform practices of gender socialization and form the basis of a religious imagination which rejects the female form as a symbol of renunciation.

The Gendered *Laukik* and Its Repercussions for the Ascetic Ideal

The Construction of Femininity

The world from which women and men 'opt out' is very differently gendered, with very different repercussions for their ability to represent the highest cultural ideal. The way in which women and men are produced as gendered beings in patrilineal, patrilocal Jain society results in renunciation being a *process of extension* for women, and heroic *rupture* for men.[3] The social environment out of which a woman 'opts out' in order to pursue asceticism is characterized by confinement to the domestic domain and by 'religious' practices centred on the management of her sexuality. Dube, in her essay on the construction of gender in India, shows how the body is the axis around which gender socialization occurs:

> The phenomenon of boundary maintenance is a crucial element in the definition of the cultural apprehension of the vulnerability of young girls and the emphasis on their purity and restraint in behaviour. This is expressed in the construction of 'legitimate' and 'proper' modes of speech, demeanour, and behaviour for young girls and in the organization of their space and time. (1988: 15)

And:

> Considerable importance is attached to the way a girl carries herself, the way she sits, stands and talks, and interacts with others. A girl should walk with soft steps: so soft that they are barely audible to others. Taking long strides denotes masculinity. Girls are often rebuked for jumping, running, rushing to a place and hopping. These movements are considered part of masculine behaviour, unbecoming to a female; however, the logic of the management of a girl's sexuality also defines them as unfeminine; they can bring the contours of the body into greater prominence and attract people's attention. A girl has to be careful about her posture. She should not sit cross-legged or with her legs wide apart. Keeping one's knees close together while sitting, standing, or sleeping is 'decent'; and indicates a

sense of shame and modesty. 'Don't stand like a man' is a common rebuke
to make a girl aware of the demands of femininity. (16)

Female socialization occurs through the imposition of a set of behavioural norms and restrictions which call forth and imply sexuality; it
revolves around a process of the 'sexualization of the female body'
(Haug, 1987). The management of sexuality informs the organization
of a woman's space and time (e.g., *parda* norms) as well as explains her
predominance in religious activities. Religion becomes the primary
means through which female honour is both privately and publicly demonstrated. It is seen as 'an essential quality of womanhood' (Reynell,
1985a: 68), and therefore, a girl's religious education begins early. Reynell writes that from the age of five a girl is instructed in religious stories
and is taught the fundamentals of Jainism by a female family member.
After the age of ten she fasts, learns the minute details about food limitations, alms giving, the *pratikraman* and *samayik* rituals, and is expected
to visit the nuns regularly (69). Reynell writes:

> [B]etween the two sexes, it is the women who are most heavily involved in
> religious activity ... [F]ieldwork results show that in terms of regular tem-
> ple going, the performance of *samayik* and *pratikraman*, the attendance of
> preachings and pujas and the observance of food restrictions, women are
> considerably more assiduous and regular in their practice than men. Fast-
> ing in particular seems to have become a female sphere of influence and
> most of the orthodox Jain women undertake quite long and complex fasts,
> regularly, which gains them both status and public admiration from the
> rest of the community. (1984: 28)

For example, the behavioural code of conduct, called the *chauda nyem*
(fourteen principles) is meant as a guideline for all Jains to follow but,
in practice, is observed almost exclusively by women. It is women who
restrict their consumption of green vegetables and fruit, who limit the
number of clothes they wear and the geographical space they move in
(see pages 93–4). Through such essentially renunciatory practices, Jain
women demonstrate their purity and honour. Holmstrom writes:

> [W]omen are perceived as the embodiment of another power, that of *sakti*,
> 'energizing principle of the universe' (Wadley 1977: 115). Both men and
> women contain *sakti*, both can increase or decrease it by specific means

including *tap*, 'heat,' but it is women who are seen as embodying *sakti* and in Hindu ideology femaleness is thus a representation of *sakti*. *Sakti* is the active power of creation; without this action, this dynamic creation cannot continue; the gods without their female consorts representing *sakti* cannot act. Women then, as uncontrolled power, are sexual beings; yet while their fertility is vital to men, in that they are *powerful* they are dangerous, they sap men's energy, they must be controlled ... They must therefore be 'cooled' (it is not for Jains the *sakti* itself which is ritually 'hot,' but the emotional energy which the power of *sakti* generates that endows women with an inner heat) (Reynell, 1985: 155). Hence the social roles available to women are centred upon this idiom of the married wife and mother of sons, defined and controlled by men, and who is therefore *channelling her inherent powers into the prosperity and well-being of her family* (Hershman 1977, Reynell 1985). (Holmstrom, 1988: 5; emphasis in original)

Lay and ascetic women are constructed as moral beings through renunciatory practices: both lay and ascetic women fast in order to demonstrate, with their bodies, their piety and honour. Reynell has demonstrated that women's religiosity is intimately construed as an extension of the nurturing role of wife and mother (Reynell, 1984, 1985a; Holmstrom, 1988: 28). In the religious imagination, the connection between female religiosity and the *pativrati* (faithful wife and mother) is so intimate that even when female religiosity reaches its acme – in the form of renunciation – the connection is not severed; it is enlarged. Holmstrom writes on ascetics:

> *Diksa* can then be seen as analogous (in that young women see it as a choice in life opposed) to marriage, and as a further extension of it, in that it is a channelling of *sakti* not for one husband but for the (male oriented) Jain community at large. (1988: 29)

The world that female ascetics stand outside of is not the abstract *laukik*; it is the narrowly circumscribed domestic domain of marriage and motherhood. Their rejection of marriage and motherhood might appear to represent a challenge to the dominant female ideology of the *pativrati*, but in practice, ascetic women operate inside, not outside, the same ideological parameters that define lay women. The following is a well-known story, told to me several times by the nuns, which demonstrates the association of female religiosity and sexual purity, as well as the view that treats a woman's decision to renounce the world as a natural progression from lay piety:

> A youth named Buddhadas from Champanagri saw Subhadra on a visit to Basantpur and was so attracted by her beauty and the serenity of her countenance that he collected information about her. He was happy to learn that she was still unmarried. However, he learned that her father was determined to give her away in marriage to a Jain family. Buddhadas belonged to a family of Buddhist tradition, and so he decided to disguise himself as a Jain house-holder. One day, he orchestrated an 'accidental meeting' with Jindas, the girl's father. Finding Buddhadas a capable youth and devout Jain, Jindas gave Subhadra to him in marriage. But when Buddhadas returned to Champanagari with Subhadra, he threw away his adopted guise of a Jain youth, because its purpose was served.
>
> When Subhadra came to know she had been deceived, she was stunned and hurt, but, because of her inner strength, faced the situation boldly and courageously. As the only Jain in a Buddhist family, she was taunted and ridiculed, but she held her head high and kept her religious resolve.
>
> One day a Jain monk came to Buddhadas's house to collect alms. Subhadra gave him alms joyfully. When he was leaving, however, she noticed tears falling from his eyes due to a straw stuck in his eye. Practicing detachment, the monk ignored the pain, but Subhadra could not bear it. She went to him and drew the straw out with her tongue. Her mother-in-law, who witnessed the incident, yelled at her, 'You have blemished our home by your indecency! You boast of your Jain religion; does your religion promote lewdness?' The whole family was furious and tried to convert her to Buddhism, yet she remained devoted to the Jain religion.
>
> When the news spread to others in the city, the situation worsened and Subhadra felt dejected. Instead of fearing the blemish on her own name, though, she worried that the Jain religion and its practitioners were being condemned wrongly because of her. She restrained herself a great deal and kept firm faith in her religion and chastity. She decided to abstain from food and drink until she cleared herself of the false charges, and absorbed herself in chanting Namaskaar Mahamantra.
>
> On the fourth day of her fast, all the four gates of Champanagari jammed mysteriously and all efforts to open them were in vain. Because all the roads to go out from the city were blocked, the inhabitants were worried. All of a sudden, a divine voice exclaimed, 'Citizens! Your efforts are in vain! Only if a chaste woman, having tied a sieve with a thin thread, draws water from the

well, and sprinkles it on the doors, can they be opened.' The voice created much discussion and deliberation among the women of the city. Some women appeared to have confidence in their chastity but doubted whether their efforts would open the door. If the door didn't open, a woman was likely to be branded as unchaste. Though most women opted not to participate because of the dilemma, a few with enough courage went to the well, tied the sieve with a thread but could not draw any water.

When Subhadra heard of the city's problem and the suggested solution to it, she thought to herself, 'What an excellent opportunity for me to get rid of the blemish wrongly cast upon me.' She said to her mother-in-law, 'If you allow me, I may go and open the door,' to which the mother-in-law looked at her with widened eyes and said, 'O wretched woman! Do you want a further defamation on our family? Have you forgotten how you acted so immodestly with that monk?' Subhadra was quiet for a moment and then again requested. When her mother-in-law did not answer, Subhadra concluded she was not protesting.

Though people stared at her with suspicious eyes as she approached the well, she paid them no heed and resolutely tied the sieve with a thin thread, mentally recited the Namaskaar Mahamantra and drew the water, which she sprinkled on three of the gates. They immediately opened. She left one closed, with the idea that if any other woman should ever be required to prove her chastity, that door would be for her.

After the event, Subhadra was given much acclaim. When Buddhadas and his family learned what happened, they all apologized and felt proud to have Subhadra as a member of their household. They adopted the Jain religion. Eventually, Subhadra became a Jain nun and attained liberation from all worldly bondages. (paraphrased from Sadhvi Visrut Vibha's [1994] story 'Chastity')

Leaving aside its negative commentary on Buddhism, the story presents the journey from lay life to nunhood as a natural progression for the pious Subhadra; it conveys a sense of continuity between the *laukik* and *lokottar* for women. In addition – and importantly – it demonstrates the importance of female sexual honour and the role of religion in establishing it.

Female renunciation does not constitute gender transgression. Instead, the women's power comes from laying claim to the female virtues of chastity and restraint and adopting them fully, thereby constructing themselves as symbols of purity par excellence.

The Construction of Masculinity

The *sadhvis*' experience of 'continuity' from lay life contrasts sharply with the monks' experience of 'rupture' and, consequently, with the male relationship to the ascetic ideal. Many of the monks of the Terapanthi order claimed that their knowledge about spiritual matters only began with *diksa*. And several spoke of the piety of their mothers as being an important factor in their decision to renounce. As boys they would observe, but not participate in, domestic religious practices. This reflects a common feature of Jain life, namely that lay men, for the most part, are far less familiar with religious matters than women (see Babb, 1996: 23; Reynell, 1985a). Men's relative ignorance is explained in terms of the gendered division of labour, which involves men in the public domain. Babb writes:

> There is a basic division of labor among temple-going Svetambar Jains: women fast, while men – too immersed in their affairs to do serious fasting – make religious donations (*dana*; in Hindi, *dan*). (1996: 25)

Reynell's research corroborates this:

> In Jain eyes, male work precludes men from extensive involvement in regular religious activity for it is important that all their time and energy should be invested in their business. By contrast, the woman, confined to the domestic sphere, is perceived by the menfolk to have more free time which she can devote to religion. (1985a: 125)

Thus, lay male religiosity and honour are demonstrated through 'performances' in the public domain. It is not centred on bodily management or behavioural practices as it is with women. Reynell writes:

> Men must also demonstrate a degree of moral uprightness, but this is accomplished less through actual behaviour and more through using their wealth in a particular way. Consequently, there is less scrutiny of their actual daily behaviour, whereas for a woman the converse is true. They continuously demonstrate their honour, and that of their family, through their behaviour, which must be impeccable. In particular, it is through their religious activities that they express their moral worth to the community. (1985a: 162–3)

Male religiosity is demonstrated through outward religious acts, most quintessentially through public charitable giving *(dan)*, which, to the Jain community, signifies a state of inner detachment and moral purity (Reynell, 1985: 165). Reynell describes female *tap* (fasting) and male *dan* (donations) as 'structural equivalents' (194). Both are concerned with family honour and with the valorization of the ascetic ideal, and both are public affairs. But their methods differ. Women's religiosity is fundamentally *deportmental or behavioural*, centred on bodily practices, whereas male religiosity is *performative*, centred on things they do in the public domain.

When a man renounces the world, he renounces the common male orientation, which is outward and worldly. In effect, he 'opts out' of the public domain.[4] There is no question of an extension of lay practices into the ascetic life. Instead, there is a sharp break with the religiosity of the 'public theatre' and, interestingly, a redirection of religiosity to focus on his bodily behaviour.

The Paradigm of Female Religiosity

Centred as it is on behavioural restraint and withdrawal from worldly life, Jain asceticism can be seen as modelled after *female* religiosity: ascetics must take care in walking, speaking, picking things up, and laying them down; they must be concerned with sexual purity, self-control, the minutiae of *ahimsa*, and 'questions of ingestion' (Banks, 1997: 229), and they should always display restraint and modesty (see Jaini, [1979] 1990: 248). Ideal ascetic behaviour corresponds with standard feminine virtues, and yet asceticism remains quintessentially a male ideal. Why this is may simply reflect an asymmetry in the cultural evaluations of male and female activities whereby male activities are, ipso facto, recognized as more important (Rosaldo, 1974: 19), but it must also reflect the fact that the *drama of renunciation* – so central to the valorization of the ascetic ideal – is largely absent in the case of female renunciation. The continuity of female religiosity across the *laukik/lokottar* boundary undermines its drama. Male renunciation represents a break with worldly life in a manner that female renunciation does not. It is the very absence of continuity (or, the creation of difference) that establishes men as renunciants. The break or rupture with the former householder life is the important thing symbolically. The fact that female renunciation is perceived as more of a continuation rather than a renunciation of lay religiosity has important and negative implications for women as symbols of the *lokottar.* Women remain associated with the worldly realm and are thus hindered from becoming cultural heroes.

The Heroism of Asceticism

The role of heroism in constituting what Babb calls the 'worship worthiness' (1996: 62) of ascetics should not be underestimated. It is the extraordinary nature of asceticism that fuels the worship of the ascetic and the glorification of renunciation. Asceticism must be perceived as an accomplishment to elicit the reverence it does. For men, it is a bold and heroic achievement. For women, it is less so, for both socioeconomic and ideological reasons.[5] External socioeconomic factors continue to motivate some women to take *diksa,* which undermines its heroism. Although today the majority of female renunciants chose asceticism as a deliberate, and often hard-fought-for, vocation (as was the case among my study group; see also Reynell, Shântâ, Holmstrom), the association of asceticism with an institution of refuge for unmarriageable women persists (see note 10, chapter 7). For instance, Padmanabh Jaini's study published in 1979 states that the majority of Jain female mendicants are widows ([1979] 1990: 247). Jaini's claim may simply reflect a common association in the Indian imagination of female ascetics with widows (Clementin-Ojha, 1988: 34), or, as Reynell suggests, it may reflect a social reality that is no longer widespread (see Cort, 1991b: 660; Holmstrom, 1988: 23–4; Goonasekera, 1986: 88). Reynell states that

> Nowadays, with the rise in the age of marriage, women are more likely to have given birth to children by the time they are widowed. This, together with the lifting of restrictions of widows' behaviour and dress, serves to militate against widows taking *diksa* quite as readily as they seem to have done previously. (1985a: 269)

A more germane and critical reason why renunciation is perceived as – and to some extent is – a form of refuge for women is rooted in the ruinous demands of the contemporary dowry system. In the lay (largely business) Jain community, a daughter's dowry is a crucial status indicator. Reynell writes:

> This creates considerable problems for the less well off Jain families who, unlike the middle income and wealthy families, are not able to open

deposit accounts for their daughters to save the required cash over the years. Such families usually only have an income of 6000 rupees a year. All of this incoming cash is used for subsistence and it is extremely difficult to save the required 50,000 rupees which is the minimum cost of a respectable wedding. Nor does the financial outlay end with marriage, as throughout a married daughter's life the parents are expected to provide gifts at various festive occasions. Thus dowry is, in a sense, a life long obligation. (1985a: 265)

Reynell suggests that although the prospect of financial distress may motivate a young woman to enter monastic life, it is difficult to prove, 'as no nun will admit to the dishonour of family poverty as a reason for taking *diksa*' (266). Reynell lists physical deformity and sexuality impurity as other possible 'external factors' motivating female renunciation, both of which would lessen a girl's chance at finding a marriage partner. In unpropitious situations, therefore, renunciation may present itself as a 'way out.' Reynell states:

A woman who is unmarriageable is a problem in that spinsterhood is virtually unacceptable, not only within the Jain community but within India as a whole. In the Jain case it is a problem, firstly, in financial terms in that women cannot work in the conservative small towns and villages. If a woman does not get married, she becomes an economic burden to her father and then to her brothers, who will have their own wives and children to support. Secondly, her moral and sexual purity will also be questioned. Where marriage is not possible, nunhood is a viable solution in that it removes a woman from financial dependence and restores her reputation to one of inviolable purity. (1985a: 264)

In such cases, it is worldly life that 'renounces' women, not the other way around. Though such cases may be few, they have a powerful and negative effect on the status of female renunciation in the social imagination. Even among contemporary nuns, the majority of whom choose nunhood as a vocation, asceticism represents an alternative to, or escape from, marriage. On the Terapanthi nuns, Holmstrom states:

[N]ow it is overwhelmingly younger women who, after their studies, take *diksa* as an oppositional choice to marriage – the reason nearly all gave, from the oldest to the youngest, was to escape the 'bondage' (*bandhan*, the same word as that of the soul enmeshed in *karm*) of marriage. (1988: 24)

As long as female asceticism is perceived as a refuge from, as opposed to renunciation of, worldly life, the raw materials for public heroism are limited. Thus, these external socioeconomic factors contribute to the popular view in India that asceticism is fundamentally a noble vocation for men (Clementin-Ojha, 1988: 34), but a sanctuary of last resort for women.

Ambiguous Symbols

Throughout the book I have argued that the ideological split between the worldly and the transcendent – between the *laukik* and *lokottar* – is fundamental to an understanding of Jainism. Although interaction and interdependence characterize the relationship between *shravaks* and *sadhvis/sadhus* in their day-to-day life, it does not undermine the significance of the ideological rupture. Jainism esteems renunciation above all else, and ascetics are its cultural heroes. Babb considers the worship of ascetics to be 'the most important fact about Jain ritual culture' (1996: 23). The ascetic symbolizes the negation of worldly existence and a way out of *samsar* (the cycle of birth and death). Through their very beings they communicate the hope of salvation: for those with unyielding courage, liberation is possible. The ascetics are worshipped because they are extraordinary beings capable of doing what the majority cannot.

Renunciation is a momentous and creative act. Through it, the 'worldly' and the 'spiritual' are delineated. The ascetic, as a symbol of liberation, represents the triumph over the worldly. As I argued in chapter 4, renunciation establishes Jain identity negatively vis-à-vis the external world. Jain moral identity is defined in terms of what it is not, and the ascetics, as symbols of negation, interdiction, and restraint, reveal another way of being. As representatives of the spiritual ideal they must be seen as 'other' – as different from those engaged in *dharma marg* (the householder's path of duty) because *dharma marg* serves as a foil against which the ascetic ideal demonstrates itself. Renunciation is about making 'real' the ideological split between the *laukik* and the *lokottar*; it is about creating difference. In the religious imagination, the act of renouncing worldly life and all its components is at least as significant as the state of renunciation. And it is the male, because of the breach renunciation brings to his life, who publicly dramatizes renunciation best.

Rules governing female ascetics reveal their continued association with the worldly and their need to be under male control. Balbir cites the Chedasutras (law book dealing with monastic offences) on the proper behaviour of nuns:

A nun is not allowed to be alone. A nun is not allowed to enter alone the house of a layman for food or drink, or to go out from there alone. A nun is not allowed to enter alone a place to ease nature or a place for stay, or to go out from there alone. A nun is not allowed to be without clothing. A nun is not allowed to be without superior. A nun is not allowed to stand in [the ascetic posture called] kayotsarga. (1994: 199)

In practice, nuns are dependent on, and subordinate to, the authority of their male counterparts (Balbir, 1994; Cort, 1991b). So, for instance, the Sadhvi Pramukha (head nun) is subordinate to the Acharya (head monk) and it is only when no monks are present that nuns take over the responsibility of lecturing to householders (in practice this does occur very often due to the greater number of nuns). Ascetic institutions mirror the structure and values of the wider patriarchal society (see Babb, 1996: 54). Cort explains:

Within the *gacch* (ascetic order) one has the *samuday* (subdivision of the gacch) and the *parivar* (family, small group). The *samuday* corresponds to the family lineage, the *kutumb*, while the *sadhu parivar* corresponds to the *kutumb* in its smaller sense, the *parivar* or immediate family … All these units, both mendicant and lay, are defined by the male members: a woman is attached to her father's, and after marriage her husband's, *kutumb*; and the *sadhvis* are always attached to the *samuday* of a sadhu. In both forms of organization, the men have absolute primacy over the women. (1991b: 662)

Both practically and symbolically, ascetic women are less able to make use of their 'renounced lives' rhetorically in the construction of difference. They are less able to contrast the *lokottar* with the *laukik* because they do not have the tools to create difference. As discussed in chapter 4, renunciation can only effectively take place in a context of abundance; one cannot renounce what one never had. We see, therefore, that renunciation is intimately connected with power – and for those members of society without power (women, the poor), their ability to renounce is undermined. Boys renounce the promise of future power. When they take *diksa*, they sever ties to their natal home. They renounce the tangibles of their family name, the possibility of carrying on their family lineage, family property, and sexual pleasure – essential elements of lay male identity. In patrilineal, patriarchal Jainism, women cannot do the same. A girl has only temporary membership in her natal home, does not carry the family name, has no decision-making powers, no autonomy, and owns no property (Dube, 1988). Other than her dowry, at the time of marriage she retains nothing of her family's wealth. Her body is her only 'property,' which is given on her wedding day as the gift of a virgin (*kanya dan*) to her affines (Reynell, 1985a: 194). And, to establish sexual purity, ascetic women tend to deny, as oppose to renounce, sexual pleasure (see chapter 5). Thus, in the public ideology, women are perceived as having less to renounce than men.

Nuns are less able to make use of the idioms of the archetypal ascetic life – of solitary pilgrimage, detachment, independence, and homelessness – in the construction of themselves as cultural exemplars. For women who have renounced the world – i.e., renounced family ties, emotional bonds, and sexuality – and pursued the Jain ascetic ideal fully as renunciants, the shadow of the worldly realm still pursues them because their ascetic lives constitute an extension, rather than a rejection, of their lay religious lives. Symbolically women are prevented from wholly embodying worldly negation and 'difference.' They are not perceived as capable of severing ties to the worldly domain completely. Ironically, therefore, not only is female nature considered more closely tied to the worldly realm, but lay women's very strategies of religiosity – because they are unequivocally renunciatory – prevent ascetic women from making their act of renunciation a statement about difference. Ascetic women are only ambiguously symbols of 'difference' and 'otherness' – the very essence of the ascetic ideal.

The Power of the Inviolable

Ascetic women carry with them the feminine virtues of restraint and modesty from the domestic domain, but these virtues are redefined within the arena of asceticism as *samiti* – that is, as rules of conduct and self-regulation having to do with nonviolence and detachment.

Ironically, as *samiti*, their comportment is less restrained, giving them a degree of forthrightness and spontaneity that they previously lacked. They do not walk 'softly,' but stride confidently. They do not assume a demeanour of modesty around men; instead, when in conversation, they look at them directly and they speak authoritatively with women and men of all ages. These behaviours, normally considered 'outside the feminine norm,' are not seen as such, due to ascetic women's greater status. By laying claim to the virtues of restraint and purity which characterize the dominant female ideology, yet divorced from sexuality and the domestic domain, ascetic women become symbols of inviolable purity and power. They see themselves, and are seen by others, as cultural exemplars of purity.

Both marriage and nunhood control female sexuality and ensure morality and family honour. Both equate religiosity with behavioural purity, demonstrated through restrained body demeanour and austerities. However, whereas lay women's religious practices are associated with the management of female sexuality and are intimately associated with the role of the *pativrati* (Reynell, 1985a), ascetic women's practices are ostensibly outside the sphere of sexuality and are unequivocally self- or soul-oriented. Renunciation allows them to redefine renunciatory practices in terms of worldly detachment, instead of in terms of sexual management. The bodily restraint of nuns does not signify modesty and humility; it demonstrates spiritual advancement. Outside the sphere of sexuality and domesticity, women become symbols of purity and are objects of veneration for the whole Jain community.

Sitting in a half-circle around Urmilla was her sister Vivek, her mother, and a group of other lay women with whom I was not familiar. 'My mother has stopped looking for a boy for Vivek,' Urmilla said with a smile as I entered the room. All appeared cheerful and anticipated a response, but such subtlety was lost on me. Forever patient, Urmilla explained, 'Vivek will take *diksa.*'

In the conservative Jain families of Rajasthan, young women have essentially only two 'career' options: marriage and renunciation. The world that ascetic women renounce, therefore, is quintessentially that of married life; it is *samsar* in its most tangible form. Because *diksa* is perceived as an alternative to married life, the *laukik* is typically discussed in terms of the tangibles and bondage of married life: wifehood, motherhood, sex, childbirth, the *himsa* activities of cooking and cleaning. This makes it distinct from male renunciation: monks are far less likely to talk of their monkhood as a renunciation of the domestic particulars of the *laukik* – for example, of marriage and fatherhood. As discussed above, because renunciation is more meaningful in a context of abundance, men tend to emphasize that which they have given up, as opposed to that which they have escaped. The bondage which men renounce is therefore rhetorically presented as 'golden' (e.g., the fortune of wealth and sensuality). Women, on the other hand, renounce the concrete 'bondage' of marriage (Holmstrom, 1988: 24).

When I first met Vivek, nearly a year earlier, she was twenty-two years old and very ambivalent about her future. Neither marriage nor renunciation appealed strongly to her. Her eldest sister, now in her forties, was married with several children and living in Gujarat. The youngest of five girls, she was the only one whose future remained undecided. Her other three sisters, including Urmilla, had already taken *diksa*. She would often sigh and say, 'It is too difficult a choice.' Today, however, she appeared self-assured and certain.

'I have thought very hard. I decided I must not waste my life,' she said. And placing her hand on her chest, she added, 'I am doing this for myself.' Just as she understood *diksa* and marriage in oppositional terms, so too did she see her future as a choice between a life dedicated to others (husbands, in-laws, children) or a life dedicated to her own spirituality. The idiom of renunciation is unequivocally and unabashedly soul-centred, and nuns can avail of it every bit as easily as monks. Female asceticism represents a continuation of the female virtues of chastity and restraint, but, significantly, it also represents a renunciation of *stridharma* (gender duty), which emphasizes *sewa* (service) to, and sacrifice for, others. Religious practices are no longer observed for the welfare of family or to demonstrate sexual purity; they are for their own liberation. They take *diksa* for themselves.

Appendix 1
The Fourteen *Gunasthanas* (Stages of Spiritual Development)

1 Mithyadrsti (perverted belief)	Non-Jain
2 Sasvadana samyagdrsti (lingering relish of right belief)	
3 Samyagmithyadrsti (right-cum-wrong belief)	Mixed View
4 Aviratisamyagdrsti (right belief attended with nonabstinence)	Laity
5 Desavirata (right belief with partial abstinence)	Laity
6 Pramatta (self-restraint unexempted from remissness)	Ascetic
7 Apramattasamyata (self-restraint with freedom from remissness)	
8 Nivrtti (dissimilar coarse passions)	Removal of Passions
9 Anivrttibadara (similar coarse passions)	
10 Suksmasamparay (subtle passions)	
11 Upasanta (subsidence of delusion)	Removal of Deluding Karma
12 Ksinamoha (extirpation of delusion)	
13 Samyogi (omniscience with actvities)	
14 Ayogikevalinah (omniscience with total cessation of activities)	Emancipation

Source: Tulsi (1985: 133–4) for list on left. The summaries on the right were commentaries from the ascetics.

Appendix 2
Rules and Regulations in the Ascetic Life

The following are some examples of rules that the *samanis* are obliged to observe, as well as some questionnaires they must respond to and submit to the *acharya*. They demonstrate how their lives are structured, scrutinized, and compared.

Daily life:
- Wake up by 4 a.m.; sleep after 9 p.m.
- Sleep side by side, lined up according to seniority
- Get permission to leave building
- Inform group leader or niojika of all activities
- Do *pratikraman,* arhat vandana in group daily
- Involve self in *pratikraman,* meditation, *jap* for 3 hours/day
- Do *swadhi* daily (memorization of texts)*
- Do vandana to elders
- General meeting with all samanis every 2 weeks
- Get permission to wash clothes, alms, water, meeting male shravaks or monks

Keep diary :
Written details about day-to-day life (e.g., how much tea drunk, how many days fasted, scriptures memorized, clothes received etc.) must be presented to Acharya at *Maryada Mahotsva.*

---

*They are tested on this constantly. Guru Dev may call on one to stand up and recite something.

A *samani* can keep:
- saris; 3 blouses, 3 choluck (bras); 2 petticoats; 2 kavatchan; 1 shawl; 1 elwan (special shawl); lunkar (thick shawl); 2 hankies, 2 small towels.
  If shawl tears, must keep it for 1 1/2 months before getting a new one
- 3 patras each
- Can borrow from *shravaks* 4 tubs, 2 *balti* (buckets) – for duration of stay in village, town etc.

Re. Education *Shiksha sutra.*
- Can't study with monk or male householder unless get permission of Guru Dev/Acharyasri
- Can't teach men, unless in a group of samanis and with permission
- Keep 1 metre distance from men
- Don't display affection with each other or with *shravaks*
- Don't wash clothes in front of *shravaks*
- Whichever *samani* borrowed 'pari hari' (items from householders) must return them
- Concerning horoscope, kundalini, palmistry. Don't give this information to *shravaks*
- Don't tell *shravaks* mantras for worldly things (e.g., getting a child).
- If having a problem and want a mantra from an outsider, first get permission to do so
- Keep no personal photos, except of Guru 'because without guru we have no existence'

Re: Contact with *Shravaks* while travelling:
- How many people did you inspire to renounce?
- How many camps were organized? How many people attended? When? Where?
- If you gave lectures, describe.
- How many did you make *anuvrati?*
- How many fasts did you encourage? how long were fasts?
- How many units of 'group fasting'?
- How many people took vows of silence? for how long?
- How many people took *santara?* Where? Who? How long did it take? Anything special? (e.g., fragrance around person, premonitions, bright lights, etc.)

Yatra (travelling):
- How many kilometres?
- How many villages with Terapanthis?

- How many villages with Jains?
- How many villages, towns, and cities in total?

Seva (service):
- How many days did you help with this *sadhvi/samani*?
- If someone was ill – Who? When? How many days?

Kala (art):
- How many pictures did you make (of Guru Dev/ historical pictures etc.)?
- How many *rajoharan* and *ojha* did you make?
- How many bowls did you make? How many polished? Painted?

Lipi (to write)
- How many special writings? (*lekan*)
- How many miniature writings? (*sukhmakshar*)

Viryachar (ethics of strength questionnaire):
- How long and how many fasts did you do?
- How many limitations did you take?
- How many *mala* did you recite in one day?

Punishments:
If take food in patra and it is living – ekhasin
If take water in pot and it is living – ekhasin
If eat living thing – upwaas
If lose/break clock, thermus, thermometer – 1 grain without water/1 day
Say bad words – 100 long breaths
Tell a lie – 100 long breaths
If sleep for more than 30 minutes during day – 100 long breaths
If break Niojikaji's rule – 100 shlok swadhai standing
If tell a secret of another person – 100 long breaths
If weep – 25 long breaths
If hurt immobiles –100 long breaths
If hurt 1–4 sensed organ beings (ants, worms etc.) – 200 *shloks swadhai*
If take something without permission (even a pencil) – 2 days consecutive
    upwaas
If hurt 5 sensed organ beings: 1–2 days *upwaas*; kill – 3 days *upwaas* consecutive*

*For example, Muniji once told me a story of how he opened a window where a lizard was resting and accidentally squashed it. For penance, he fasted for three days.

If one keeps more than prescribed limits (e.g. 3 instead of 2 pairs of glasses) –
    2 days *upwaas*
If eat during night – 1 day fast
If go out during night – 6 long breaths
If still doing *pratikraman* after the prescribed 48 minutes after sunset – 25 long
    breaths
If keep anything of own outside at night – 12–25 long breaths
If miss *pratikraman* – *ekhasin* (one meal in a day)
If dream of violence, or of eating etc.   100 long breaths
If vomit during night – 25 long breaths
If wring water out of clothes – 2 *logus* (14 lines) meditation
If take anything before sunrise – 1 day fast

Appendix 3
Examples of Sarala's Poems (Abridged)

'Circulation'
After every birth
Comes a rain of death
Just as the night follows
the run of the day
Never can one stop
This motion of destiny
They are necessary actions
Of Nature
Which changes the spring
To autumn
And autumn to spring.

'Glorious Death'
Death is better
Restraint and renunciation,
Than Life
Of Lust and luxury.

'Great Terapantha'
We are peaceful in this Terapantha
We are blissful in this Bhikshu Sangh

Never can come near
Darkness or fear
Only the flow of sweet air
In this Terapantha

Product of dedication
Product of legislation
Product of instruction
That is the Terapantha

We are peaceful in this Terapantha
We are blissful in this Bhikshu Sangh.

Appendix 4
The Ascetic Ideal

The Utopia: Characteristics of the Ideal Monk

(1) A monk's life shall I lead, perceiving the truth,
   Wishing well, upright, tearing off intents deep;
   Abandoning acquaintance, longing not for objects sensual,
   Who begs from families strange, he is indeed the ideal monk.

(2) With affection ceased, and vivacious,
   Abstaining, knowing the lore, self-protected,
   Wise and conquering, perceiving all,
   Who is attached not anywhere, he is indeed the ideal monk.

(3) Overcoming abuse and injury, steadfast,
   Vivacious ever, the sage travels self-protected,
   Undistracted in mind, not elated,
   Who endures all, he is indeed the ideal monk.

(4) Using beds and seats lowly,
   Cold and heat diverse, gnats and mosquitoes,
   Undistracted in mind, not elated,
   Who endures all, he is the ideal monk.

(5) Desires not treatment respectful, nor homage,
   Nor reverence, let alone praise;
   Self-restrained, keeping the vows, ascetic,
   Wishing well, who introspects the self, he is indeed the ideal monk.

(6) For whom one gives up life,
     Or falls into delusion deep;
   Such women ever the ascetic avoids,
     And is not enamoured, he is indeed the ideal monk.

(7) The rent (in garment), tones, (portents) earthly and celestial,
     Dreams, science of signs, staffs and building-sites,
   Defects physical, and the science of cries,
     Who lives not on sciences such, he is indeed the ideal monk.

(8) Charms strange and doctor's prescriptions,
     Emetics, purgatives, fumigation, and bathing.
   The patient's asylum and treatment medical,
     Eschewing, who renounces, he is indeed the ideal monk.

(9) Kṣatriyas, guilds, Ugras, princes,
     Mahanas, Bhogas, and artisans of all sorts;
   Who praises not, nor honours,
     And avoiding them, renounces, he is indeed the ideal monk.

(10) The householders whom, after renouncing, he met,
      Or, ere renunciation, was acquainted with;
    With them, who, for gains earthly,
      Cultivates not acquaintance, he is indeed the ideal monk.

(11) Beds and seats, drink or food,
      Dainties various, and spices, by others,
    Refuses to partake of, the Nirgrantha,
      Who gets not angry, he is indeed the ideal monk.

(12) Food and drink of kind any,
      And dainties various, and spices, by others,
    (Being offered), who blesses them not in the triple way,
      Restrained in thought, word, and deed, he is indeed the ideal monk.

(13) Rice-water and barley-pap,
      Cold sour gruel, and barley-water,
    Insipid alms, who despises not,
      And visits the houses lowliest, he is indeed the ideal monk.

(14) Sounds manifold there are in the world,
    Of gods and men, and of beasts too,
  Dreadful, frightening and awful ones;
    Who bears them unperturbed, he is indeed the ideal monk.

(15) Knowing doctrines, different in the world,
    Wishing well, griefless, and learned;
  Wise, conquering, and perceiving everything,
    Tranquil and inoffensive, he is indeed the ideal monk.

(16) Not living on craft, without house and friends, ,
    Subduing his senses, free from ties all;
  With passions minute, eating light and little,
    Homeless and living alone, he is indeed the ideal monk.

Source: Tatia and Kumar (1981)

Appendix 5
Examples of the *Nivrtti-Marg*: Jainism's Public Face

Paul Dundas depicts the ascetic path as one of total withdrawal and restraint:

In the widest sense, the entire range of ascetic behaviour is aimed towards both the imposition of mental and physical constraints in order to ward off the influx of new karma and the cultivation of ascetic practices which, if exercised with sufficient intensity, will destroy karma which is already clinging to the soul. These two areas are defined as being 'restraint' (*samyama*) and 'asceticism' (*tapas*). (1992: 138)

The *Tattvartha Sutra (TS)*, the only text considered authoritative by all Jain sects, likewise describes the ascetic path as one of restraint:

Progress in spiritual development depends on progress in inhibition ... Psychic inhibition is when the mind disengages from worldly action. Physical inhibition is when karmic inflow actually ceases because of this mental detachment. (1994: 213)

And:

Inflow is inhibited by guarding, careful movements, morality, reflection, conquering hardships, and enlightened conduct. (219)

Jaini's description of asceticism similarly centres on the importance of restraint:

The purpose of assuming the mahavratas [at the time of initiation] is to reduce to a minimum the sphere of activity and frequency of activities that would otherwise generate the influx of karmas and the rise of fresh passions. The stopping of karmic influx, called samvara, is achieved by various methods; these basically involve control of the senses and the development of extreme mindfulness. ([1979] 1990: 247)

The *Tattvartha Sutra* emphasizes the importance of *detachment* in the ascetic path:

> Absolute renunciation of all possessions and passions including the body is the aim of ascetic practice ... The ascetic has to be free of the sense of mineness. Whatever he seeks for the bare maintenance of life is to be used with absolute detachment. The feeling of detachment from the body is an integral part of compulsory daily practice. (1994: 236)

Acharya Tulsi writes:

> Righteousness consists in complete self [i.e., soul] -absorption and in giving up all kinds of passions including attachment. It is the only means of transcending the mundane existence (Bhava-pahuda, 83). (Tulsi, 1985: 88)

Discussion of ascetic life typically centres on the rules governing this 'realigned way of life.' Jaini writes that the ascetic is distinguished from that of the householder 'by the manner of his observance of *ahimsa* in daily practice' ([1979] 1990: 242):

(1) He must refrain from all acts of digging in the earth, in order to avoid the destruction of earth bodies;
(2) he must refrain from all forms of bathing, swimming, wading, or walking in the rain, thus showing proper concern for water bodies;
(3) he must protect fire bodies by never extinguishing fires; nor may he light a match or kindle any flame, for such is the evanescent nature of the fire bodies that the very act of producing them is virtually equivalent to causing their destruction;
(4) he must refrain from fanning himself, lest he injure air bodies by creating a sudden change of temperature in the air;
(5) he must avoid walking on greenery or touching a living plant, since either action might injure certain vegetable bodies. (242–3)

And Jhingran writes:

> The search for liberation requires a complete breaking away of the mind from the outer world and its direction towards the innermost reality of the self, culminating in the total absorption of the former (mind) into the latter (self). This is the *nivrtti-marga* which seeks to forcefully curb the outgoing tendency of the human mind and is supposed to be the *sine qua non* of self-realization or *moksa*. (1989: 114)

Jaini goes on to describe the mechanics of withdrawal, embodied in the three 'restraints' (*guptis*) and the five rules of conduct (*samitis*) which 'prepare an ascetic for the advanced meditational states through which kamic matter is finally eliminated from the soul' ([1979] 1990: 247):

> The term *gupti* refers to a progressive curbing of the activities of mind, body, and speech; hence the monk undertakes long periods of silence, remains motionless for hours on end, strives for one-pointedness that stills the intellective process, and so forth. (247)

The *samitis* include:

(1) care in walking (*irya-samiti*) – a mendicant must neither run nor jump, but should move ahead slowly, gaze turned downwards, so that he will avoid stepping on any creature no matter how small;
(2) care in speaking (*bhasa-samiti*) – in addition to observing the vow of truthfulness, he should speak only when absolutely necessary and then in as few words as possible;
(3) care in accepting alms (*esana-samiti*) – only appropriate food may be taken, and it should be consumed as if it were unpleasant medicine, i.e., with no sense of gratification involved;
(4) care in picking up things and putting them down (*adana-niksepana-samiti*) – whether moving a whisk broom, bowl, book or any other object, the utmost caution must be observed lest some form of life be disturbed or crushed;
(5) care in performing the excretory functions (*utsarga-samiti*) – the place must be entirely free of living things. ([1979] 1990: 248)

Jaini continues, stating that an ascetic is

> encouraged to reinforce his practice of the *guptis* and *samitis* by constantly manifesting the ten forms of righteousness (*dasa-dharma*):

(1) perfect forbearance
(2) perfect modesty
(3) perfect uprightness
(4) perfect truthfulness
(5) perfect purity
(6) perfect restraint
(7) perfect austerity
(8) perfect renunciation
(9) perfect non-attachment
(10) perfect continence (248)

The aspirant must also continuously contemplate the twelve mental reflections (*anupreksa*) which will lead to detachment from the world:

(1) the transitoriness of everything that surrounds one,
(2) the utter helplessness of beings in the face of death,
(3) the relentless cycle of rebirth, with its attendant suffering,
(4) the absolute aloneness of each individual as he moves through this cycle,
(5) the fact that soul and body are completely separate from each other,
(6) the filth and impurity which in reality permeate a seemingly attractive physical body,
(7) the manner in which karmic influx takes place,
(8) how such influx can be stopped,
(9) how karmas already clinging to the soul can be driven out,
(10) fundamental truths about the universe, namely, that it is beginningless, uncreated, and operates according to its own laws – thus each person is responsible for his own salvation, for there is no divinity that might intervene,
(11) the rarity of true insight (*bodhidurlabha*), and the number of creatures who, because they have not been so fortunate as to attain human embodiment, are currently denied the wonderful opportunity to attain *moksa*,
(12) the absolutely true teachings of the Jinas (*dharma-svakhyatatva*), how they are the most fundamentally expressed through the practice of *ahimsa*, and how they can lead one to the ultimate goal of eternal peace. (248–9)

Appendix 6
The Daily Routine of the *Sadhvis*

Holmstrom (1988: 24–8), who spent several months travelling with the Terapanthi *sadhvis* in 1987, provides a sketch of the daily routine of the *sadhvis*. I quote at length:

The structure of the day itself hardly ever changes, though here it is not explicit rules which order it but an undeclared rhythm of action ... The sadhvis rise at 4 a.m., the last quarter of night, and meditate or recite a list of *acarya* Bhiksu's rules for the order. At 4:30 they gather and chant the *arhat vandana* together, the most fundamental Jain prayer, and then the *pratikraman*, which covers roughly one *muhurta* [48 minutes], a long Prakrtit list taken from the Pratikrman Sutra ... When light is adequate to make out the finger-print on one's hands, they start on the day's first *pratilekhna*, checking their belongings and changing into their day clothes, and pack up their possessions into bundles of white cloth.

At sunrise (c. 5:30 a.m.) they sling their bags and rolled-up mat over one shoulder, fill their gourds with water from householders, straining it through cloth (this they have not taken since sunset), and set off on the road. The group I was with stopped off to pay *darsan* on the *acarya*, though they can only enter the place where the *munis* are staying after the shout has gone up inside that the sun has actually risen. The daily journey, through relatively well-populated Harayana, was usually 13–18 km, taking some two hours; they travel in twos or threes, striding rapidly through the early morning countryside. Since our group was so big we stayed often in village schools (especially suitable if separate wings for girls and boys) or, in larger places, in *dharmsalas* or private houses.

Immediately they arrive there are jobs to be done; it is about 8 a.m. and morning begins. If there are enough houses, they go in pairs for alms of breakfast, to collect water which is poured into *matkas*, large clay jars borrowed from householders for the day, and there are informal classes and other work to attend to. If the village is reasonably sizeable, the *acarya* when he gets in gives a public lecture to the local community; a few monks generally go to support and sing *bhajans*, but normally the *sadhvis* do not bother to go unless they are specifically taking notes from the *acarya*'s speeches for editing and publication ...

At 11 a.m. or so it is time for pairs to go for *gotceri* or *bhiksa*, alms. The *sadhvis* in this large group are divided into three smaller groups only for the purpose of collecting and eating alms; as many pots as are needed are collected from the various members of the group and stacked one on top of the other in the *jholi*, a sling of white cloth knotted. As they can only take a little from many places ('like bees'), collecting alms enough can take a lot of trekking around; women often come to ask the *sadhvis* to come to their houses, or the *sadhvis* will go to local Terapanth houses, then other Jain sects (though some of these too come to offer alms), or vegetarian Hindu houses. Eventually the three pairs return, full *patras* skilfully balanced, and 'show' the *sadhvi pramukha* or the most senior *sadhvi* what they have collected before settling down to eat. They all eat more or less together, squatting in three circles, sharing out everything equally within groups, sometimes between groups, as far as possible. Eating times are the only times when they can legitimately shut the doors to householders and approach anything like 'privacy' in a collective sort of sense. The *sadhvi pramukha* eats separately, cross-legged on her mat. It is a mark of respect to her authority (and also affection) first to share out her meal onto a separate *patra*, rather than diving into the joint ones like everyone else.

After eating everyone wipes their *patra* as clean as possible with their fingers and swills a little water around, drinking what is left. The idea is not to leave any remains of food as it would bring insects wherever the *patra* is washed; I think this is also to do with non-reciprocity; you cannot leave anything given to you, nor give it back to a householder (unless it was an unacceptable e.g. 'live' article and, realizing, you hand it back at once – books are exempt too, once they are read they are given away, too heavy to accumulate, the bodies of dead *sadhvis* are also handed back of course). Nothing of a *sadhvi*'s is to serve the purpose of a householder (old clothes must be torn first into strips and then little squares, and buried in earth). Every day two *sadhvis* take it in turns to finish washing everyone's *patras*, and in the evening they also wash the cloths used for making *jholis* and straining water.

The midday meal marks the beginning of afternoon; some take a short nap if they have been travelling, though if they have not then they should not sleep unless they are over 50 or sick or fasting. (The ideal is to do 30 days' fast a year; most fast every 15 days, on the eve of the full moon and the dark moon, but it usually works out more sporadically, especially whilst travelling; those who get sick when fasting are not directly pressed.) It is a case of the emphasis on constant awareness, control over one's sense and actions, wakefulness which is the whole mode of renunciatory conduct. Many women come for *darsan* at this time, bringing assorted children.

At about 4–4:30 p.m. the *sadhvis* start on the second *pratilekhna* which marks the third quarter of the day, the start of evening. It includes unwrapping and rewrapping the *rajoharan*, the woollen broom each one owns, flicking through both sets of clothes to rapidly check for insects or dust, and changing into one's 'night' set, usually the slightly dirtier or more torn set. This is the lull before the rush for collecting alms and water which immediately precedes sunset. At 5:30 or so they set off, and by about 6:30 p.m. have usually finished eating; then each *sadhvi* takes a brimming *patra* of water with which to clean her teeth, face, hands and feet, and to get as much inside herself as possible before the long hot night. Meanwhile the two will be washing out *patra*-cloths with a little water and washing powder (begged along with dollops of toothpaste with the evening alms), hastily hanging them out to dry.

Quick, quick, the shout goes up: 20 minutes to sunset – 10 minutes to sunset – 5 minutes to sunset – the sun has set! The cloth-washers immediately empty out what water is left (carefully, in a place free from grass or insects); water gourds are emptied and wiped dry. No spot of water is to be left, nor food; you can keep food from the midday to evening meal, but not overnight. The *matkas* are emptied and overturned. Even medicines are handed over to householders for safekeeping and asked for again at sunrise. It is extremely important, and seen as a definite act of *tyag*, to renounce food and water at night. (Also they try to avoid going outside at night and sleep on a roof or balcony only if shaded by a parapet or similar – this stops 'germs' (English word) or insects falling out of the sky onto them and hence being injured. Another frequently given reason for not eating at night is that they might eat one of these beings unknowingly.)

Immediately after sunset the *sadhvis* gather for *pratikraman*, the repetition of rules in their form of the renunciation of sinful acts and meditation upon any sins one may have committed. Whereas the morning *pratikraman* is uttered immediately before sunrise, the night one is immediately after sunset; these times are the meeting points, *sandhyas* when the deities visit earth and categories are confused. For one *muhurta* (48 minutes) either side of the *sandhyas* no other scriptures may be recited, as they are in (Ardha Magadhi) Prakrit, which would irritate and provoke the gods, whose language it also is. The *pratikraman* itself would not do so being a list of rules rather than preaching, and is in any case a purifying strengthening of boundaries in the repetition of right conduct. The *pratikramans* also punctuate the year; every 15 days (the full moon and dark moon) they are 3 times their usual length, every four months they are 5 times their usual length, and once a year at *samvatsari* during the week of *prayusan* they are a mammoth – 10 times their usual length, with meditation upon the sins committed during the intervening period, and the mutual asking for and granting of pardon. After the *pratikraman*, the *sadhvis* each pay homage to all those senior to themselves in *diksa* terms ... Finally they gather once more for the *arhat vandana* and then sit in the cool evening chatting; this was when most of this dissertation was created, in the discussions as the light faded until around 10:30 p.m., one quarter into night, when they spread their mats, drew their *caddars* over themselves and at last slept.

Glossary

Acharya	spiritual leader of order
Agam	canonical literature, scripture
Ahimsa	nonviolence, nonharm
Ajiva	non-soul, matter, that which is not alive, insentient
Anuvrat	'small vows'
Anuvrat Movement	a movement of moral rehabilitation launched by Acharya Tulsi in 1949
Aparigraha	vow of nonpossession
Arihant	one who is worthy of worship; one who has attained omniscience
Atman	soul
Bania	merchant caste
Bhakti	devotion
Bhiksha/bhiksa	alms
Bhikshu/Bhikanji	first Acharya of Terapanthis
Bhut	souls of unhappy *deva* (ghosts), demons, *preta*
Brahmacarya	vow of celibacy
Camatkar	miracle
Chappals	sandals, thongs
Chaturmas/caturmas	four-month rainy season retreat
Dana/dan	donations
Darshan	to be in the guru's presence; to see and be seen by the guru
Daya	compassion
Dharma	duty/religion/righteousness
Dharma Marg	path of duty (*shravaka*'s path)
Dharmasangh	ascetic community
Dhyan	meditation

Digambara	Jain sects whose ascetics are 'sky clad' – i.e., naked
Diksarthi	initiate (n.)
Diksha/diksa	initiation
Fordmaker	one who has created a ford (passage) to cross the ocean of *samsar*, used synonymously with Tirthankara and Jina
Gali	path, road
Gan	an organized group of ascetics, a religious order
Gautam Shalla	name of *samanis'* residence in Ladnun
Gochari	alms collecting
Gotra karma	karmas that determine family and status
Gunasthana	stages of spiritual purification
Harijan	individual of an 'untouchable' caste, literally 'people of god'
Himsa	violence
Jholi	sling to carry stacked *patras*
Jina	epithet of the Tirthankaras, 'one who has conquered'
Jiv jiva	sentient being, soul
Kavatchan	tunic worn by *upasikas, mumukshus,* and *samanis*
Kayotsarga	body abandonment (a technique of meditation)
Kevalin	one who has attained omniscience
Kheer	sweet rice porridge
Kurta pyjama	long top and trouser suit
Laukik	of the world, of society, worldly, mundane
Laukik daya	social compassion
Laukik dharm	societal resonsibilities
Laukik punya	social merit
Lokottar	transcendent, spiritual, other-worldly
Lokottar daya	spiritual compassion; that leading to liberation
Lokottar punya	religious merit
Maan	ego
Maharaja	king; honorary term used for the *munis*
Maharani	queen; honorary term used for the *sadhvis*
Mahavratas	'great vows' of an ascetic
Mala	rosary beads
Maryada Mahotsva	annual Terapanthi Jain 'festival of restraint'
Moksa	liberation from cycle of birth and death
Moksa Marg	path of spiritual liberation/release
Muhpatti	mouth covering worn by Sthanakavasi and Terapanthi ascetics
Mumukshu	'one who is desirous of emancipation,' a student training to be an ascetic at the PSS

Muni	monk, male ascetic, *sadhu*
Murtipujak	idol-worshipper; Jain sect that worships in temples
Nama karma	karmas that determine body and life-span
Namaskar mantra	the most basic Jain mantra paying homage to the five holy beings: Jinas, liberated souls, mendicant teachers, mendicant leaders, all mendicants of the world
Namaste	a greeting: 'I bow to the divinity within you'
Nigodas	the simplest form of life
Nivrtti-marg	ascetic path, path of turning away from the world
Paap	bad karma
Pappadum	crispy bread
Patra	bowl/vessel/container used for carrying alms
Prapatti	devotional surrender
Pratikramana	a ritualized confessional prayer
Pratilekhna	careful checking of clothes, books, etc. for insects before use
Pravachan	sermon, lecture
Pravrtti-marg	path of worldly life
Preksha-Dhyana	'insight meditation,' associated with Terapanthis
PSS	Parmarthik Shikshan Sanstha (training school for girls who aspire to be ascetics) in Ladnun
Punya	good karma, merit
Rag	desire
Raj	group of ascetics who travel with Acharya
Rajoharan	a whiskbroom carried by ascetics
Rishabdwar	name of *sadhvis'* residence in Ladnun
Roti	bread
Sadhana	spiritual practices (meditation, fasting, prayer, etc.)
Sadhvi	nun
Sadhvi pramukha	chief female ascetic, appointed by the acharya
Saman	male semi-ascetic category created by Terapanthi
Samani	female semi-ascetic category created by Terapanthi
Samavasaran	divinely created assembly hall from the centre of which the Jinas preach
Samnyasi	ascetic, renunciant, hermit
Samsar	worldly existence, cycle of birth, death, and rebirth
Samyag darsan	true inner religious experience
Sangh	assembly
Santhara or santara	ritual fast until death
Shakti	creative energy/power
Shishya	pupil

Shramana	ascetic
Shravak	householder
Singharpati	leader of small group, *agrani*
Slokas	religious verses
Sthanakavasi	dweller in halls; Jain sect that does not worship in temples
Stotra	religious stanza of praise
Stridharma	woman's duty/destiny
Sutra	canonical scripture
Svetambara	Jain sect whose ascetics wear white garments. Terapanthis are a subsect of the Svetambaras.
Tap/tapas	austerities, fasting
Tapasvini	someone who performs heroic austerities, usually long fasts
Tirth	passage/ford
Tirthankara	one who has created a passage to cross the ocean of *samsar,* omniscient teacher; used synonymously with Jina and Fordmaker
Tonga	horse and cart
Tyag	renunciation
Upasika	'worshipper' – term used for first-year student at the PSS
Vairagya	state of complete detachment
Vandana	devotional salutation
Varna	one of four main categories of brahmanical social system
Vihar	ritualized annual itinerary; ascetic wandering
Yuvacharya	assistant and designated successor to *Acharya*

Notes

1: Introduction

1 When, in March 1994, Tulsi renounced his position as acharya after fifty-eight years, his successor Mahaprajna bestowed upon him the title of *Gana-dhipati*, meaning 'leader of the order.' *Guru Dev* means 'godly teacher' and is used with affection. On 23 June 1997, at the age of 82, Guru Dev died.

2 Although I studied Hindi prior to leaving for India, and enlisted the help of a Hindi teacher in Ladnun, my ability to communicate in that language was seriously limited in the early stages of my fieldwork. Originally I had hoped to immerse myself in the local dialect, but that was somewhat naïve. Upon my arrival, the leader of the ascetic order assigned me the role of English teacher. In addition, many of the ascetics and lay individuals with whom I worked were proficient in English. Therefore, my fieldwork was throughout a hybrid of English and Hindi. The verbatim dialogue presented here is in English only.

3 This is the traditional Svetambar dating. The Digambar claim he died 510 BCE (Dundas, 1992: 21).

4 *Jina* is used synonomously with *Tirthankara* and Fordmaker to denote one who has made the 'crossing' (Folkert, 1987) or passage over the ocean of *samsar* to liberation.

5 Truths are dependent on favourable eras of the cosmic cycle for their dissemination. In the middle eras of each half-cycle, twenty-four *Jinas* appear consecutively and propagate the eternal truths to receptive listeners. Mahavir was the twenty-fourth, and final, *Jina* of the present cycle. No *Jinas* will appear during the 'Corrupt Age' (the *Kaliyuga*), in which we are presently living, when religion, culture, knowledge, human nature, etc., are in decline. The ensuing age will bring the complete demise of truth and Jain

teachings will die out. But since it is a continuous cycle, another twenty-four *Jinas* will appear in future cycles to again propagate the universal truths (see Babb, 1996, for a detailed description of Jain cosmography and time).

6 Dumont's analysis of world renunciation parallels Victor Turner's notion of liminality in that he treats renunciation as a method of 'release' for the caste structure, as a 'social state apart from society proper' (Dumont, 1980: 273). Turner depicts the state of liminality as a suspension of social structures and the inversion of norms, eventually culminating in social harmony. His concept of liminality has been described as a 'moment of suspension of normal rules, a crossing of boundaries and violating of norms, that enables us to understand those norms' (Bynum, 1994: 30). In a similar way, Dumont sees the renunciant as an embodiment of social guardianship and elucidation: by renouncing hierarchically organized caste society, the ascetic represents purity 'outside the world' but parallels and legitimates the Brahman priest, who represents purity 'within the world.' The ascetic, in Dumont's words, becomes the 'safety-valve of the Brahmanic order' (1960: 52).

7 In 1996 there were 539 nuns (*sadhvis*), 142 monks (*munis*), 81 semi-nuns (*samanis*), 4 semi-monks (*samans*), 51 nuns-in-training (i.e., 36 *mumukshu* and 15 *upasika* sisters [*bahan*]), and 4 monks-in-training (*mumukshus* brothers [*bhai*]) in the Terapanthi order. The Tapa Gacch, predominant in Gujarat, has the greatest number of ascetics of any single Jain order, with 1,246 monks and 4,226 nuns (Babb, 1996: 54). But this group is broken down into sixteen subgroups called *samudays* (see Cort, 1991b for a detailed account of Svetambar ascetic lineages). In the Tapa Gacch, the *samuday* is the primary organizational unit, and the number of nuns in these units is smaller than that of the Terapanthi.

8 The institute is also open to boys as a day school. A few boys take classes at the institute but spend most of their time with the monks within the grounds of the JVB.

9 In 1991 the government of India notified the JVBI of its 'deemed to be university' status.

10 *Raj* = the group of *sadhvis* and *munis* that travel with the leaders of the order.

11 I write 'approximately' because the *samanis* are a very mobile order. Small groups would often be sent off to another village or city for some event, while others would return.

2: Ethics and the Ascetic Ideal

1 This is the argument put forward by the Terapanthi ascetic order, which accepts minors for initiation.

2 While I would maintain that Jain *ahimsa* is primarily concerned with non-injury, it has a sociocentric dimension and application among lay Jains, who comprise the overwhelming majority of Jains. Here ahimsa is also interpreted to mean offering help and support to other living beings, such as rescuing animals and maintaining panjapoors (animal shelters). But to understand how the ethos of world renunciation and ahimsa form one ethic, one must realise that ahimsa is primarily an ethic of non-injury for both lay and ascetic Jains; what James Laidlaw describes as an 'ethic of quarantine.'

3 Because other species are believed to lack some essential human characteristic, most are denied moral consideration.

4 Jains classify living beings in a myriad of ways, but there is no category that humans occupy alone. One division is between birth 'by womb' and by 'agglutination' (an asexual reproduction or gathering of materials). Interestingly, human beings fall into both categories! In comparison with the Judaeo-Christian view of humans as 'created in the image of God,' Jain writings often reflect a rather modest and sober view of the human incarnation The *Tattvartha Sutra* states: 'The humans born of agglutination originate in human excreta such as faeces, urine, sputum, mucus, vomit, bile, pus, blood, semen, etc. Their lifespan is very short (the tiniest lifespan is 2 *avalikas*)' (1994: 54).

5 More precisely, Jains believe there exist two types of worldly souls: those that are capable of emancipation, called *bhavya*, and those incapable of it, *abhavya*. Although consciousness exists in each living being, only *bhavya* souls are capable of developing their internal powers fully. Most souls are endowed with this potential. P.S. Jaini writes that the quality of *bhavyatva* 'is a sort of inert catalyst, awaiting the time when it will be activated and thus trigger an irrevocable redirection of the soul's energy: away from delusion and bondage, towards insight and freedom' (1990: 139).

6 Just as plants and animals are moral symbols and represent varied states of bondage, so too does the human body. The Jain conception of the human body as a moral template is, therefore, intimately connected with its view of the universe as a moral order.

7 The heavens and hells represent the realms of 'just deserts' – that is, where rewards (*punya*) and punishments (*paap*) come to fruition due to past life events. But the beings within them – the gods and hell-beings – are not part of this metonymical scheme (above) because they are outside of the realm of moral discourse (the *karmbhumi*). Babb writes that 'The value of world renunciation transcends mere questions of sin and virtue,' and that '[N]o karma is ever really 'good' and these rewards are of no ultimate value' (1996: 32). Gods and hell-beings are not represented in the stages of spiritual devel-

opment (*gunasthanas*). They are liminal beings, and the heavens and hells represent liminal periods. They must return to the area of *karmbhumi*, the 'land of endeavour' to become karmically active again, because it is only from the human form that liberation can occur. (See Babb's discussion of the Cosmos in Jainism, 1996: 38–52.)

8 Gods, like hell-beings, are outside of this hierarchical scale because they are outside the *karmbhumi*, the realm of moral discourse. See endnote 7 above.

9 See Lynn White's 1967 classic paper on the Judaeo-Christian roots of our ecological crisis.

3: Creation through Negation: The Rite of *Bhiksha*

1 The terms householder, lay person, and *shravak* are synonomous, and I use them interchangeably.

2 Samani Urmilla (not her real name), my closest friend within the Samani order, explained that when Guru Dev wants the order to be more disciplined, he will often encourage it through his own behaviour. In that way, he humbles the others to do the same.

3 *Patra* literally translates as 'container' or 'vessel.' When used by the ascetics, it refers to their alms bowls.

4 The ascetics could never return the food, since it is not theirs to give away. It was given as a sacrifice to them by generous householders and it would be sinful to distribute it to non-ascetics. I once asked 'Samanji' [Saman Stithprejna] why the ascetics are compelled to bury excess food, and why they could not leave it outside for beggars or hungry animals. He explained that to leave it outside would result in tremendous violence. Insects would come to eat, dogs would also come and eat the insects. Perhaps dogs would fight over the food. He could imagine a number of potentially violent scenarios. The ascetics would then be implicated in that violence. But it is a very rare occurrence indeed when food has to be so disposed. In fact, the ascetics are obliged to finish every last scrap of food given in alms. If food is left over, it must be redistributed within the group until it is all eaten. It is only on rare occasions when too much food is gathered that they are required to dispose of it. Usually, the mendicants know in advance how much milk, kheer, or rice (for example) they should collect, because they have inquired of their fellow mendicants how much they can eat.

5 The Great Vows are nonviolence, truth, nonstealing, celibacy, and non-possession.

6 'Correct manner' refers to that which is approved by monastic rules for avoiding injuring any form of life while performing the duties necessary for religious life.

7 Although Muni Nathmal was described as living as a hermit – and was exempt from daily lectures and meetings with householders – he must have continued to collect *bhiksha* from a community of lay Jains since he could not prepare food himself.

8 Yuvacharya Mahaprajna explains: 'The word *preksa* is derived from the root *iksa*, which means "to see." When the prefix *"pra"* is added, it becomes *pra + iksa = preksa*, which means "to perceive carefully and profoundly." Here "see-ing" does not mean external vision, but careful concentration on subtle consciousness by mental insight. Preksa Dhyana is the system of meditation engaging one's mind fully in the perception of subtle internal and innate phenomena of consciousness' (1993: 1). In addition, he writes that the terms *preksa* and *vipasyana* are synonomous, but that since the latter is commonly used in Buddhism, he adopted the former for his system. He claims that the Jain canonical aphorism 'See you thyself' (*Sampikkhae Appagamappaaenam*) forms the basic principle for *preksa* meditation. It is a method aimed at per-ceiving the most subtle aspects of consciousness by one's own conscious mind. He continues: 'In *preksa*, perception always means experience bereft of the duality of like and dislike. When the experience is contaminated with pleasure or pain, like and dislike, perception loses its primary position and becomes secondary. Impartiality and equanimity are synonymous with *preksa*. *Preksa* is impartial perception, where there is neither the emotion of attach-ment nor aversion, neither pleasure nor displeasure' (3).

9 A number of Preksa Dhyana centres have been established in India. The Adhyatma Sadhna Kendra (ASK) in New Delhi is the largest and attracts individuals of all faiths with its promotion of Preksa Dhyana as a secular, health-promoting practice. The ASK holds special meditation camps for asthma, cancer, and heart disease patients. There is also a centre in the United States (Orlando, Florida), where *samanis* and *samans* are sent by Acharyasri to instruct both the Jain and non-Jain communities in the tech-niques of preksa meditation.

10 *Anuvrat* means 'small vows' and refers to the code of conduct followed by *shravaks*. In 1949 Acharya Tulsi initiated a national social reform movement based on the observance of the *anuvrats*.

11 A booklet written by two Terapanthi monks on Acharya Mahaprajna's life, entitled *A Living Legend*, describes his early life with Guru Dev: 'Born in Tamkor a very small village in District Jhunjhunu, Rajasthan, on 14th June, 1920, and baptised as "Nathmal," this child, on 29th January, 1931, renunci-ated the family and worldly pleasures and started on the thorny path of ascet-icism. He was taken as a disciple by Acharya Kalugani, the eighth Acharya of "Terapanth" of Jainism and the child dedicated his whole Being at the feet of his Master. Acharya Kalugani then entrusted this child to the care of his

young and talented disciple Muni Tulsi, and by his simplicity and unaffected-
ness, the child instantaneously endeared himself to his new teacher. With
Muni Tulsi, the child's intellectual development accelerated and he memo-
rised thousands of sermons and verses in Hindi, Sanskrit, Prakrit and Rajasthani' (Prashant Kumar and Lokprakash Lokesh, 1995: 12).

12 Most fruits and vegetables require boiling (killing) to be rendered *ajiv* (not
alive) and therefore suitable for the ascetics to consume. Bananas and
oranges need only be peeled.

13 The twelve vows include the five *anuvrats* (small vows) that are modelled
after the *mahavratas* (great vows of the ascetics). The *anuvrats* are: nonviolence, truth, nonstealing, celibacy (understood at nonadultery), and nonpossession. The seven supplementary vows are: refrain from moving outside
a limited area so as to restrict the sphere of activity; restrict movement; avoid
wanton thoughts and actions; keep aloof from sinful conduct for a set
period; observe sacred days by fasting and not bathing etc. (eighth, four-
teenth, or fifteenth day of the fortnight); limit consumable and nonconsum-
able goods; offer alms to ascetics (*Tattvartha Sutra* [hereinafter *TS*], 1994:
176–7).

14 The *Tattvartha Sutra* (*TS*) was written in the second century CE by the Jain
philosopher-monk Umasvati. It translates as 'A Manual for Understanding
All That Is.' It is accepted as authoritative by both the Svetambars and
Digambars, though some sutras and their commentary are interpreted somewhat differently by them. These sectarian variations are dealt with in the
1994 translation of the TS: The SS refers to the 'Sarvarthasiddhi,' a commentary considered by the Digambars to be a faithful rendering of Umasvati's
sutras. The SBT is the 'Svopajna Bhasya Tika,' a Svetambar commentary on
sutras they believe to be of Umasvati's own writings.

15 Sangam was reborn as Shaalibhadra in the Gobhadra family, the richest family in town. The family was so rich that even the king could not compete with
them. Shaalibhadra grew up in luxury and was married to thirty-two beautiful women, but eventually realized the pointlessness of worldly life,
renounced the world, and attained *moksa*.

16 This is Samani Urmilla Prajna's spoken version of the well-known tale.

17 They are 'one-time' or 'former' relations in the sense that they no longer
(officially) recognize familial ties. The family represents the most tangible
form of worldliness that is renounced at the time of *diksa* (ascetic initiation).

18 For example: Flügel writes: 'The various forms of Jainism and other religions. ... are rationalisations of the socio-psychological processes involved'
(1995–6: 169). Jains, however, would likely see it conversely: that is, socio-
psychological processes are outcomes, not determining factors; they are

products of the phenomenon of *vyanjana paryaya* (the mutual influencing of *jiv* and *ajiv*), which combine and tranform (*srstivada*) to create all we know of worldly existence.

19 *Nibbana* = nirvana, emancipation.

20 Time is understood cyclically, as a wheel with twelve spokes: six inclining and six declining, called the *utsarpini* and the *avasarpini* respectively. In the sixth spoke of the *avasarpini*, Jainism is unknown and it is a period of utter bleakness. It will be followed by the first *utsarpini*, the beginning of renewal. We are now in the fifth spoke of the *avasarpini* – called the *Kaliyuga* – a period of decline. Dundas elaborates: 'The Jains share with the Hindus the notion of Kaliyuga, the Corrupt Age, which for them involves a gradual diminishment of culture, religion and eventually even human stature. This age, in which we are living now, has been continually invoked by Jain writers from the early medieval period and provides an overarching principle with reference to which the tradition can explain the course of its own immediate fortunes after the death of Mahavira ... as involving a continual tension between decline and attempted reform' (1992: 12).

21 The ascetics are generally more careful than householders in distinguishing between spiritual and worldly rewards. For example, whereas they acknowledge that wealth, intelligence, and beauty are likely the result of spiritual merit, they insist that a spiritual person would never yearn for such things. Instead, by leading a spiritual life aimed at salvation, these may result as beneficial 'side-effects' (see Babb, 1996).

22 Cf. Folkert (1993) for an opposite view. He writes: 'When one looks more carefully at the actual history of Jain asceticism, one sees that the Jains have been far more willing to be "mathavasis," or temple dwellers, than our standard sketches indicate. The ideal sadhu, eternally wandering, staying no more than a day or two, must be adjusted' (171). He adds, however, that 'modern groups, especially the Terapanthis, have sought to break this pattern [of a monastery-dwelling askesis] (172).

23 Carrithers traces the pattern of the *sangha* development in its agrarian environment in Sri Lanka, whereby monks who are dispersed throughout the rice-growing valleys have little choice but to spend their time with the lay community.

24 It should also be noted that it was the issue of what constitutes the true ascetic path that prompted a number of Terapanthi ascetics to leave the order to form the Naya Terapanthi in 1981.

25 See Flügel (1995–6). He describes, for example, how the Terapanth Mahasabha national council 'provides a centralized organizational framework for the Terapanth laity, parallel to the religious organization of the ascetics' (147).

26 Later called 'Sudhari,' the town is now a pilgrimage site for religious Tera-panthis.

27 The five *mahvratas* are nonviolence, truth, nonstealing, celibacy, and nonpos-session; the five *samitis* are careful conduct in walking, speaking, seeking alms, handling objects, and disposing of excreta; the three *guptis* are control of the mind, body, and speech.

28 The salient features of the constitution are: (1) there will be only one *acharya* in the Terapanthi order; (2) all disciples will remain under one *acharya*; (3) *caturmas* (travelling etc.) will be done according to the direction of the *acharya*; (4) the present *acharya* will nominate his successor, who will be accepted by all; (5) no monk or nun will initiate his or her own disciples; (6) all books and manuscripts will remain under the control of the *acharya*.

29 Consider the story of the wayward Jain monk: Greedy for food, he resolves his dilemma by becoming a Buddhist monk! (see Granoff, 1993). A story which is critical of a Jain monk does so in a circuitous way that avoids criti-cism of the institution of Jain asceticism itself.

30 *Adharma* glosses as 'not religion.'

31 Because ascetics take a vow of nonviolence daily, and are vigilant in its obser-vance, any life that may be lost (e.g., trampling to death a tiny invisible being) is not defined as 'violence' and will not lead to the accumulation of karma. The reverse is also true, however: if an ascetic is careless, karma will accrue even if no violence has occured.

32 Flügel interprets Bhikshu's doctrinal innovations as an attempt 'to eradicate the legitimacy of religious property once and for all' (1995–6: 123). He argues that by distinguishing social acts of charity from religious acts of pen-ance, 'popular puja-rituals of material gifts were thus deprived of religious value' (ibid.).

33 Anekantavada is the Jain epistemological doctrine of 'many-sidedness.' It states that truth is not singular. Instead, truth is multiplex and depends on a variety of viewpoints. Ekanta, meaning 'one view,' is its antithesis.

34 Jains believe that there are three essential and interdependent components of the spiritual path: Right Faith, Right Knowledge, and Right Conduct. Right Faith, or 'Enlightened Worldview,' brings forth Right Knowledge and then Right Conduct. Right Faith means a belief in the categories of truth (see chapter 2). A person with Right Faith is full of compassion, believes in the transmigration of the soul, and has a 'fear of, and distaste for, worldly life' (*Tattvartha Sutra*, 1994: 6).

35 Muniji's interpretation is the official Terapanthi assessment of lay–ascetic interaction. Nevertheless, on many occasions the *samanis* would interpret the

relationship in a more reciprocal way, saying that since the householders 'do so much for us,' they felt that they ought to make themselves available to the householders.

36 During my stay, I would throw scraps of bread to hungry dogs who had entered the monastery and made it their home. One day during the morning sermon, when I was sitting among the *samanis*, Guru Dev announced to the large gathering that he was happy to learn that I had been helping the dogs. By this he did not mean that I was gaining *punya* for my deeds, but rather that I was – in his mind – acting according to the duties of a householder. It must be said, however, that Guru Dev appeared more willing than most ascetics to implicate himself in social affairs. The gentle and elderly Muniji, for instance, adopted a more purist approach. He explained that he would never praise a householder for performing social duties because in so doing he would be tacitly approving of violence. This view may have been the dominant one within the sect before the leadership of Acharya Tulsi (Guru Dev), leading to its reputation for rigidity.

37 As mentioned earlier, the distinction between worldly and spiritual boons is not at all easy to make. Jains assume an indexical relationship exists between the two, so that an individual may be *materially* blessed because of a *spiritually* pure past life.

38 The ascetics claim that because we are living in the fifth cycle, the *kaliyuga*, the human body is relatively weak in comparison with earlier epochs. For example, our bones and joints are less well formed, and less able to withstand ascetic rigours. I was shown illustrations depicting the changes in the human skeletal system. Whereas we have poorly formed joints connecting our bones, human joints in earlier epochs were literally nailed together. In addition to a decline in physical might, human will and mental strength have also deteriorated.

39 Cf. Folkert (1993b: 172).

40 Interestingly, unlike Carrithers (1979) and Tambiah (1976), Strenski takes a rather positive view of ascetic 'domestication.' He states, 'domestication is no fall, no decline in the fortunes of Buddhism; it is a legitimate and natural development of ancient strands of the Buddhist tradition. It ought then to be seen as part of the process of expressing and achieving certain Buddhist goals – in particular that of Buddhist culture, society or civilization ... or what Tambiah calls ... a "world religion." Domestication is first of all part of the formation process of Buddhist *society*, growing slowly into the early *sangha* itself, then expanding to embrace ever larger spheres' (1983: 470). Likewise, Folkert writes, '[T]his phenomenon [of *caityavasi*, i.e., monastery-dwelling

ascetic order] has commonly been portrayed as "decay" in the Jain community. I would propose that it was more likely an innovation that put and kept
the community and the *sadhus* together in ways that, had there been no *cai-
tyavasis*, they would not have been bonded. One must note here the specific
place this institution allows for a prolonged lay–guru relationship' (1993b:
172).

41 Other modifications to ascetic conduct are also of considerable importance.
Unlike full ascetics, the 'semis' are allowed to travel by means other than by
foot, and are allowed to use flush toilets. The vow of *ahimsa* prevents the
ascetics from engaging in these activities. Travelling by any means other than
by foot results in the killing of innumerable life forms; flush toilets are inherently destructive devices due to their considerable use of water – which itself
is alive. And to accept alms prepared for them specifically would implicate
them in the violence committed in its preparation.

42 The ascetics refer to their rounds of alms collection as *gochari* from the Hindi
cognate *gao* meaning 'cow.' Like grazing cows, the ascetics only 'nibble' (or
take tiny amounts of food) from many householders.

43 The *saman* category is not seen as a stepping stone for monks as it is for
nuns. Instead, only those male aspirants who can speak English and are good
public speakers are considered for it. Because there are far fewer monks
than nuns in the order (approximately one-third), the Terapanthi leadership has been less inclined to delay full initiation for them.

44 Since ascetics are prevented from using electricity – because of its violence to
fire-bodied beings – householders turn lights on and off for them. The
housekeeper at the Guatam Shalla (an unassuming man in his early fifties),
is responsible for this task and, for the sake of convenience, usually leaves on
a light in the main room the whole night.

45 That is, we paid homage to Guru Dev and Acharyasri. Those responsible for
alms collection have no time to wait to hear the morning blessing (the *mangal path*). Many homes must be visited before sufficient alms are collected for
the group.

46 The Terapanthi Jains are unique within the larger Indian Jain community in
their proselytizing aspirations.

47 When instructing me in its usage, the ascetics explained it to mean 'I bow
before your greatness.' 'Matthayena' or 'Matthaen' Vandami literally translates as = 'I honour you with my head bowed down.'

48 The nuns make the *patras* and the *rajoharan* for the entire ascetic community,
monks and nuns. Also, they mend the robes of the monks and nuns alike.
Here is one instance where we see the domestic role of women carried over
to the ascetic domain.

4: The Making of an Ascetic: The Construction of Difference

1 Prayer of penance that the ascetics are required to recite twice daily, after sunrise and before sunset. See note 3, chapter 5.

2 Reynell's study demonstrates that Jains equate moral purity with sexual purity and are deeply concerned with the need to control female sexuality (1985: 176–82). As ascetics, the nuns renounce their sexuality and demonstrate their moral purity through the absence of sexual desire.

3 'Dulha' means 'groom.' 'Dulharaji' therefore (and interestingly) denotes his former householder status.

4 'Guru Dev' is the term of affection. He was *Acharya* (leader) of the Terapanthi order from 1936 until he relinquished his position to then-successor Yuvacharya Mahaprajnaji (now Acharya Mahaprajna) in 1994. After 1994, his official title became Ganadhipatti – leader of the order – (Guru Dev) Tulsiji.

5 *Harijans* ('people of god') – Mahatma Gandhi's term for the 'scheduled castes,' or so-called untouchables. 'Scheduled castes' are those castes scheduled by the government to receive affirmative action.

6 The *samanis* instructed me in the appropriate comportment. I learned to memorize the required terms of respect for *samanis, sadhvis,* and *munis,* and for Guru Dev and Acharya Sri – each increasingly deferential – and to kneel and touch my forehead on the floor before them. This 'performance' of veneration was eased as time went on. It was almost totally abandoned with those *samanis* with whom I became very close. But when we were 'in public,' I would always be expected to play my deferential part.

7 *Jinas* = those who have 'conquered themselves' – i.e., their passions – and attained omniscience.

8 'Fragrances' include scents from food.

9 All Tirthankaras – and other emancipated beings – are depicted as male, though the image is genderless. The 19th Tirthankara (Malli), believed by the Svetambaras to have been a woman, is depicted like all the rest.

10 For a discussion of lay and ascetic women's comportment, see chapter 8.

11 A yearly quota of *rajoharan* and alms bowls is imposed on the *sadhvis.* The brooms are made from yarn, and the bowls are made from coconut shells. The *sadhvis* are responsible for making these essentials for both themselves and the monks. The monks, for their part, are required to transcribe a certain number of texts per year. A point system, with bonuses and penalties, keeps track of each ascetic's efforts. I will explain this in Part Three, in the context of the rules and regulations of monastic life.

12 I.e., before sunset, since no ointment (or food, water etc) can be taken after sunset.

13 All ointments, creams, medicines, etc. belong to the householders, who lend them to the ascetics for a limited time. The ascetics 'return' them each night (to a caretaker) and 'borrow' them again in the morning.

14 Guru Dev himself was an exception to the mendicant's ideal demeanour, but it may have been that his position of ultimate power provided him with room for divergence, without upsetting the order itself.

15 My friend Samani Urmilla read to me from Bhikshu's book. She summarized the main points as follows: An ascetic's celibacy is like a field with nine thorn fences around it, and one solid wall. The fences are: (1) A celibate should live in a solitary place without any females, animals, or ennuchs; (2) A celibate should not be concerned or talk about the physical attributes of a woman. He should not notice how she walks, talks, her hands, legs, wrists, stomach, ponytail which is like a snake, her nose which is like a flame, her pink lips, her voice sweet like a cuckoo, her walk which is like a swan, her narrow waist, her lotus-like navel, her beautiful belly etc. He should not praise a woman for these things; (3) A celibate should not sit on a seat with a woman, otherwise the sex desire will be stimulated. Like a jug of *ghee*, if it is near a flame, it will turn to liquid. A monk should wait forty-eight minutes and then clean it as some sexual 'pudgal' (matter) may be left from a women's lower end; (4) A celibate should not observe the beauty of a female. Lord Mahavir said one should not even observe a painting of a woman. Like seeing the sun, one must avert one's eyes; (5) A celibate should not stay in such a place where the wall between him and a couple is thin. He may hear sounds of the couple which will arouse him; (6) A celibate should not recall the enjoyments of food and sex that he may have had as a *shravak*. If he does, he may fall ill; (7) A celibate should not take delicious food daily because they will stimulate his sexual desire; (8) A celibate should not overeat for it will lead to many diseases and increase his sexual desire; (9) A celibate should not beautify or decorate himself. If he does, he will attract intense karma and will take birth again and again. The final boundary is the self. One must have neither aversion nor attachment, and then sensual objects will have no power. Objects are neither attractive or disagreeable in and of themselves; it is the individual's emotions which determine such things. Thus if one can have equanimity, the outer wall, or tenth boundary, will never be violated.

16 *Niyojik/Niyojika* is the term used for the leader of the *saman/ samani* group respectively.

17 'Prajna' is added like a suffix to all *samanis*' names. It means 'wisdom' or 'wise.'

18 Of the eight attributes that an *acharya* is expected to possess, physical beauty

is one. Jains treat the physical body as an index or sign of one's level of spirituality.

19 The *Namaskar Mantra,* alternatively called the *Namokara Mahamantra,* is recited by Jains throughout India, irrespective of sect. It gives respect to the *Arihantas* (ones who are worthy of respect), the *Siddhas* (liberated and perfected souls), the *Acharyas* (leaders of the Jain orders), the *Upadhyays* (teachers of the scriptures), and to all *sadhus* (mendicants).

20 *Jyoti* means 'light' or 'enlightenment' and therefore is an appropriate ascetic name.

21 Since their whole life is considered to be an act of *samayika* (equanimity), ascetics do not actually 'perform' it as a distinct ritual, in the way householders do (see Laidlaw 1995: 195–204).

5: Death, Demons, and Desire

1 It translates roughly as 'I bow before your greatness' and is used when bowing before *munis* and *sadhvis.* When meeting a *samani* or *saman,* one says *'Vandami Namansami.'*

2 Householders are not solely perceived as 'temptations' to the ascetics; they can also be vigilant monitors of ascetics' conduct.

3 *Pratikraman* is one of the most important obligatory actions incumbent upon ascetics. In brief, it is an act of repentance. The word means 'going back,' and it involves the recitation of a list taken from the *Pratikraman Sutra,* renouncing sinful acts. It is a process of internal cleansing for any wrong action committed intentionally or unintentionally. It is performed twice daily (before sunrise and just after sunset). Paul Dundas writes, 'As well as involving meditative elements, *pratikramana* revolves around the recitation of six passages enumerating faults, each ending with the expression *miccha mi dukkadam,* "may evil which has been done by me be in vain"' (1992: 148).

4 Fire-bodies along with earth-, air-, and water-bodies are considered to be one-sensed microscopic life forms, called *nigodas.*

5 *Kinnara, Atikaya, Agnisikha, Sughosa* respectively.

6 See Kakar (1996: 56) for a description of the pantheon of spirits in popular Hinduism.

7 Oblivious to most of what they were saying, I could rely on the keeper of the residence, who delighted in teasing Bapu, for translations.

8 According to Jains, eggs are alive and sentient beings.

9 Unlike demons in Buddhist Sri Lanka, where, according to Kapferer, 'demonic attack contradicts the order of the cosmos in which demons are

subjugated and restrained' (cited in Boddy, 1994), demonic attack in Jainism is expected and serves as a means to demonstrate spiritual strength.

10 The *samanis* wished to shield Asha's condition from the monks and especially from Guru Dev because possession is considered shameful and a sign of weakness. Guru Dev takes pride in the members of his order and would be embarrassed by Asha's behaviour. He may even have expelled her for it, deeming her not suitable for ascetic life. Kakar describes possession as a 'stigma' and claims that it is usually the weak and morally suspect who are susceptible to possession (1996: 84).

11 Ascetics commonly claim to have 'light' karma. The karmic load of demons would be very dense.

12 Maryada Mahotsva = 'Festival of Restraint.' It is a yearly festival where as many Terapanthi ascetics (and householders) as possible congregate to take stock of the past year and plan for the next. See Flügel (1995–6).

13 One mantra that is considered especially effective to exorcize or deter a *bhut* is: '*Om A Bhi Ra Shi Ko*,' taken from the names of *tapasmunis* (monks of great spiritual power) at the time of the fourth Acharya: Jaiacharya. Their names are Ami Chandji (A); Bhimraj ji (Bhi); Ramsukhaji (Ra); Shiraji (Shi); Kodaraji (Ko).

14 *Amrit Kalash* is a three-volume Terapanthi compilation of essential scriptures, stories, sutras, and blessings. See Jinprabha and Swarnrekha (1990: Book 1, page 71) for mantras to exorcize demons.

15 Kakar describes malignant spirits as '*atripta*' – ghosts of 'unsatisfied desires' (1996: 56). He claims that they are spirits of individuals who did not fulfil their life's potential and therefore seek to possess another in order to do so.

16 Both nuns and monks claim that nuns, more often than not, are the objects of demonic attack. (See Kakar's [1996: 76] discussion of female possession.) I accept their statements as tentatively true, since during my time at the monastery I did not learn of any attacks against *munis*. However, given the secrecy surrounding Asha's difficulties, it is unlikely that I would have ever learned of a monk's possession.

17 *Bhuts* are notorious for their 'sweet tooth.' Indeed, an individual's senseless craving for sweets may signal their presence.

6: The Worldly Life of Renunciants

1 The ideas for this chapter were formed during my visits to Delhi in long and delightful discussion with Professor A.N. Pandeya.

2 A number of the *Harijan* villagers discounted this when I went to meet with them. They claimed that athough some among them ate meat and drank

liquor, others were strict vegetarians. They said that by labelling them all as meat eaters was just an excuse by the ascetics to justify never going to their homes for *bhiksha*.

3 During his leadership, Guru Dev Tulsi initiated changes to allow the ascetics to maintain a certain standard of hygiene and the appearance of cleanliness. For example – and not without controversy – he allowed them to wash their clothes weekly (of course, using *ajiv* water). He argued that if they were interacting with householders, and if they wanted to give a good impression to all about the ascetic life, they ought to appear clean. Prior to this arrangement, ascetics were not allowed to wash their clothes at all.

4 Flügel (BEI 1995–6) provides an excellent historical analysis of this process.

5 For example, since Terapanthi ascetics cannot stay in purpose-built residences, they rely on the homes of their lay followers for accommodation, giving the laity more influence (Flügel, 1995–6: 135). And because the Terapanth abolished the role of the *yati* (a resident ascetic, or one who owns property), there exists no intermediary between the *shravaks* and ascetics. Rather, it is the *acharya* who has total responsibility for all aspects of lay–ascetic interaction and lay socioreligious events.

6 Indeed, to *not* have had the ascetics – even lowly *mumukshus* – intervene earlier was evidence of my peripheral status. This lesson in cross-boundary power was brought home to me even more forcefully just days later. During one large afternoon ceremony, Guru Dev called on me to stand up. He said that he had been observing me since my arrival six months earlier, and was now convinced that I was a Jain *sadhvi* in my past incarnation. The audience was delighted and from that day on, there was neither a monk nor nun who wouldn't smile when our paths crossed, nor a householder who didn't invite me to eat at her home.

7 In conversation with me, many ascetics attributed incredible powers of concentration to their gurus: e.g., 'Between questions from householders, Acharyasri is deep in meditative thought' 'Though he is concerned with everyone, he remains detached from everything' ...

8 The ascetics cannot correspond with householders in writing unless it is absolutely urgent. It is seen as a frivolous exercise and potentially harmful (*himsa*) if such writings are misunderstood or misused.

9 According to Flügel, the Terapanthi order had 149 *munis* and 554 *sadhvis* in 1991, organized into the 126 *singhars* (1995–6: 130).

10 The positions of *mahasamani, mahasaman, yuvacharya,* and *acharya* are semi-permanent, changing only with promotion, demotion, or death.

11 A cursory examination of some of these methods reveals the centrality of discipline to Terapanthi spiritualism. The following is a common method – a

game called 'Roj Ki Kamai' (daily earnings). In front of a large audience, the ascetic will explain the game and encourage all to join in. Each *shravak* must close her/his eyes and pick a number. Each number corresponds to a type of renunciation that they must observe for one full day. Among those who successfully complete their day of renunciation, there is a 'lottery' to choose the winner who then gets a prize (e.g., some Terapanthi literature). Examples of 'renunciations' are: take no food or water after sunset; don't watch any TV or see any movies; give food to ascetics (if none are present, close eyes before meal and say 'I want to give this to the ascetics'); be celibate for one day and night; don't gamble; limit quantity of food; don't drink living water (*katcha pani*); don't eat green vegetables; don't walk on grass; don't sleep on soft bed, and so forth.

12 The following is the *samanis/samans' lekh patr or likhat*, containing the basic rules of the order (it is nearly identical to that of the *sadhvis* and *munis*), and is recited daily:

1. I have faith in Lord Mahavira and in his tradition, in Acharya Bhikshu, and all those who followed until the present Guru Dev Tulsi and Acharya Mahaprejna. I accept their discipline. I believe Guru Dev, you are the whole and soul of our organization. I have supreme faith in you.
2. I will not break your discipline.
3. I will not break the discipline of my Niyojikaji.
4. I practice the rules of *saman* training as my own witness.
5. I will be very humble towards the whole ascetic order.
6. I will be very humble to my elders and affectionate to my juniors.
7. I will treat all equally within the *saman* order.
8. I follow your indication about where I will travel (and all else).
9. I will not initiate any member into the *saman* order according to my own will.
10. I will not say negative things about my fellows.
11. If I have some problem or complaint, I will speak directly to the individual or to an authorized person.
12. If there is a disagreement, I will accept your opinion as truth, or the decision of the person you support.
13. I will accept your choice of successor without question.

I accept this letter faithfully, not by any influence, nor compulsion. I accept it by my own reasoning mind. [They then state the day, month, and year using the Indian calender.]

At an earlier period, the ascetics signed the a copy of the *patra* each morning to demonstrate allegiance. Today the pledge is verbal.

13 They are also responsible for mending all the robes – both of the *munis* and other *sadhvis* – though this is not typically understood as part of their annual obligations; it is done on a 'needs be' basis.

14 In his dissertation, Goonasekera writes that, given the restriction on going outside after sunset, 'Ideally, it is better to finish Panchami before sunset' (1986: 148). But of course, this ideal is rarely met by each ascetic each day, so the ascetics use cans or buckets and dispose of the waste in the appropriate place and manner at sunrise.

15 Shanta and I would meet and talk on several more occasions. By the time I was departing, she claimed that she would stay and make the best of her life in the order. Although she wasn't sure how it would be received, or if there might be negative repercussions, she was considering making a formal request to be allowed to remain a *samani* indefinitely, and therefore to avoid becoming a *sadhvi*.

7: Devotion and Divinity

1 The *samans* (male semi-monk order) are less adept at perfectly timing the covering of their mouths. Their occasional awkwardness stems from their inexperience. All were initiated as *samans* after a short period of training (usually a few months) and unlike the *samanis* do not attend long-term training school where they can learn all the minutiae of being an ascetic.

2 Her numerology was based on the transliterated alphabetic spelling of her name from Hindi.

3 'We have so many!' the ascetics would say, showing me piles of posters of their gurus. Unlike with alms, they can and do pass these devotional items along to householders. Technically, they have not 'received' them from the householders – they never 'begged' for them – nor was it a sacrifice for a householder to give them. Many lay devotees, on short visits to Ladnun, buy dozens of posters and pens and simply leave a few extra in the ascetics' residences. From these, I was often offered to take what I wanted.

4 The Terapanthis and the Sthanakvasis are opposed to image making and idol worship. Their rejection can be traced to a man by the name of Lonka, who lived in Gujarat in the fifteenth century, and whose anti-image stance was based on the violence inherent in creating them. It has been suggested that his rejection of image worship may have stemmed from the influence of Islam (Dundas, 1992: 213).

5 The 'gifts' that Jain ascetics bestow upon their followers are explicitly *unintentional*, otherwise they might be seen to be a form of exchange for alms, shelter, etc., and implicate them in worldly life. See chapter 3.

6 See Appendix 5 for examples of the *nivrtti-marg*.

7 The four main birth destinies (*gati*) are *deva* (god), *manusya* (humans), *naraki* (hell beings), and *triyanca* (animals and plants). They are represented as four spokes in the symbolic wheel of life, the *svastika* (Jaini, 1990: 108).

8 *Sants* are popular 'poet-saints' of the devotional tradition. *Sant* is derived from the Sanskrit *sat* ('truth' or 'reality'), meaning 'one who knows the truth' (Schomer and McLeod, 1987).

9 Both *bhakti marg* and *nivrtti marg* are critical of the violence and externality of Vedic ritualism and emphasize inner attitudes rather than external conformation. They share a rejection of external rituals, place an emphasis on self-realization and renunciation of worldly desires (see Jhingran, 1989: 147–68).

10 Families often talk of 'donating' a child to the order out of deep devotion; and Guru Dev himself asked householders to demonstrate their commitment by giving a child. However, at least since the term of Guru Dev, entry into the order is entirely voluntary – and often hard fought for. The vast majority of new initiates are young and have not been married. In previous times (e.g., under the leadership of all the preceding acharyas before Acharya Tulsi, who became acharya in 1936), a large number of nuns were widows or were forced into the order because the family could not marry them, for financial or other reasons (Goonasekera, 1986). Although this reason for renunciation still exists, today it is rare. The vast majority have to battle (and often fast) to gain the permission from their parents, who, though honoured by their daughters' choice, do not want to be separated from them. In 1996, none of the 81 *samanis* and 36 *mumukshus* had ever been married.

11 Goonasekera also met with Muniji (Muni Dulaharaji) when he visited Ladnun. However the account he tells of Muniji's life is somewhat different – he writes that Muni Dulaharaji's desire for renunciation was as a consequence of the death of his wife (1986: 114). While this version may strike us as more likely, Muniji was very careful to emphasize to me that his spiritual awakening occurred when his wife was alive, shortly after marriage.

12 Devotion *does* have utilitarian functions within the order, in addition to that of spiritual purification. In the hierarchically organized monastic structure, its practice is a sort of currency in that it enables the ascetic to secure a place of privilege. As discussed in chapter 6, the ascetics compete among themselves for the guru's affection.

13 Guru Dev Tulsi writes: 'Mind tainted with attachment is filled with the emotion of love whereas one tainted with aversion is filled with hatred. Love, in its turn, produces avarice. Avaricious mind becomes deceitful, lustful and possessive' (Tulsi, 1995: 69).

14 The ascetic path is one of 'knowledge' *(jnana)*, whereas the devotional path is the path of attachment and emotion. Knowing and feeling are opposed.

15 Nuns and monks are forbidden to be in the same place in darkness. The sun must be up before the two groups can gather.

16 'Three times from right to right circumambulating I adore, make obeisance, revere and respect you, the auspicious, the absolute good, the embodiment of religion and the truly learned. I wait upon you, honour you with head bowed down.' Usually only the words *'Matthayena Vandami'* are spoken aloud, the rest is said to oneself.

17 Although my contact with monks was more limited than it was with nuns, the differences I describe above were conspicuous. The monks freely admit that devotion forms an imporant part of their ascetic lives, but they did not provide it the same centrality as did the nuns in their 'public' narrative accounts to me.

8: Conclusion: Ascetic Women – The Link in the *Laukik* and *Lokottar*

1 Reynell writes that not only is fasting a demonstration of female honour, 'it is a source of prestige for the woman's husband in that it gives him a chance to demonstrate his wealth to the community' (1985a: 191) (e.g., through his well-jewelled wife, and by holding lavish feasts).

2 The Digambar position is typical of Indian attitudes to female asceticism. Clementin-Ojha describes female ascetics in the Hindu tradition as 'outside the norm' (1988: 34) and subordinate to men. In Buddhism, nuns are similarly subordinate to monks (see Nissan, 1983). It is well known that the Buddha established a female order only with the greatest of reluctance.

3 As we saw in chapter 4, Terapanthi girls go through a training period, often up to ten years, during which time they 'learn' to be ascetics. By contrast, the process through which boys become ascetics is much shorter and, hence, more dramatic.

4 If the male ascetic aspirant is young, it would be more appropriate to say that he renounces the 'promise' of the public domain.

5 That asceticism is perceived as much more of an achievement for men than for women resonates with Rosaldo's (1974) thesis, which states that, cross-culturally, masculinity must be *achieved* whereas femininity simply comes to pass 'naturally.' (See also Chodorow 1974.)

References

Agrawal, A.K. 'Jain Ethics and the Spirit of Capitalism: A Critical Reappraisal of Weber.' Paper presented to a seminar on Jain Religion and Society, Rajasthan University, Jaipur, August/September 1984.

Agrawal, B.C. 'Diksha Ceremony in Jainism: An Analysis of Its Sociological Ramifications.' *Eastern Anthropologist* 25(1) (1972): 13–20.

Asad, T. (Ed.). *Anthropology and the Colonial Encounter.* London: Ithaca Press, 1973.

– 'Anthropological Conceptions of Religion; Reflections on Geertz.' *Man* 18 (1983) 237–59.

– *Genealogies of Religion: Discipline and Reasons of Power in Christianity and Islam* Baltimore and London: The Johns Hopkins University Press, 1993.

Babb, L. 'Sathya Sai Baba's Miracles.' In *Religion in India,* ed. T.N. Madan, 277–292. Delhi: Oxford University Press, 1991.

– 'Monks and Miracles: Religious Symbols and Images of Origin among Osval Jains.' *The Journal of Asian Studies* 52(1) (1993): 3–21.

– *Absent Lord: Ascetics and Kings in a Jain Ritual Culture.* Berkeley: University of California Press, 1996.

Balbir, N. 'Observations sur la secte jaina des Terapanthi.' *BEI* 1 (1983): 39–45.

– 'Women in Jainism.' In *Religion and Women,* ed. A. Sharma, 121–38. Albany: State University of New York Press, 1994.

Banks, M. 'Caste, Sect and Property: Relations in the Jain Community of Jamnagar, Gujarat.' Paper presented to a seminar on Jain Religion and Society, Rajasthan University, Jaipur, August/September 1984.

– 'Defining Division: An Historical Overview of Jain Social Organization.' *Modern Asian Studies* 20(3) (1986): 447–60.

– *Organising Jainism in India and England.* Oxford: Clarendon Press, 1992.

– 'Representing the Bodies of Jains.' In *Rethinking Visual Anthropology,* ed. M.

Banks and H. Morphy, 216–39. New Haven and London: Yale University Press, 1997.

Bhatnagar, R. (Ed.). *Acharya Tulsi*. Ladnun: Jain Vishva Bharati, 1985.

Boddy, J. 'Spirit Possession Revisited: Beyond Instrumentality.' *Annual Review of Anthropology* 23 (1994): 407–34.

Bynum, C.W. *Fragmentation and Redemption: Essays on Gender and the Human Body in Medieval Religion*. New York: Zone Books, 1994.

Caillet, C., A.N. Upadhye, and B. Patel. *Jainism*. Delhi: The Macmillan Company of India, 1974.

Cantlie, A. 'Aspects of Hindu Asceticism.' In *Symbols and Sentiments: Cross-Cultural Studies in Symbolism*, ed. I.M. Lewis, 247–69. London: Academic Press, 1977.

– 'The Moral Significance of Food among Assamese Hindus.' In *Culture and Morality: Essays in Honour of Christoph von Furer-Haimendorf*, ed. A. Mayer. Delhi: Oxford University Press, 1981.

Carrithers, M. 'The Modern Ascetics of Lanka and the Pattern of Change in Buddhism.' *Man* (N.S.) 14 (1979): 294–310.

– *The Forest Monks of Sri Lanka: An Anthropological and Historical Study*. London: Oxford University Press, 1983.

– 'The Domestication of the *Sangh*.' *Man* (N.S.) 19 (1984): 321–2.

– 'Jain Ideals and Jain Identity.' In *The Assembly of Listeners: Jains in Society*, ed. M. Carrithers and C. Humphrey, 15–17. Cambridge: Cambridge University Press, 1991.

Carrithers, M., and C. Humphrey (Eds.). *The Assembly of Listeners: Jains in Society*. Cambridge: Cambridge University Press, 1991.

Chodorow, N. 'Family Structure and Feminine Personality.' In *Woman, Culture and Society*, ed. M.Z. Rosaldo and L. Lamphere, 43–66. Stanford, CA: Stanford University Press, 1974.

Clementin-Ojha, C. 'Outside the Norms: Women Ascetics in Hindu Society.' *Economic and Political Weekly*, (30 April 1988): 34–6.

Clifford, J. 'Introduction: Partial Truths.' In *Writing Culture: The Poetics of Ethnography*, ed. J. Clifford and G.E. Marcus, 1–26. Berkeley, CA: University of California Press, 1986.

– 'Reply to Roth.' *Current Anthropology* 30(5) (1989): 561–3.

Corin, E. 'Refiguring the Person: The Dynamics of Affects and Symbols in an African Spirit Possession Cult.' In *Bodies and Persons*, ed. M. Lambek and A. Strathern, 80–102. Cambridge: Cambridge University Press, 2001.

Cort, J.E. 'Recent Descriptive Accounts on Contemporary Jainas.' *Man in India* 66(2) (1986): 180–7.

– *Liberation and Wellbeing: A Study of the Svetambar Murtipujak Jains of North Gujarat.* Ph.D. dissertation, Harvard University 1989.
– 'The Svetambar Murtipujak Jain Layman.' *Journal of Indian Philosophy* 19 (1991a): 391–420.
– 'The Svetambar Murtipujak Jain Mendicant.' *Man* (N.S.) (1991b): 26, 549–69.
– 'Introduction: Kendall Folkert and the Study of the Jains.' In *Scripture and Community: Collected Essays on the Jains,* by Kendall Folkert, ed. J. Cort, xiii–xxiv. Atlanta, GA: Scholars Press, 1993.
– 'Murtipuja in Svetambar Jain Temples.' In *Religion in India,* ed. T.N. Madan, 212–23 Delhi: Oxford University Press, 1995a.
– 'Defining Jainism: Reform in the Jain Tradition.' The 1994 Roop Lal Jain Lecture. University of Toronto, Centre for South Asian Studies, 1995b.
Descola, P., and G. Pallson. *Nature and Society: Anthropological Perspectives.* London and New York: Routledge, 1996.
Douglas, M. *Implicit Meanings: Essays in Anthropology,* 210–29. London and Boston: Routledge and Kegan Paul, 1975.
Dube, L. 'On the Construction of Gender: Hindu Girls in Patrilineal India.' *Economic and Political Weekly* (30 April 1988), 11–19.
Dumont, L. 'World-Renunciation in Indian Religions.' *Contributions to Indian Sociology* (N.S.) 4 (1960): 33–62.
– *Homo Hierarchicus: The Caste System and Its Implications.* Complete revised English edition. Chicago: The University of Chicago Press, 1980.
Dundas, P. 'Food and Freedom: The Jain Sectarian Debate on the Nature of Kevalin.' Paper presented to a seminar on Jain Religion and Society, Rajasthan University, Jaipur, August/September 1984.
– *The Jains.* London and New York: Routledge, 1992.
– 'The Meat at the Wedding Feasts: Krsna, Vegetarianism and a Jain Dispute.' The 1997 Roop Lal Jain Lecture. University of Toronto: Centre for South Asian Studies, 1997.
Dwivedi, R. 'Social Significance of Jain Ethics.' Paper presented at the UCG seminar on Jain Religion and Society, August/September 1984.
Flügel, P. 'The Ritual Circle of the Terapanth Svetambara Jains.' *BEI* 13–14 (1995–6): 117–76.
Folkert, K. 'Jainism.' In *A Handbook of Living Religions,* ed. J. Hinnels, 256–77. Middlesex, England: Penguin Books, 1987.
– 'Jain Studies.' In *Scripture and Community: Collected Essays on the Jains,* by Kendall Folkert, ed. J. Cort, 23–33. Atlanta, GA: Scholars Press, 1993a.
– 'The Jain *Sadhu* as Community Builder.' In *Scripture and Community: Collected*

Essays on the Jains, by Kendall Folkert, ed. J. Cort, 167–74. Atlanta, GA: Scholars Press, 1993b.

– 'Monastic Ideals and the Lay Community in Religion.' In *Scripture and Community: Collected Essays on the Jains,* by Kendall Folkert, ed. J. Cort, 177–86. Atlanta, GA: Scholars Press, 1993c.

Fuller, C.J. *The Camphor Flame: Popular Hinduism and Society in India.* Princeton University Press, 1992.

Geertz, A. 'On Reciprocity and Mutual Reflection in the Study of Native American Religions.' *Religion* 24 (1994): 1–7.

Ghurye, G.S. *Indian Sadhus.* Ghurye Birth Centenary Commemoration Issue. Bombay: Popular Prakashan PVT Ltd. [1953] 1995.

Goldman, R. 'Foreword.' In *Gender and Salvation. Jaina Debates on the Spiritual Liberation of Women,* by P.S. Jaini, vii–xxiv. Berkeley: University of California Press, 1991.

Goonasekera, S.A. *Renunciation and Monasticism among the Jains of India.* PhD thesis, University of California, 1986.

Granoff, P. (Ed.). *The Clever Adulteress and Other Stories.* Delhi: Motilal Banarsidass, 1993.

Grimshaw, A. *Servants of the Buddha: Winter in a Himalayan Convent.* Cleveland, OH: Pilgrim Press, 1994.

Haug, F. *Female Sexualisation,* trans. Erica Carter. London: Verso, 1987.

Holden, P. (Ed.). *Women's Religious Experience.* London: Croom Helm, 1983.

Holmstrom, S. *Towards a Politics of Renunciation: Jain Women and Asceticism in Rajasthan.* M.A. thesis, University of Edinburgh, 1988.

Howell, S. (Ed.). *The Ethnography of Moralities.* London and New York: Routledge, 1997.

Humphrey, C., and J. Laidlaw. *The Archetypal Actions of Ritual: A Theory of Ritual Illustrated by the Jain Rite of Worship.* Oxford: Clarendon Press, 1994.

Ingold, T. 'Humanity and Animality.' In *Companion Encyclopedia of Anthropology: Humanity, Culture and Social Life,* ed. T. Ingold, 14–32. London and New York: Routledge, 1994.

Jackson, M. *Paths towards a Clearing: Radical Empiricism and Ethnographic Inquiry.* Bloomington: Indiana University Press, 1989 .

– (Ed.). *Things as They Are: New Directions in Phenomenological Anthropology.* Bloomington: Indiana University Press, 1996.

Jacobi, H. *Jaina Sutras, Sacred Books of the East,* vol. 22. Delhi: Motilal Banarsidass, 1994.

Jain, J.C. 'Status of Women in Jain Literature – An Analysis.' Paper presented to a seminar on Jain Religion and Society, Rajasthan University, Jaipur, August/September 1984.

Jain, P. *Women Images.* Jaipur: Rawat Publications, 1996.

Jain, R. '"Jain-Osval" of Calcutta as an "Ethnic Group." A Socio-Historical Perspective.' *Man in India* 67(4) (1987): 383–403.

Jaini, P.S. *The Jaina Path of Purification.* Berkeley: University of California Press, [1979] 1990.

– 'The Pure and the Auspicious in the Jaina Tradition.' In *Purity and Auspiciousness in Indian Society,* ed. J.B. Carmen and F.A. Marglin, 84–93. Leiden: E.J. Brlll, 1995.

– 'Is There a Popular Jainism?' In *The Assembly of Listeners,* ed. M. Carrithers and C. Humphrey, 187–99. Cambridge: Cambridge University Press, 1991a.

– *Gender and Salvation. Jaina Debates on the Spiritual Liberation of Women.* Berkeley: University of California Press, 1991b.

Jhingran, S. *Aspects of Hindu Morality.* Delhi: Motilal Banarsidass, 1989.

Jineshkumar, Muni. *A Primer of Jain Philosophy.* Udaipur: K. Jain Publishers, 1990.

Jinprabha, Sadhvi, and Sadhvi Swarnrekha. *Amrit Kalash,* 2 vols. Ladnun: Adarsh Sahitya Sangh, 1990.

Johnson, W.J. *Harmless Souls. Karmic Bondage and Religious Change in Early Jainism with Special Reference to Umasvati and Kundakuna.* Delhi: Motilal Banarsidass, 1995.

Kakar, S. *The Inner World. A Psycho-Analytic Study of Childhood and Society in India.* Delhi: Oxford University Press, 1981.

– 'Lord of the Spirit World,' chap. 3 in *The Indian Psyche.* Delhi: Oxford University Press, 1996.

Kapashi, V., A. Shah, and K. Desai. *Text Book of Jainism,* Level 1. Middlesex: Institute of Jainology, 1994.

King, U. (Ed.) *Religion and Gender.* Oxford, UK, and Cambridge, MA: Blackwell, 1995.

Kumar, Prashant, and Lokprakash Lokesh. *Acharya Mahapragya: A Living Legend.* Bombay: Shri Bhikshu Foundation, 1995.

Laidlaw, J. 'Prophet, Salvation and Profitable Saints.' *Cambridge Anthropology* 9(3) (1985): 50–70.

– *Riches and Renunciation: Religion, Economy and Society among the Jains.* Oxford: Clarendon Press, 1995.

Lambek, M. 'Taboo as Cultural Practice among Malagasy Speakers.' *Man* 27(2) (1992): 245–66.

Lannoy, R. *The Speaking Tree.* London: Oxford University Press Paperback, 1974.

Leiss, W. *The Domination of Nature.* New York: George Braziller, 1972.

Linzey, A. *Animal Theology.* Urbana and Chicago: University of Illinois Press, 1995.

Lutz, C. 'Depression and the Translation of Worlds.' In *Culture and Depression,*

Studies in the Anthropology and Cross-Cultural Psychiatry of Affect and Disorder, ed.
A. Kleinman and B. Good, 63–100. Berkeley, Los Angeles, and London: University of California Press, 1985.

Lynch, O. *Divine Passions: The Social Construction of Emotion in India.* Berkeley: University of California Press, 1990.

Macpherson, C.B. *The Political Theory of Possessive Individualism.* Oxford: Oxford University Press, 1962.

Mahaprajna, Yuvacharya. *Preksha Dhyana: Basic Principles,* trans. Muni Mahendra Kumar and Jethalal S. Zaveri. Ladnun: Jain Vishva Bharati, 1993.

– *Steering the Wheel of Dhamma (A Biography of Acharya Tulsi),* trans. R.K. Seth. Ladnun: Jain Vishva Bharati, 1994.

Mason, J. *An Unnatural Order.* New York: Continuum, 1993.

Mauss, M. 'A Category of the Human Mind: The Notion of Person; the Notion of Self.' In *The Category of the Person: Anthropology, Philosophy, History,* ed. M. Carrithers, S. Collins, and S. Lukes, 1–25. Cambridge: Cambridge University Press, 1987.

– *The Gift. Forms and Functions of Exchange in Archaic Societies,* trans. I. Cunnison. London: Routledge, 1988.

McManners, J. *The Oxford History of Christianity.* Oxford: Oxford University Press, 1990.

Mellor, P., and C. Shilling. 'Reflexive Modernity and the Religious Body.' *Religion* 24 (1994): 23–42.

Meneley, A. *Tournaments of Value: Sociability and Hierarchy in a Yemeni Town.* Toronto: University of Toronto Press, 1996.

Metcalf, B. *Perfecting Women: Maulana Ashraf Ali Thanaan's Bihishti Zewar.* California: University of California Press, 1990.

Midgely, M. *Beast and Man, The Roots of Human Nature.* London: Methuen Press, 1979.

Miles, M. *Augustine on the Body.* Missoula, MT: Scholars Press, 1979.

Nair, V.G. *Jainism and Terehpanthism.* Bangalore: Shri Adinath Jain Swetambar Temple, 1969.

Narayan, K. *Storytellers, Saints and Scoundrels: Folk Narrative in Hindu Religious Teaching.* Philadelphia: University of Pennsylvania Press, [1989] 1992.

Nevaskar, B. *Capitalists without Capitalism: The Jains of India and the Quakers of the West.* Westport, CT: Greenwood Publishing Corporation, 1971.

Nissan, E. 'Recovering Practice: Buddhist Nuns in Sri Lanka.' *South Asia Research* 4(1) (1983): 32–50.

O'Connor, J. 'On Studying and Being the Other: An Open Letter to Armin Geertz.' *Religion* 24 (1994): 8–11.

O'Flaherty, W.D. *The Origins of Evil in Hindu Mythology.* Delhi: Motilal Banarsidass, [1976] 1988.

Oldfield, K. *Jainism Today: A Study of the Jain Community in a Rajasthani Village in 1982.* M.A. thesis, University of Lancaster, 1982.

Olivelle, P. 'A Definition of World Renunciation.' In *Vasudevasrama Yatidharmapraksha: A Treatise on World Renunciation,* ed. P. Olivelle, 75–83. Delhi: Motilal Banarsidass, 1975.

Pagels, E. *The Origin of Satan.* New York: Random House, 1995.

Parry, J. 'The Gift, The Indian Gift and the 'Indian Gift.' *Man* (N.S.) 21 (1986): 453–73.

– 'On the Moral Perils of Exchange.' In *Money and the Morality of Exchange,* ed. J. Parry and M. Bloch, 64–93. Cambridge: Cambridge University Press, 1989.

Regan, T. *The Case for Animal Rights.* Berkeley and Los Angeles: University of California Press, 1983.

Reynell, J. 'Equality and Inequality.' Paper presented to a seminar on Jain Religion and Society, Rajasthan University, Jaipur, August/September 1984.

– *Honour, Nurture and Festivity: Aspects of Female Religiosity amongst Jain Women in Jaipur.* PhD thesis, University of Cambridge , 1985a.

– 'Renunciation and Ostentation: A Jain Paradox.' *Cambridge Anthropology* 9 (1985b): 20–33.

– 'Prestige, Honour and the Family: Laywomen's Religiosity amongst the Svetambar Murtipujak Jains in Jaipur.' *Bulletin d'Études Indiennes* 5 (1987): 313–59.

– 'Women and the Reproduction of the Jain Community.' In *The Assembly of Listeners,* ed. M. Carrithers and C. Humphrey, 41–65. Cambridge: Cambridge University Press, 1991.

Robinson, S. 'Hindu Paradigms of Women: Images and Values.' In *Women, Religion and Social* Change, 181–201. Albany: State University of New York Press, 1985.

Rosaldo, M.Z. 'Woman, Culture, and Society: A Theoretical Overview.' In *Woman, Culture and Society,* ed. M.Z. Rosaldo and L. Lamphere, 17–42. Stanford, CA: Stanford University Press, 1974.

Said, E.W. 'Orientalism Reconsidered.' In *Europe and Its Others,* vol. 1, ed. F. Barker, P. Hulme, M. Iversen, and D Loxey, 14–27, Colchester: University of Essex, 1985.

Sangave, V. *The Jaina Path of Ahimsa.* Solapur, Maharashtra: Bhagwan Mahavir Research Centre, 1992.

Schomer, K., and W.H. McLeod. (Eds.). *The Sants: Studies in a Devotional Tradition of India.* Delhi: Motilal Banarsidass, 1987.

Schubring, W. *The Doctrine of the Jainas.* Delhi: Motilal Banarsidass, 1978.

Schweitzer, A. *Indian Thought and Its Development.* Bombay: Wilco Publishing House, 1980.

Sen, A.C. 'Ahimsa in Jainism: Viewed in Historical Perspective.' In *Jainthology*, ed. G. Lalani, 61–71. Calcutta: Jain Bhawan, 1991.

Settar, S. *Inviting Death: Indian Attitudes towards the Ritual Death.* Leiden: E.J. Brill, 1989.

– *Pursuing Death*, Leiden: E.J. Brill, 1990.

Shântâ, N. *La voie Jaina: Histoire, spiritualité, vie des ascètes pèlerines de l'Inde.* Paris, OEIL, 1985.

Sharma, A. (Ed.). *Religion and Women.* Albany: State University of New York Press, 1994.

Shilling, C. *The Body and Social Theory.* London, Newbury Park and New Delhi: Sage Publications, 1993.

Sinclair, K. 'Women and Religion.' In *The Cross-Cultural Study of Women. A Comprehensive Guide*, ed. M.I. Dudley and M.I. Edwards, 107–24. New York: City University of New York: The Feminist Press, 1986.

Stevenson, M.S. *The Heart of Jainism.* New Delhi: Mushiram Manoharlal, [1915] 1970.

Streng, F. *Understanding Religious Life*, 3rd ed. California: Wadsworth Publishing Company, 1985.

Strenski, I. 'On Generalized Exchange and the Domestication of the *Sangha.*' *Man* (N.S.) 18 (1983): 463–77.

Tambiah, S.J. *World Conqueror and World Renouncer: a study of Buddhism and Polity in Thailand against a Historical Background.* Cambridge/New York: Cambridge University Press, 1976.

Tatia, N. *Aspects of Jaina Monasticism.* Ladnun: Jain Vishva Bharati, 1981b.

– 'Lectures on Jainism.' Annual Lecture Series No. 1. Madras: The Department of Jainology, University of Madras, 1988.

Tatia, N., and Muni M. Kumar (Trans.). *The Utopia and the Utopian.* Delhi: Today and Tomorrow's Printers and Publishers, 1981a.

Tattvartha Sutra. Trans. N. Tatia. The Sacred Literature Series. HarperCollins Publishers, 1994.

Taylor, C. *Sources of the Self.* Cambridge, MA: Harvard University Press, 1989.

Tester, K. *Animals and Society.* London: Routledge, 1995.

Thomas, K. *Man and the Natural World.* New York: Pantheon Books, 1983.

Tobias, M. *Life Force: The World of Jainism.* Berkeley, CA: Asian Humanities Press, 1991.

Tulsi, Acharya. *Illuminator of Jaina Tenets (Jaina Siddhanta Dipika).* Trans. S. Mookerjee. Ladnun: Jain Vishva Bharati, 1985.

Tulsi, Ganadhipatti. *Bhagavan Mahavira.* Ladnun: Jain Vishva Bharati, 1995.

Turner, V. *The Ritual Process.* Chicago: Aldine, 1969.

Tyler, S. *The Said and the Unsaid: Mind, Meaning, and Culture.* New York: Academic Press, 1978.

– *The Unspeakable: discourse, dialogue, and rhetoric iun the postmodern world.* Madison, Wis: University of Visconsih Press, 1987.

Vail, L.F. *Renunciation, Love and Power in Hindu Monastic Life.* Unpublished PhD dissertation, University of Pennsylvania, 1987

Van Maanen, J. *Tales of the Field. On Writing Ethnography.* Chicago: The University of Chicago Press, 1988.

Visrut Vibha, Sadhvi. *Journey Into Jainism: A Collection of Short Stories.* New Delhi: B. Jain Publishers Pvt. Ltd., 1994.

White, L. 'The Historical Roots of Our Ecological Crisis.' In *Science* 155 (1967), 1203–7.

Williams, R. *Jaina Yoga.* London/Delhi: Motilal Banarsidass, 1963.

Index

ANTHROPOLOGICAL HORIZONS

Editor: Michael Lambek, University of Toronto

Published to date: